Hollywood's World War I

Hollywood's World War I:
Motion Picture Images

edited by

Peter C. Rollins
and
John E. O'Connor

Bowling Green State University Popular Press
Bowling Green, OH 43403

Copyright © Bowling Green State University Popular Press

Library of Congress Cataloging-in-Publication Data

Hollywood's World War I : motion picture images / edited by Peter C.
    Rollins and John E. O'Connor.
            p.   cm.
        Includes bibliographical references.
        ISBN 0-87972-755-1. -- ISBN 0-87972-756-X (pbk.)
        1. World War, 1914-1918--Motion picture and the war.
    2. Motion picture industry--California--Hollywood. I. Rollins, Peter C.
    II. O'Connor, John E.
    D522.23.H65   1997
    791.43'658--dc21   97-26062
                                                                        CIP

Cover design by Dumm Art

Contents

Acknowledgments

Many of the writers contributing to this volume attended a wonderful conference on "Film and the First World War" at the University of Amsterdam during the summer of 1993 under auspices of the International Association for Media and History (IAMHIST). Special thanks to David Ellwood, president, and to number of University of Amsterdam staffers including Pim Slot, Piet van Wijk, Karel Dibbets, and Bert Hogenkamp who made the meeting a wonderful experience. (With an international focus, some of the conference papers were published under the title of *Film and the First World War,* ed. Karel Dibbets and Bert Hogenkamp [Amsterdam: University of Amsterdam Press, 1995].)

An earlier version of Andrew Kelly's essay appeared in the *Historical Journal of Film, Radio and Television* 13.2 (1993): 215-27 as "The Brutality of Military Incompetence: 'Paths of Glory' (1957)." We thank IAMHIST for permission to reprint this fine article.

Many thanks to John O'Connor for permission to print the essay by Michael Eisenberg; it first appeared in *American History/American Film: Interpreting the Hollywood Image* (New York: Ungar, 1979) 17-37.

Introduction:
The Great War (1914-1918) in the American Mind

Peter C. Rollins and John E. O'Connor

On August 30, 1993, close to one hundred of the nearly 48,000 living American veterans of World War I (along with 700 family members and friends) convened near Chicago to celebrate the 75th anniversary of the Armistice which brought the Great War to an end. Reah Hollinger had some humorous memories of the first Armistice on November 11, 1918: "The cease-fire came at 11:00 A.M. When we finished up at about 3:00 P.M., we walked up to the front and began talking to some German soldiers. I don't know what we talked about, but I traded some socks for some German sauerkraut, the first fermented cabbage I had tasted since leaving home" (Veteran interviews).

Not every serviceman was within walking distance of the front when the war ended. Ed Schultz had wanted to see action with the Marines, but his medical skills were needed in Brooklyn because a worldwide influenza epidemic had hit during the winter of 1917. Working nights at a "contagious hospital," Schultz remembered the grim chore of wheeling one or two corpses to the morgue each morning at the end of his shift. (Official records of the army list almost 23,000 troops lost to the contagion.) When Armistice Day arrived, Schultz was still tending the sick.

For some of the younger soldiers, the war was a "great adventure," but it could be a traumatic one. George Brummell of Woodburn, Oregon, remembers: "You lived constantly with the fear of whether you would stay in Paris or be sent to the front. The Germans were only twenty miles outside Paris at one time while I was there. The shellings with Big Berthas [long-distance artillery] had a great psychological effect." Yet the same war could be pure tedium. A. I. Stevens of Texas, a member of an African American unit, remembers long days building roads, unloading ships, salvaging battlefields, and repairing railroad tracks: "We didn't have much chance to see anything; they kept us busy. It wasn't pleasant." Looking back, most of the living veterans stood in awe of the changes accelerated by the Great War. Winston Roche, a 94-year-old veteran from Dallas, reflected: "We made America a world power. We saw

1

America from the days of horses and mules, handguns, a few machine guns, and a few outdated field pieces, all the way to jet fighters and the moon landing. We have lived in a wonderful generation of American history."

The experience of battle gave many a new perspective on life. Speaking for many veterans from the Civil War to Vietnam, Orville Rummell (age 93) observed: "It put a different value on what you did, how you did it, how you enjoyed what you got, how you lived each day." But not every veteran emerged from the war with such philosophical calm. An Oklahoma veteran spoke to us about his sense of guilt. As a machine gunner, he had killed hundreds of German infantrymen as they charged toward his pillbox. Answering in faltering tones as if the experience had happened yesterday, this 85-year-old man sat on the edge of his bed at the Claremore Veterans Center crying throughout our twenty-minute interview. On the eve of the 75th anniversary of the Armistice, he was worried about the fate of his eternal soul.

After studying the literature, films, and memorials connected with World War I, we have concluded that there are two contradictory ways of remembering the Great War. On one hand, some veterans, officials, monuments, and movies have promoted the heroic version, celebrating the unselfish service of our fighting men; from a contrasting viewpoint, other veterans, artists, writers, and filmmakers have argued that the war needlessly sacrificed the youth of a generation. With the benefit of hindsight, our introduction will survey both angles of vision.

The Heroic Vision: "They Came on the Wings of Eagles"

Not surprisingly, the heroic vision prevailed at the 75th anniversary celebration of the World War I armistice at Cantigny, millionaire Robert McCormick's estate (now a World War I museum) five miles south of Chicago's O'Hare airport. In fact, the celebrations were conducted under an upbeat rubric: "A Grateful Nation DOES Remember." For the event, the McCormick Foundation created a special commemorative medal, a replica of the World War I Victory Medal given after the war to every American soldier, sailor, and marine. On the front of the medal is a drawing of Nike, the classical Greek messenger of victory. The reverse side of the medal carries an inscription "They Came On the Wings of Eagles"—borrowed from a battlefield memorial in France. All living World War I vets were eligible for the medal, a gesture to the veterans lauded by the Veterans of World War I of the U.S.A, partially because a less-than-grateful nation—perhaps still suffering from what George Bush described as the Vietnam syndrome—seemed to have forgotten the 75th anniversary.

During the 1920s, Hollywood contributed to the heroic image. *The Big Parade* (1925) was the first financially successful postwar film about the conflict. The famous battle scenes (re-enacting American actions in the Argonne forest of France) employed innovative visual and editing techniques. The director, King Vidor, asked his actors to walk, shoot, and fall to the cadence of an on-set metronome, thereby creating a visual rhythm which—to the surprise of everyone except the director—gave the battle scenes a strange, balletic quality. (Those who have not seen *The Big Parade* need to be told that the title of the film does not refer to a military ceremony, but to America's march to victory on the Western Front.) When the doughboys fight and die in this film, they do so as heroes for their nation's democratic cause. Not surprisingly, veterans were delighted with Vidor's patriotic tale. Michael T. Isenberg's essay explores a major paradox about *The Big Parade*: how could such a heroic and awe-inspiring epic be characterized by filmmaker Vidor as an antiwar film? (chapter 3).

In *Wings* (1927), William Wellman followed the development of two aviators from their first days of flight training. Wellman, himself, had been a pilot in the war and sought to make the Army Air Corps look every bit as romantic as the Army infantry in *The Big Parade* and the Marine Corps in *What Price Glory?* (1927). The War Department provided a cast of thousands for a film which, even with government help, cost over $2 million. No expense was spared; for example, reenactment of the St. Mihiel offensive cost Paramount over $250,000. All aerial duels were filmed aloft with cameras mounted on the planes. Distributed soon after Charles Lindbergh crossed the Atlantic, *Wings* exploited America's fascination with the military potential of aviation. Indeed, Lindbergh was quoted in the film's heraldic titles in a dedication "to those young warriors of the sky, whose wings are folded about them forever." America's young pilots could have had no memorial more noble than this monument in celluloid. (*Wings* is an action film that still rents well.)

A week after the Armistice was signed, *Stars and Stripes* (the service newspaper still published today for the armed forces) carried a poem entitled "Your Soldier," which presaged the heroic themes of *The Big Parade* and *Wings*:

> It is for you. Through endless nights
> Of mud and rain he stubbornly
> Plods on, head down, back bent beneath
> His pack—on towards the shell-streaked sky
> And maddening roar where truth and lies

4 Hollywood's World War I

And love and hate and life and death
All meet in war, red war! He loves
And hates, and so he fights. To all
His love be true. Guard well your heart
And keep the faith. He fights for you!
(Veterans of World War I)

The poet was anonymous, but he captured the proud spirit of the warriors' self-image. That heroic image of World War I aviators in *The Dawn Patrol* is explored by Dominick A. Pisano (chapter 4); the aerial heroics of *Hell's Angels* are further examined by Robert Baird (chapter 5). All three authors—Isenberg, Pisano, and Baird—highlight the complexities of the heroic image for all war films, an issue more intricate than it may appear. Daniel J. Leab's close reading of *The Fighting 69th* further identifies the difficulty in labeling films "prowar" or "antiwar" (chapter 6).

The Versailles Treaty was signed in the palace's Hall of Mirrors at the end of May, 1919. A year later, England buried its unknown soldier in Westminster Abbey and France buried her unknown beneath the Arc de Triomphe in Paris. On November 11, 1921, then known as Armistice Day, America's Unknown Soldier was buried with elaborate ceremony in Arlington National Cemetery. In one of the country's first nationwide radio broadcasts, President Warren G. Harding tried to focus America's thoughts on current issues of war and peace. (The ceremony was taking place one day before the convening of the Washington Arms Limitation Conference, which sought to prevent a postwar arms race.) At Arlington, however, the retrospective view prevailed. Lord Beatty, Admiral of the British Fleet, presented the Victoria Cross to the Unknown. Marshal Ferdinand Foch, advocate of "indomitable will" in battle, pinned the *Medaille Militaire* and the *Croix de Guerre* to the display. Arthur Balfour, Aristide Briand, and even Prince Iyesato Tokugawa were in respectful attendance—in part because the arms conference was to begin the next day. Congressman John C. McKenzie of Illinois assured the audience that there was "a lesson of patriotism to be learned" from the ceremony. Secretary of War, Newton D. Baker, emphasized the symbolic importance of the tomb in terms of national memory: "In the long run of history, the names of individuals fade, but the great movements which have been inspired and defended by the mass of virtue, which we call the national spirit, remain as solid achievements and mark the advance which civilization attains" (Veterans of World War I).

The tomb of 1921 is today called the Tomb of the Unknowns: it now preserves the remains of the Unknown Soldier of World War I, the

Unknown American Serviceman of World War II, the Unknown Serviceman of the Korean War, and the Unknown Serviceman of the Vietnam Era. Located on a plaza down the steps from the Arlington Memorial Amphitheater, this hallowed place is guarded twenty-four hours a day by members of the First Battalion, Third Infantry, U.S. Army of Fort Myer. On Memorial Day 1993, President Bill Clinton spoke at the ceremonies in a former antiwar protester's gesture of respect to the martial spirit.

Popular outside of Washington has been a heroic statue titled *The Spirit of the American Doughboy*. Designed by Ernest M. Viquesney of Indiana and copyrighted in 1920, the metal statue depicts an American infantryman in the act of crossing no man's land (evidenced by tree stumps and some barbed wire at his feet) ready for battle. In his left hand, he holds his Springfield rifle, with its characteristic long bayonet, parallel to the ground. His right hand is aloft in the act of throwing a hand grenade in the direction of the German trenches. He wears a full cartridge belt around his waist; a gas mask pouch hangs from his neck and rests on his chest. This heroic statue seems clearly to have been inspired by a statue of Mercury by Giovanni Bologna, housed in the Louvre, Paris. (Mercury's hands are doing similar things; all that is needed is a set of fatigues, a gas mask, and a slightly more soldierly stride.) T. Perry Wesley, editor emeritus of the local paper of Spencer, Indiana—and the world's lone expert on the doughboy statue—estimates that there are at least 150 replicas scattered around the country in at least 32 states.

To promote the statue, artist Viquesney sent out scores of 12-inch miniature models to Commanders of American Legion Posts: "In the early days, the copper sheet statue was about $1000 FOB whereas cast versions would be in the $9000-11,000 range. Ground preparations, base, plaques, of course, would be additional" (Wesley). Clearly, Ernest Viquesney's *Doughboy* touched the American imagination at a mythic level, updating Mercury as a heroic Everyman.

The record of heroic memorialization can be summed up by the Tomb of the Unknown Soldier at the Arlington National Cemetery complemented by the many copies of doughboy statues across the nation—plus a few trend-setting films. (There are four doughboys in Oklahoma alone.) Perhaps there would have been a more pervasive interest in memorials if there had not been a competing vision of the war.

The Nightmare Vision: World War I As Meaningless Slaughter

The statistics from the Great War would give anyone nightmares: the Allies (France, England, and the United States) reported a total of 2.3

million battle deaths, while the Central Powers (Germany, Austria-Hungary) lost some 2.7 million. The machine gun, the tank, poison gas, the airplane, barbed wire, and the submarine thrust mechanized warfare into a horse-and-buggy era. The dimensions of the nightmare were registered as early as the Battle of the Somme in 1916, a six-month struggle which S. L. A. Marshall has described as "the most soulless battle in British annals. . . . It was a battle not so much of attrition as of mutual destruction" (258). A feature-length documentary called *The Battle of the Somme* was released in late summer of 1917. According to Paul Fussell, by this time the war had become "a hideous embarrassment to the prevailing Meliorist myth which had dominated the public consciousness for a century. It reversed the Idea of Progress" (8).

After the Versailles Treaty, a host of exposés convinced many Americans that their country had been seduced into the European conflict. As James Welsh explains, Director D. W. Griffith certainly attempted to produce a work of propaganda for the British in a film entitled *Hearts of the World* (1918) (chapter 2). Using all the tricks in his melodrama kit, and employing both of the beloved Gish girls, Griffith dramatized the evils of Hun occupation. Focusing on print media, George Creel described his role in *How We Advertised America* (1920). Creel, who had been America's chief propagandist, gleefully explained how he and his colleagues had sought to mobilize public support. African American audiences in the United States were not ignored during World War I. Thomas Winter has uncovered a film about the service of black troops in the U.S. Army, a film designed to promote enthusiasm for the war among a segregated minority (chapter 1). Larry Ward documents many other cinematic ploys by the Film Division of George Creel's Committee on Public Information (chapter 12).

Pondering the various forms of media persuasion, Walter Lippmann's *Public Opinion* (1922) voiced a sardonic evaluation of what he called "the myth of the omnicompetent citizen." Lippmann's reading of the war record led him to advise the nation to give up its traditional democratic model of government. America would be better served by a government of experts—professionals who were not susceptible to the wiles of propaganda. Within this context, Erich Maria Remarque's *All Quiet on the Western Front* (1928) crystallized an existing disillusionment. The protagonist, Paul Baumer, enters the struggle as an idealist, but months of shelling and death convince him that "We are little flames poorly sheltered by frail walls against the storm of dissolution and madness" (275). Some critics scrutinized Remarque's war record in an attempt to challenge the book's authenticity, but no one could deny that the German author had captured the mood of a "lost generation." Robert

Baird gives the antiwar thrust of the cinematic version of *All Quiet* close scrutiny (chapter 5). Stanley Kubrick added a cynical layer of Marxism to the criticism in his class-conflict exposé of the war, *Paths of Glory* (1957); this powerful film is evaluated by Andrew Kelly (chapter 8). A Vietnam-era sequel to Milestone's 1930s protest film is *Johnny Got His Gun* (1971), directed by Dalton Trumbo—who was also the author of the 1939 novel. Martin Norden shows that philosophical nihilism and cinematic pathos could go no further than this story of a mute torso kept alive in the name of clinical research (chapter 9).

Paul Fussell believes that the imagery of postwar writing came directly from the battlefront: "T. S. Eliot's 'Waste Land' with its rats' alleys, dull canals, and dead men who have lost their bones and the 'Valley of Ashes' in *The Great Gatsby* are only a few of the literary images which would spring to consciousness after the war to represent not just the war, but the post-war world" (23). Hemingway's protagonist, Frederic Henry, spoke for late 1920s Americans when he rejected wartime shibboleths in a famous passage from *A Farewell to Arms:* "I was always embarrassed by the words sacred, glorious, and sacrifice and the expression in vain . . . I had seen nothing sacred, and the things that were glorious had no glory and the sacrifices were like the stockyards in Chicago if nothing was done with the meat except to bury it" (184). Hemingway would turn this kind of alienation into a stoic code, a pose after which Americans—including a fictional detective named Sam Spade—would model themselves.

Lewis Milestone's screen adaptation of *All Quiet on the Western Front* (1930) shared the nightmare vision with mass audiences across the globe. During a famous battle segment, Paul Baumer finds himself trapped for the night in a muddy shell crater with a dead French soldier. As a result of this claustrophobic experience, Baumer—and presumably each audience member—comes to realize that the world's ordinary people are victims of bureaucracy, the nation state, industrialism, and "progress." The fact that *All Quiet* won awards for best picture and best director was a sign that the nightmare vision was (at least temporarily) *au courant* in Hollywood. In Germany, Nazis under Joseph Goebbels first disrupted screenings of the "American propaganda," and then found legislative methods to prevent distribution. By 1933, Remarque's anti-heroic books were being burned in Berlin—tragically, in the courtyard of the national library. Robert Baird's study analyzes some key scenes from Milestone's classic adaptation, providing an original insight into America's ambivalence toward both the war and the evolving wonders of motion pictures (chapter 5). War may have been hell, but *All Quiet* was a film not to be missed!

In volume two of his trilogy entitled *USA*, John Dos Passos addressed the meaning of World War I in terms of the burial ceremony for the Unknown Soldier. "The Body of an American" can serve as an example of the dark retrospection:

In the tarpaper morgue at Chalons-sur-Marne in the reek of chloride of lime and the dead, they picked out the pine box that held all that was left of
enie menie minie mo plenty other pine boxes stacked up there containing what they'd scraped up of Richard Roe
and other person or persons unknown. . . .
and Mr. Harding prayed to God and the diplomats and the generals and the admirals and the brasshats and the politicians and the handsomely dressed ladies out of the society column of the *Washington Post* stood up solemn
and thought how beautiful sad Old Glory God's Country it was to have the bugler play taps and the three volleys made their ears ring.
. . . Woodrow Wilson brought a bouquet of poppies. (462-67)

Dos Passos had been to the war. As he looked back from the vantage point of 1932, he saw—in the symbolic return of America's first Unknown Soldier—only pain and political manipulation. (Indeed, the depressing vision of Dos Passos seems to be more common among returning veterans than Americans realize; James I. Deutsch draws surprising parallels between the post-war experience of WWI vets and their later comrades [chapter 13].) How unlike the positive Secretary of State Newton Baker (quoted above) was Dos Passos in this chilling literary account of the ceremony at Arlington!

The Heroic Version Returns—in the Nick of Time

The cynical version of World War I was wheeled off the set as World War II approached. Back in New York, Louis de Rochemont's newsreel staff at *The March of Time* produced a feature-length docudrama entitled *The Ramparts We Watch* (1940). A plea for military preparedness, the film tried to establish parallels between World War I and the conflict threatening in 1939-1940. Fast-moving events in Poland and France reenforced lessons about unpreparedness. Hoping to win battles before they were fought, the Nazis distributed impressive documentaries about the successes of their *blitzkrieg*. As experts in the editing of newsreels, de Rochment's crew made full use of both World War I and Nazi footage to put the fear of God into the American audience. De Rochement's message was that Americans needed to stop watching from their protected ramparts, and should start building their own war machine so that they would not be caught off guard again—as they had been in 1914.

In 1941, Warner Bros. came forward with *Sergeant York*, a landmark picture for the new American mood. Alvin York was a Tennessee boy who killed 20 Germans at the Argonne forest in 1918 and captured another 132—a spectacular feat on any battlefield. For these exploits, the sergeant from Tennessee was awarded a host of medals including the Congressional Medal of Honor. Director Howard Hawks took this story about a man of natural virtue and exploited it to expose the flaws of isolationism. York's "conversion" scene (powerfully reenacted by Gary Cooper) was aimed directly at those who said we should remain out of the coming fray. (As late as July 1941, polls showed that this meant 70 percent of Americans.) Here was a spin on the war that flashed back to 1917 when President Woodrow Wilson spoke idealistically about "a war to end all wars."

Sometime near the premier of the film, the real Sergeant York—who joined FDR and Warner Bros. in endorsing the film's propagandist messages—called for aid to Britain. Concerned Citizen York explained that Americans must stand up for democracy; if they did not, "then we owe the memory of George Washington an apology, for if we have stopped, then he wasted his time at Valley Forge." In a speech to the Veterans of Foreign Wars, York noted that the last war had been fought to make the world safe for democracy "and it did—for a while." At such a moment, we can safely say that the memory of World War I had come full circle—back to the heroic version.

The films of transition deserve attention. Michael Birdwell shares his research into the production history and messages of the hagiographic film *Sergeant York* (chapter 7). Daniel Leab's reading of the political climate for *The Fighting 69th* further enhances our understanding of the forces swirling around key movies—forces that shape media images.

How Do We Remember the Great War Today?

The 1993 reunion of World War I vets, mentioned at the opening of this introduction, took place at Robert R. McCormick's Chicago estate, Cantigny. As a member of General Pershing's staff, McCormick was with the First Army Division during the Battle of Cantigny (Near Montdidier, France; May 28-29, 1918). The untested American unit lost 1000 soldiers in the attack, but took and held its objective in the face of counterattacks by some of Germany's most seasoned troops. The outcome was both a moral and a military victory for "the big parade" of American doughboys. The 1993 reunion on the McCormick estate provided the veterans touring the displays and reconstructed battlefield with a moment to remember their service to country.

Yet, just a month prior to the Chicago reunion, a world conference on *Film and the First World War* (held at the University of Amsterdam) revealed that scholars of many disciplines—history, English, communications, film, television, sociology—are just now "rediscovering" the war as a subject for interdisciplinary study. Most scholars agree that World War I marked the end of one vision of the world and the beginning of something new; but agreement seems to stop at that point. Was World War I a heroic crusade, or was it a traumatic nightmare? We are beginning to discern that it was both—and more.

Retrospective films for television such as the CBS series entitled *World War I* (1964-1965) were undertaken with dual interests in history and cinematic impact; Richard Bartone examines the tensions (chapter 11). Peter C. Rollins argues that productions for classroom audiences—such as *Goodbye Billy* and *The Frozen War*—have addressed some profound linguistic, cultural, and archetypal ripple effects from the war, aftershocks which continue into our own time (chapter 10). Larry Ward, as a participant in a compilation film project entitled *The Moving Picture Boys in the Great War* (1975), speculates on the competing demands of content and style in a mass medium driven to keep audiences glued to their screens (chapter 12). In a comprehensive filmography, Gerald Herman provides a broad overview of the total cinematic record (chapter 14).

Certainly more work needs to be done before we fully understand how a nation's stories are written with a cinematic pen. For the films of World War I, as for other historical periods, scholars need to consider the reigning interpretations of the past, the ideological pressures of the present, and the values filmmakers—consciously and unconsciously—share with their audiences. In fourteen essays, the contributors to *Hollywood's World War I* provide models of scholarship for exploring how motion pictures have inscribed their vision of the past.

Works Cited

Creel, George. *How We Advertised America.* New York: Harper, 1920.

Dibbets, Karel, and Bert Hogenkamp, eds. *Film and the First World War.* Amsterdam: Amsterdam UP, 1995.

Dos Passos, John. *1919.* New York: Scribner, 1932.

Fussell, Paul. *The Great War in Modern Memory.* New York: Oxford UP, 1975.

Hemingway, Ernest. *A Farewell to Arms.* New York: Scribner, 1929.

Lippmann, Walter. *Public Opinion.* New York: Macmillan, 1922.

Marshall, S. L. A. *World War I.* Boston: Houghton Mifflin, 1987.

Remarque, Erich Maria. *All Quiet on the Western Front*. Trans. A. W. Wheen. 1928. New York: Fawcett Crest, 1991.

Veteran Interviews at Cantigny Celebrations. Aug. 1993.

Veterans of World War I of the U.S.A. Various newsletters and ephemera supplied by this veterans group—help gratefully acknowledged.

Wesley, T. Perry. Personal interview. June 1993.

1

The Training of Colored Troops:
A Cinematic Effort to Promote National Cohesion

Thomas Winter

The years from the turn of the century to World War I represented a period of ambivalence, characterized by an upsurge of a reform spirit during the Progressive Era, and yet a simultaneous intensification of racism (Fredrickson 283-319). After the United States government entered the war in April of 1917, the pressure to find solutions in the name of national cohesion increased. Race and racial discrimination potentially affected the fighting effort and, therefore, played an important role in the United States government's attempt to promote national unity and cohesion (Schaffer 13-30, 75-90).

Practice, however, too often failed to follow theory, and racism was widespread in the United States armed forces. In Brownsville, Texas, in 1906 and in Houston in 1917, black soldiers resisted racial harassment and rigidly enforced Jim Crow laws. In both incidents, the military authorities placed the blame solely on the black troopers. In the Browns-ville case, the soldiers indicted were dishonorably discharged from the army. Twenty-nine of the soldiers involved in the so-called Houston Mutiny received death sentences, ten of which President Wilson commuted to imprisonment for life. Forty-two received life sentences, four shorter jail terms, and four were acquitted (Wynn 178; Shapiro 93-110).

Despite such treatment, African Americans contributed to the war effort, sensing an opportunity to tear down racial barriers at all levels of society. The prominent African American leader and author W. E. B. DuBois used his editorials in *The Crisis* to rally blacks to the cause. He urged African Americans "to seize the opportunity to emphasize their American citizenship because out of this war will rise, too, an American Negro with the right to live without insult" (Wynn 175). When in April 1917 the United States declared war on Germany 2,290,525 African Americans answered the call to arms. Of those, 367,410 actually served

13

in the armed forces, but only about 42,000 actually participated in combat operations. While the collapse of the all-black 368th regiment during the Argonne offensive received much publicity at the time, these men proved to be capable, determined soldiers (Franklin and Moss 294, 301-02; Nalty 107, 112).

However, the news media largely ignored the successes of black soldiers. In newsreels and alleged films of record dealing with African Americans in the United States armed forces during World War I, demeaning stereotypes abounded (Leab 48-49; Cripps 8). African American newspapers, such as *The New York Age*, owned by T. Thomas Fortune and the conservative African American spokesman Booker T. Washington, led in the protest against the stereotypical, racist depiction of blacks on screen (Sampson 1). Lester Walton, a writer for *The New York Age*, described a "typical" scene from a Hearst-Pathé newsreel (Leab 48). On August 24, 1918, Walton wrote that "after showing white Americans in the trenches at their best," the newsreel "portrayed a colored soldier, a most dumb specimen of humanity, sitting with book in hand trying to learn French." The newsreel gave a rather unflattering portrayal of the black soldier who "was scratching his head and gazing into the book in a bewildered fashion." Disappointed with the efforts to portray African Americans and their contributions to the war effort on film, Walton added that "nothing could be worse for America at this time than to pursue a policy of belittling the Negro." He appealed to the government to help correct the course taken by private newsreel companies, which perpetuated derogatory stereotypes of the nation's black citizens. Walton wrote: "I respectfully refer this matter to Mr. George Creel, head of the Committee of Public Information, Washington, D.C., with the request that it be regarded as important and worthy of immediate consideration" ("Colored Soldier" 6).

Committee on Public Information, Film, and Wartime Propaganda

The Committee on Public Information played a key role in the United States government's first significant attempt to use film to promote national unity in a time of war (Campbell 25; Ward 53, 59). President Woodrow Wilson had created the Committee on Public Information (CPI) through Executive Order 2594 on April 13, 1917, to promote participation in the war as a defense of American democratic ideals. Filmmaking became one of the CPI's primary means of informing the public and galvanizing opinion. However, the CPI had to fulfill its role as a filmmaking agency under haphazard conditions. Receiving its raw material from the Army Signal Corps, the CPI had little influence on what kind of film the Signal Corps camera men would provide. On September 25, 1917, President Wilson issued Executive Order 2708, creating a Division of Films to better coordinate the cinematic efforts of the CPI and to combine Army Signal Corps footage into coherent movies. During the final six months of the war, the Division of Films used this material to produce a series of feature-length films and shorter documentaries. On June 1, 1918, the Division of Films added a Scenario Department, to further facilitate the effort. Frequently cooperating with private producers to guarantee wide distribution and to cut costs, the Scenario Department planned a series of one-reel pictures (Creel Report 56; Ward 45-46, 76-90, 101, 110).

The Training of Colored Troops:
Government Filmmaking and Racial Attitudes

One of those films was *The Training of Colored Troops* (1918).[1] Meant to win African American support for the war effort, *Training* reflected the intention of the filmmakers to make military service appealing to blacks, while it also reflected white prejudices about African Americans, prominently among them anxieties about blacks receiving training in the use of arms. In comparison with the typical presentation of African Americans in newsreels and feature films in a time of widespread racism and xenophobia, *Training* represented an attempt to treat blacks with some more dignity. However, the film did not overcome previously existing traditions of racism and frequently perpetuates them. In this ambivalence, the film fits into a succession of films reaching from early efforts involving black soldiers during the Spanish-American War to World War II productions such as *The Negro Soldier* (1944) and *The Negro Sailor* (1945).

Training is very likely identical with the film *Our Colored Fighters*. Available information on the distribution, profits from sales and rental, and possible exhibition sites of *Fighters* allows us to draw some tentative conclusions about how widely *Training* was distributed and seen.[2] *Fighters* was distributed by a private African American distributor, the Downing Film Company to target black audiences. Judging by the sales and rental profits, which amounted to $640, the film was not immensely popular. However, the Division of Films charged cinemas and distributors according to a sliding scale. Small distributors and cinemas were charged less than their larger competitors (Mock, Larson 137-38). In November of 1918, Henry F. Downing, director of the Downing Film Company that distributed *Fighters*, announced that due to the great demand from African American churches and social organizations, additional copies of the film had to be made (*The Motion Picture World* 750).

Thus, the film was possibly shown quite widely in smaller theaters of about 150 seats, catering mostly to African American audiences. In some cases, a film such as *Training*, may have been shown in larger theaters holding up to 2,000 seats and catering to both black and white audiences in a segregated setting (Sampson 18-24).

Produced under the auspices of the Division of Films of the Committee on Public Information, *Training* follows the military career of Edward Johnson from Louisville, Kentucky. The film begins with Johnson going off to boot camp. After basic training, he goes with the Engineering Corps to France, sending a letter back home to his family, describing his experience. However, no reference is made to Johnson other than in the opening and closing scenes. Except for the staged material at the beginning and the end, focusing on Johnson and his family, the film consists of actuality footage showing black recruits at boot camp. Depictions of the registration process at the camp are followed by scenes of soldiers going in and out of the barracks, and repeated depictions of drill exercises. While the film was meant to appeal to African Americans, they are depicted throughout in stereotypical ways.

Filmmaking and Racial Stereotypes in American Culture

Cinematic stereotypes about African Americans had been a staple of filmmakers before World War I. The most notorious example was D. W. Griffith's *The Birth of a Nation* (1914). This film, "an impressive peace of film propaganda," in Donald Bogle's words (12), featured blacks as brutal, oversexed creatures ready to wreak havoc. Several feature films dealt with the alleged consequences of mixing of the races. This was the theme of films such as *The Nigger* (1916), in which a southern governor found out that he has African American blood in his veins. This realization prompts him to resign from his office and to leave the woman he loves (Klotman 378). The same theme is found in *The Bride of Hate* (1917) in which a southern doctor seeks revenge on an enemy by encouraging marriage between him and a light-skinned African American woman. Once the doctor's enemy realized his bride's racial origins, he begins to drink and eventually dies (Klotman 77). These films reflected the racism in the years before and during World War I, fed by a strong undercurrent of cultural pessimism that found its expression in pseudoscientific tracts, such as Madison Grant's best-selling *The Passing of the Great Race* (Gossett 339-69).

Race and Wartime Film to World War I

Films relating to war and military service represented in some ways an exception to the pattern. In 1898, during the Spanish-American

War, cinema audiences witnessed armed black soldiers arriving on Cuba in the film *Colored Troops Disembarking*. In *The Ninth Negro Cavalry Watering Horses*, American viewers "saw crisp armed black men outside their prescribed 'place.'" The film showed "black troopers in smart order pass before a fixed camera shooting at a cloudless sky broken by a single tall pine." Films such as *The Battle of Mt. Ariat* showed the all-black Twenty-fifth Infantry, and the *Colored Invincibles* depicted African American soldiers "fighting with 'as much zeal as their white brothers'" (Cripps 12). In the 1917 production, *Jim Bludso*, the main character, a white man, and a black man form a bond by mutually saving each others lives during the Civil War. In addition, the black man saves the hero's faithless wife from drowning. In the end, the African American man becomes part of Bludso's family. While *Jim Bludso* seemed to give a more positive and courageous portrayal of blacks, it also reiterates paternalistic stereotypes as the faithful African American becomes part of Bludso's household, entering into his patriarchal care (Campbell 75).

For the sake of wartime cohesion, even Griffith somewhat revised his earlier, outright racist depictions of African Americans. In *The Greatest Thing in Life* (1918) the experience of war changed a southerner, who shared a foxhole with an African American soldier and receives water from the African American's canteen. Eventually, the white hero comforts the black soldier in his final hour with an "extended kiss on the lips" when he calls out "Mammy-good-bye-Mammy—kiss me!" In Griffith's film, the experience and dangers of war redeem the hero, who gained a broader sense of humanity (Campbell 75, 106-07; Klotman 213). While films such as *Jim Bludso* or *The Greatest Thing in Life* seemed to treat African Americans with more dignity, if compared to Griffith's own *Birth of a Nation*, they often reinforced a notion of white paternalism in race relations.

African American Filmmakers and Military Propaganda

Films produced by African American filmmakers and companies represented an exception to a pattern of excluding and ignoring contributions by African Americans in battle. In the 1916 Lincoln Motion Picture Company production, *Trooper of Company K*, the main character, "Shiftless" Joe, is transformed through his experience with the 10th Cavalry in the battle of Carrizal in June of 1916. Joe distinguishes himself in battle and rescues his wounded captain in the face of enemy fire. Upon return, his sweetheart, who read about Joe's exploits in the paper, welcomes him with open arms. Although the plot was somewhat contrived, it was well received by black reviewers and the audience (Leab 326-27; Klotman

544-45; Sampson 92-93). Another exception was *The Heroic Black Soldiers of the War*. A World War I documentary, consisting of U.S. War Department footage filmed in France, it was first shown by the black-owned Frederick Douglass Company at the Douglass Theatre in New York City, but it seems that no copy has survived (Sampson 71). On occasion, African American–made movies would take a comical bent on the war and wartime hysteria. In the 1918 Ebony Film Corporation production, *Spying the Spy*, the main character, Sambo Sam, dreams of becoming a hero by catching German spies. Sam's efforts are soon crowned with dubious success, when he "captures" Herman Schwartz, who turns out to be a "'respectable colored gentleman'" ("schwarz," spelled without a *t* is German for "black"). To reward Sam for his efforts, black lodge members, dressed in black-hooded robes, scare him out of town by threatening to behead the poor soul (Sampson 94-95).

Government Films and the Portrayal of Race Relations

Government films about African Americans in the nation's war effort painted a more ambiguous picture. In the 1917 production *The Slacker* representatives of every race were shown, their faces grouped together and merging into a composite that becomes an American flag (Campbell 75). *How Uncle Sam Prepares*, released in April of 1917, showed immigrants and African Americans joining other Americans enlisting in the armed forces. Later, the film had shots of a regiment of black soldiers. As in World War II, when feature films or government documentaries promoted cooperation across boundaries of race, they did so in the name of national unity, and not to promote desegregation or equal rights (Campbell 54, 231).

Other wartime propaganda films continued to reinforce stereotypes. In the 1918 CPI-sponsored production, *America's Answer*, one scene showed four black soldiers dancing in uniform. The scene is preceded by the title, "music moves the feet in France as in our sunny South." *America's Answer*, which made $185,144.30, was among the more popular films made by the government during the war (Isenberg 73-74).

Where films transgressed boundaries of race, problems would occur. One of the longer films produced under the auspices of the CPI, the seven-reel film *Pershing's Crusaders,* broke records. By September of 1918, the movies had been booked by 3,749 cinemas. However, due to the inclusion of black troops, the film did not do very well in the southern states (Campbell 78-79, 235). In its initial form, *The Lost Battalion* (1919) went even further in its attempt to give a more inclusive, though unrealistic, depiction of black soldiers in the armed forces. The movie features a story of American troops under siege by the Germans.

The American battalion, miraculously integrated, included blacks. As Craig Campbell has pointed out, the African American soldiers shown in *The Lost Battalion* "were lost on the cutting room floor soon after the initial release" (75, 129). Government filmmakers, then, felt the need to accommodate prevailing ideas about issues of race and racial equality.

The Training of Colored Troops

While *Training* avoids the worst excesses of racial stereotyping, it nonetheless reflects widely held prejudices about blacks. To deflect anxieties about African American soldiers trained in the use of arms, the film attempts to demonstrate the harmlessness of African Americans as soldiers through racist imagery. Two scenes convey the image that even under the disciplined order of boot camp, blacks retain stereotypical behavior patterns. In the first of these scenes, several black soldiers are shown eating watermelons. Eventually, the camera focuses on one of them, who starts smiling while biting large chunks out of his slice. Although the soldier in all likelihood acted out of his free will, the result on screen is reminiscent of the demeaning depiction of blacks in the 1899 film *Watermelon Contest*, in which "four grinning Negroes wolfed melons and spat seeds with a will" (Cripps 12). A second scene shows a group of soldiers sitting together and making music. A black man enters the scene and starts dancing while looking into the camera. The result reminds viewers of the stereotypical depiction of African Americans as inherently rhythmic, a virtual staple in films at that time and later (Cripps 22). The scenes may not have been staged, but the selection of the material and the way the scenes were edited played to white stereotypes.

As Daniel Leab points out, the white-owned movie industry refused to handle films that did not conform to stereotypes. Even most cinemas that catered to black crowds were owned by whites, who believed that their black audiences enjoyed burlesque depiction of their own (328). *Training* tried to appeal to its black audiences through the use of stereotypes. One scene shows a friendly boxing match between two black recruits, a reference to the popularity of the African American boxer Jack Johnson. The filmmakers most likely inserted the boxing, dancing, and watermelon scenes with the belief that these pictures would make army life look more appealing to potential black recruits. Of course, the rationale that blacks found such stereotypes appealing and would accept them as accurate representation of their own was self-serving. Believing not only that blacks conformed to certain stereotypes but accepted them as accurate portrayal helped whites to affirm their own beliefs as to the innate inferiority of blacks (Toll 202).

The overall message of *Training* is clear: African Americans, even if trained for soldierly duties, would remain harmless, content denizens at the lower rungs of America's social ladder. Once removed from the direct surveillance of their Caucasian superiors, the film suggests, African Americans will backslide into predictable behavior patterns. It most likely comforted the makers of *Training* that black recruits could be nurtured into becoming disciplined soldiers, but once relieved from guidance and supervision, the same recruits would relapse into childish, harmless behavior patterns.

The attempt to appeal to African American audiences through the stereotypical depiction of members of that same group resulted in ambiguous, contradictory images. For example, *Training* focuses exclusively on soldier's activities in the training camp, but avoids showing African Americans in battle. It is not that overseas or combat footage (albeit often staged) was unavailable. In the same year the one-reeler *Our Hell Fighters*, depicting the all-black 369th Regiment and its contribution to the war effort, was released (Klotman 399). Indeed, a good amount of combat footage existed and was later included in the 1986 production, *Men of Bronze* (1986), a documentary on the history the 369th Regiment. The availability of combat and battle footage, showing black soldiers in arms at the front, suggests that the selection of boot camp footage was not dictated by the scarcity of other material, but reflected the deliberate choice of the filmmakers.

The depiction of African Americans, primarily unarmed and in noncombat functions, may have served several purposes. The filmmakers, who most likely shared prevailing stereotypes about blacks as cowardly, may have felt that showing African Americans footage of battle actions would have scared them away from the enlistment bureaus. But the depiction of noncombat activities and pointing out that Edward Johnson went to France with the Engineering Corps—probably as part of a labor battalion—may have also played a propagandistic function. By June of 1918, rumors had spread according to which black troops were being used as cannon fodder (Schaffer 79). Depicting blacks in noncombat function, then, did not simply reflect white prejudices but also served as an appeal to black audiences, giving proof of the unfoundedness of such hearsay.

In the process, however, *Training* also manages to gloss over serious problems and conditions existing in many of these boot camps for African American soldiers. Camp life, as depicted in *Training*, does not fully represent reality: while in boot camp, African American soldiers were housed in inferior facilities and received virtually no medical attention. In many camps, the accommodation for black troops consisted of tents without floors and stoves. In the winter of 1917-1918, men froze to death in those tents (Foner 119). Focusing exclusively on the portrayal of camp life, then, not only enabled the filmmakers to deflect rumors about the use of African American soldiers as cannon fodder, but also to preempt possible rumors about the conditions in boot camp.

Training made every attempt to appeal to African Americans to support a war that had been proclaimed as a crusade "to make the world safe for democracy" and join the army. The final scene of the film shows how the Johnson family received their son's letter from France. The letter is read out by a family member with several others standing by, gesturing enthusiastically. The excited, enthusiastic body language, however, also reminds viewers of the comical conduct of the happy and content plantation slaves in such films as *Birth of a Nation*.

In the final scene, the film gets its message across by connecting African American support for the United States involvement in World War I to past wars and the role blacks took in them. After hearing about the young man's exploits, one of the bystanders, an older black man, goes back into the house and gets his sword out of the closet. His age and the sword suggest that he has probably served as a noncommissioned officer in the Civil War. He goes to the backyard and frantically sharpens the sword over a grindstone with the help of a black woman. The couple remind the viewer of the Old Uncle and Auntie image that dominated post–Civil War imagery of African American life on the plantation (Toll 208). Once finished sharpening the sword, he swings it in the air fighting imaginary enemies. Apparently he, too, feels ready to go into battle.

The meanings of the scene may have been ambiguous, depending on the viewing audience. White audiences may have found the old man's childish, burlesque, Uncle Remus-like behavior reassuring that blacks in the armed forces did not represent a threat. Black audiences certainly did not fail to pick up on the racist, demeaning depiction of the man. However, they may have nonetheless appreciated other meanings conveyed in that same scene. White Americans believed that African Americans were cowardly by nature and inept as soldiers (Wynn 179). Therefore, seeing a black man ready and eager to engage an enemy, instead of being scared by the mere thought, was a rare sight in the films of the time. Second, the sword, indicating past service in the nation's wars, served as a reminder that since colonial times African Americans had helped to fight and win America's wars, a fact unacknowledged by the dominant culture of the time. While the old man's behavior appears as stereotypically childish, it nevertheless also served as an appeal to African Americans to serve their country as they have done in the past. The filmmakers tried to link World War I, sold to the public as a crusade for democracy, back to the Civil War, which freed blacks from the yoke of slavery. As the film implicitly linked both wars to a common motive of freedom, it at the same time suggested that African Americans had as much a part and stake in this war as in the Civil War.

Conclusion

How successful and persuasive the film was in the African American community is impossible to determine. Lester Walton never even mentioned it in his film and entertainment column in the *New York Age*. Instead, Walton continued to accuse the film industry of neglecting the accomplishments and contributions of African Americans to the war effort ("French War Pictures" 6, "Colored Heroes" 6). Other black newspapers, such as the *Cleveland Gazette*, the *Chicago Defender*, or the *Washington Bee* never mentioned the film in their pages—either under the title *Training of Colored Troops* or as *Our Colored Fighters*.

Training, then, had at best a mixed impact on racial ideologies and race relations. Though *Training* never questioned Jim Crow practices in the armed forces and ignored the daily racism blacks had to face in civilian life, the film did represent an attempt to treat African Americans with more respect than many movies previously had done.

This does not mean that the film had no legacy. *Training* can be regarded as a distant predecessor of the 1944 production *The Negro Soldier* and the 1945 film *The Negro Sailor*. There are both similarities and differences between *Soldier*, or *Sailor*, and *Training*, partially owing to the development of filmmaking technology. Whereas *Training* simply appeals to African American men to serve in the army by invoking themes of family, community, and freedom, *Soldier* and *Sailor* actually portrayed blacks as a part of American society. However, like *Training*, *Soldier* and *Sailor* also included appeals to blacks' race pride by reflecting on their contribution to earlier American wars (Cripps, Culbert 115, 119; Callahan).

Not until such films as *Soldier* and *Sailor*, then, would American government films portray the complexity of the African American experience of war, which included two battlefronts. *Training of Colored Troops* would remain for the time being only a first, reluctant effort to grapple with the complexity of the issues involved. Only when the stakes were higher, would the cinematic image change and filmmakers become more receptive to the notion of racial harmony, if not yet equality. *Training of Colored Troops* can be seen as an indicator of white filmmakers' ambivalence about the contribution of African Americans to a nation at war and the possible consequences of the experience.

Notes

1. A copy of the film is located at the National Archives and Records Administration, Motion Pictures, Sound, and Video Branch, Rm. 3340, 8601 Adelphi Road, College Park, MD 20740, from which copies can be purchased.

2. A government report, which mentions *Fighters*, nowhere refers to *Training*. Furthermore, *Training* contains some staged, fictional footage, which makes the film likely to be a production of the Division of Films of the Committee on Public Information. *Fighters*, like *Training*, emphasized the role of African American soldiers as laborers in the American Expeditionary Force (Klotman 398). In addition, all of the CPI's short films were newsreel style documentaries with actors added to raise interest. The similarities suggest that *Training* and *Fighters* are one and the same film. The difference in titles is most likely due to the fact that the Signal Corps reedited most of its films in 1936 (Ward 103). Because of these difficulties, *Training* has received virtually no attention from historians. It is only briefly mentioned by Neil A. Wynn (188, 194-95 n. 57).

Works Cited

Barbeau, Arthur E., and Florette Henri. *The Unknown Soldiers: Black American Troops in World War I*. Philadelphia: Temple UP, 1974.

Barsam, Richard Meran. *Non-Fiction Film: A Critical History*. Rev. ed. Bloomington: Indiana UP, 1992.

Bogle, Donald. *Toms, Coons, Mulattoes, Mammies, and Bucks: An Interpretive History of Blacks in American Films*. New York: Viking, 1973.

Callahan, Patrick. *"The Negro Sailor."* Unpublished essay, 1993.

Campbell, Craig W. *Reel America and World War I: A Comprehensive Filmography and History of Motion Pictures in the United States, 1914-1920*. Jefferson, NC: McFarland, 1985.

Creel, George. *How We Advertised America*. New York: Arno, 1972.

Cripps, Thomas. *Slow Fade to Black: The Negro in American Film, 1900-1942*. New York: Oxford UP, 1977.

———, and David Culbert. *"The Negro Soldier* (1944): Film Propaganda in Black and White."* *Hollywood As a Historian: Film in a Cultural Context*. Ed. Peter Rollins. Lexington: U of Kentucky P, 1983. 109-33.

Fielding, Raymond. *The American Newsreel, 1911-1967*. Norman: Oklahoma UP, 1972.

Foner, Jack D. *Blacks and the Military in American History: A New Perspective*. New York: Praeger, 1974.

Franklin, John Hope, and Alfred A. Moss, Jr. *From Slavery to Freedom: A History of Negro Americans.* New York: Knopf, 1995.

Fredrickson, George M. *The Black Image* in the *White Mind: The Debate on Afro-American Character and Destiny, 1817-1914.* New York: Harper, 1971.

Gossett, Thomas F. *Race: The History of an Idea in America.* Dallas: Southern Methodist UP, 1963.

Isenberg, Michael. *War on Film: The American Cinema and World War I, 1914-1941.* Rutherford: Fairleigh Dickinson UP, 1981.

Klotman, Phyllis Rauch. *Frame by Frame: A Black Filmography.* Bloomington: Indiana UP, 1979.

Leab, Daniel L. "'All Colored'—But Not Much Different: Films Made for Negro Ghetto Audiences, 1913-1928." *Pylon* 39.2 (1975): 321-39.

——. *From Sambo to Superspade: The Black Experience in Motion Pictures.* Boston: Houghton Mifflin, 1975.

Men of Bronze: The Black American Heroes of World War I. Pacific Arts Video, 1986.

Mock, James R., and Cedric Larson. *Words That Won the War: The Story of the Committee on Public Information, 1917-1919.* Princeton: Princeton UP, 1939.

Nalty, Bernard C. *Strength for the Fight: A History of Black Americans in the Military.* New York: Free Press, 1986.

O'Connor, John E., and Martin A. Jackson, eds. *American History/American Film: Interpreting The Hollywood Image.* New York: Continuum/Ungar, 1988.

"'Our Colored Fighters' in Demand." *The Motion Picture World* 16 Nov. 1918: 750.

Rollins, Peter, ed., *Hollywood As Historian: American Film in a Cultural Context.* Lexington: U of Kentucky P, 1983.

Sampson, Henry T. *Blacks in Black and White: A Source Book on Black Films.* Metuchen: Scarecrow, 1977.

Schaffer, Ronald. 1991. *America in the Great War: The Rise of the War Welfare State.* New York: Oxford UP, 1991.

Shapiro, Herbert. *White Violence and Black Response: From Reconstruction to Montgomery.* Amherst: U of Massachusetts P, 1988.

Toll, Robert C. *Blacking Up: The Minstrel Show in Nineteenth-Century America.* New York: Oxford UP, 1974.

United States Committee on Public Information. *The Creel Report: Complete Report of the Chairman on Public Information, 1917:1918:1919.* New York: Da Capo, 1972.

Walton, Lester A, "The Colored Soldier on the Screen." *New York Age* 24 Aug. 1918: 6.

——. "French War Pictures." *New York Age* 19 Oct. 1918: 6.

——. "Our Colored Heroes in the Movies." *New York Age* 30 Nov. 1918: 6.

Ward, Larry Wayne. *The Motion Picture Goes to War: The U.S. Government Film Effort During World War I.* Ann Arbor: UMI Research, 1985.

Wynn, Neil. *From Progressivism to Prosperity: World War I and American Society.* New York: Holmes & Meier, 1986.

2

The Great War and the War Film as Genre: *Hearts of the World* and *What Price Glory?*

James M. Welsh

As those familiar with film history will understand, basic proto-types of the major American genre films had already been established before 1920. For example, the first American masterpiece of feature filmmaking, *The Birth of a Nation* (1915) was, after all, a war film that traced the fortunes of its characters from before the Civil War through the war to its aftermath. Moreover, the first feature-length gangster film, *Regeneration,* based on an autobiographical novel by Owen Kildare and directed by Raoul Walsh, was also released in 1915, and the western had established stars such as Tom Mix, William S. Hart, and Bronco Billy Anderson by 1920. The formulas governing such films would be further embellished during the 1920s, but the basic pattern for the war film had already been established before 1920 by D. W. Griffith with *The Birth of a Nation* and *Hearts of the World* (1918).

Even so, it is difficult to define the war film as a genre. Is the war film a genre that celebrates national honor and victory through specta-cles of heroic action, and if so, should the war film in America include stories of the Revolutionary War, the War of 1812, the Civil War, and the Spanish-American War, or would such films be better described as his-torical epics? In the twentieth century does the category encompass the Great War, World War II, the Korean conflict, and the holding action in Vietnam as well, even though the messages of such films vary substan-tially? Are war films primarily combat films, or should the genre also include homecoming stories and problems of readjustment? Is William Wyler's *The Best Years of Our Lives* (1946) something other than a war film, for example, or Oliver Stone's *Born on the Fourth of July* (1989), or Michael Cimino's *The Deer Hunter* (1978), for that matter? Is Stanley Kubrick's *Paths of Glory* (1957), which has a great deal to say about stress under combat and military justice in World War I a war film or an antiwar film? Should such films be classified under a separate category?

27

Is the war film a fully developed genre, after all, or merely a catch-all category for disparate kinds of war stories, each governed by its own rules and expectations?

For the purpose of this discussion, the war film will be defined restricted to the warfare of the twentieth century, focused upon selected silent films, starting with D. W. Griffith's *Hearts of the World* (1918), a film that went into production before the Armistice. In other genre films such as the western, creative credit is usually ascribed to directors such as John Ford and Howard Hawks, who appropriated the basic elements of the genre, involving stereotyped characters and repeatable situations, from an already developing body of pulp fiction. In the early war films, however, much of the shaping credit goes to a writer, Laurence Stallings, who adapted his play *What Price Glory?* (1924) to the screen and also wrote the scenario for King Vidor's *The Big Parade* (1925). Stallings had served in the war, and like the John Gilbert character in *The Big Parade*, lost a leg in France. The first and most popular World War I films were shaped by his direct experience. The early war films were influenced by the specific war that had dominated the headlines of the times, just as, a bit later, the gangster film would be shaped by the public's fascination with legendary gangster types during the Great Depression. The early films of the genre told stories of unquestioning sacrifice, serving the popular myth of "the war to end all wars." Later films widened the context and offered new formulas (such as the "great escape" plot, for example, and the homecoming motif) in a far more sophisticated political and sociological setting.

The war film did not build upon a cohesive mythic structure already formulated, as was the case with the western, which incorporated popular myths and legends developed by pulp fiction writers of earlier decades. The western was informed in particular by the myth of the frontier as articulated by Frederick Jackson Turner in his thesis concerning the disappearance of the frontier, and its importance in the development of the American national character, involving a belief in progress, westward expansion that displaced and generally destroyed Native American cultures, and the presumed building of the national character by pioneers forced to meet the challenge of taming the wilderness. The classic western involved larger-than-life heroes whose resourcefulness triumphed, in comparison to the soldier heroes of the combat films who were more ordinary men capable of courageous heroic action. The western myth was later to be questioned by revisionist attitudes that came to regard the Indian wars as genocide, but—by the time the climate of opinion had changed—the western had already developed well beyond its classic statements into more complicated, baroque modifications that resulted in psychological and political westerns such as *High Noon* (1952) and *The*

Searchers (1956), rendering action and characterization more realistically and paying the price of turning erstwhile heroes into antiheroes, blurring earlier simplistic notions of good and evil.

The myth of the West was open to revisionist treatments in a way that World War I and World War II were not. The war film was stuck throughout the 1920s in its primitive stages, then stuck again in its classic statements during the World War II that were made for the most part to serve or justify wartime propaganda and patriotic values. This impeded development continued through the Korean conflict and the 1950s, with a few notable exceptions, such as Stanley Kubrick's *Paths of Glory*, until the films of the Vietnam era, which involved more ambiguous values politically and morally and therefore allowed revisionist approaches that would question the purpose of the war. As a developing genre, the war film did not hit its stride until the 1970s, when filmmakers began to find new mythic patterns that would energize and transform a tired genre, filmmakers such as Francis Ford Coppola, Michael Cimino, and Oliver Stone, addressing more ambiguous issues.

Until that point, psychological realism was underdeveloped, though battle "realism" became well advanced to provide spectacles of combat —in *The Big Parade* (1925) on the ground, for example, and in *Wings* (1927) in the air—that were considered convincing to contemporary audiences, and for some viewers, are still powerful. The shape of the story, involving basic training and the turning of men into warriors, male bonding, trial by combat leading to loss and suffering, and the homecoming evolved in the service of ideology celebrating national honor and victory. The pattern established during the 1920s in *The Big Parade* was still operating effectively in *Thirty Seconds over Tokyo* in 1944. In Vietnam, however, there was no victory to be celebrated and national honor was clouded by the ambiguity of the American involvement in what many came to regard as a civil war in a third-world country and a further advance of imperialism in the name of democracy. Since the Vietnam war lacked a unified and mutually agreeable sense of purpose, filmmakers were forced to innovate and mythicize in order to find a purpose that would somehow make sense of the suffering.

Hearts of the World

In approaching his film *Hearts of the World* (1918) while the Great War was still in progress, D. W. Griffith (1875-1948) had little reason to question his purpose or the rationale for the war. Griffith had seen a bit of the war firsthand in May of 1917 and was invited to make a propaganda film by Lord Beaverbrook, chairman of the War Office Cinematograph Committee, but the film that resulted wraps the propaganda around a typically melodramatic Griffith story. As a celebration of American innocence, particularly in terms of old-fashioned values and domestic virtue, *Hearts of the World*—made just as the war was in its concluding stages—certainly is resonant with the director's personal style but also tinged with anti-German hysteria. Ultimately, in consideration of timing and taste, the film's propaganda was toned down before its final release by deleting a great deal of heavy-handed anti-Hun material. Robert M. Henderson reports that the film was reduced from twelve reels to eight, partly to reflect the changing world situation after the Armistice but also partly for artistic reasons (187). The extant version is still obviously anti-German and reduces a complex political conflict to a morality play of Manichean absolutes. This is the film's most serious flaw.

The print of *Hearts of the World* circulated by the Killiam Collection in America runs to just two minutes over two hours. In this version the action is broken down into three major movements: 1) the village in peacetime; 2) war and the German occupation; and 3) liberation and the restoration of order and civilized values. Fully one-third of the film (subtitled "The Story of a Village") is devoted to the first movement, as Griffith takes his time to establish the nature and character of this particular, anonymous French village. In fact, the first portion of *Hearts of the World* could easily stand on its own as a self-contained vignette telling the story of young love and courtship as it develops between "The Boy" (Robert Harron) and "The Girl" (Lillian Gish), both of whom are transplanted Americans living on the "Rue de la Paix" in this peaceful, idyllic French village. When war threatens the village, the boy joins the French army.

Apart from the fanciful melodramatic story the film contains elements of verisimilitude. It starts, for example, with a prologue that shows Griffith himself at No. 10 Downing Street, shaking hands with British Prime Minister Lloyd George; it then shows Griffith "in the British front line trench at Cambrin, fifty yards away from the enemy's lines." Such *tableaux vivants* as one finds in this film have an eerie authenticity, as when, Lloyd George, Winston Churchill, Asquith, and Gray are seen waiting dramatically in London, on the brink of the war. Such apparent documentary footage has an authentic "feel" that will remind viewers of the chronological closeness of the artifact to the event.

But ultimately Griffith is not dealing with world leaders. The film shows how the war affects ordinary people, suggesting in broad dramatic strokes how it indiscriminately destroys villages and villagers. In telling this story of death and destruction, Griffith is at his most powerful. As

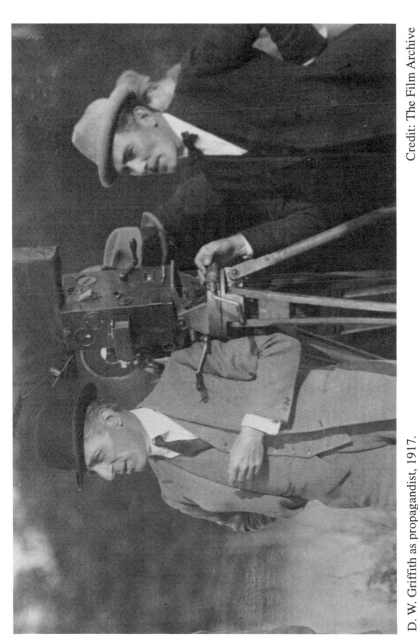

D. W. Griffith as propagandist, 1917.

Credit: The Film Archive

the war comes to the village, the girl, having witnessed the death of her mother, goes into a state of shock. She wanders off, unhinged, into the blue-tinted night. Approaching the battle zone, she discovers the wounded body of the boy and spends the night with him, locked in a pathetic embrace with her unconscious lover who has fallen "under the risen moon" and appears to be dead (though he will later recover). After several hours the wounded soldier is found by the Red Cross and taken away for medical treatment. Still in a state of somnambulant shock, the girl returns to the village, not totally aware of where she has been or what she has experienced. She is eventually nursed back to sanity by her friend, known only as the "Little Disturber" (Dorothy Gish).

Thereafter, as Richard Schickel observes, "the film begins to deteriorate to melodrama of a creaky and unpersuasive sort" (356), as the Germans turn the villagers into slave laborers, the boy's mother dies of exhaustion, and the girl gets brutally beaten by a German sergeant. Nursed back to health by the Red Cross, the boy volunteers for duty behind enemy lines, disguised as a German officer. He makes his way back to the village and finds the girl, but they are discovered by the sergeant who had beaten her and who attacks the boy. As they struggle, the girl stabs the sergeant. At the last minute they are rescued by the advancing French army.

Even though the story becomes melodramtically overheated, it is told effectively and with some intelligent restraint, apart from the way the Germans are portrayed. In Griffith's world the family is sacred, yet here it is threatened by a war that claims its casualties, one by one. The survivors respond heroically, attempting to hold the social unit together. When the boy's mother dies, for example, his younger brothers—mere children—bury her, performing this sacred rite themselves. The acting is generally understated, and all the more touching for that. Beyond the rather ponderous opening, subtitles are used minimally and efficiently.

In this film Griffith claimed to be working toward two ends, one moral, the other artistic. (A third, unstated, end was obviously patriotic and propagandistic.) *Hearts of the World* begins with a statement concerning the destruction and futility of war: "God help the nation that begins another war of conquest or meddling! Brass bands and clanging sabers make very fine music, but let us remember there is another side of war. After all, does war ever settle any questions? The South was ruined—thousands of lives were sacrificed by the Civil War; yet did it really settle the Black and White problem in this country?"

After editorializing in this way, Griffith goes on quickly to establish the immediate setting for his action: "Peaceful days in the year of 1912. The Village at the time of spring, where people love and hate, cry and laugh, sin and are forgiven—even as you and I." The director's moral point is made more eloquently, however, later in the film through the images, when slain and wounded soldiers are seen on the field of battle, intercut with the simple and ironic subtitle "War's peace," a subtitle Griffith had earlier used in *The Birth of a Nation*. *Hearts of the World* can in fact be regarded as an updated remake of the earlier Civil War film, which it resembles in its plot and structure; as William K. Everson maintains, it displays "the same family structure, the same separations and reunions [and] the same editing patterns" (98).

Ultimately, the brutality and inhumanity of the war is presented more as background than foreground in this film. The war provides a continuing source of menace and destruction that efficiently complicates the plot and sustains tension; it separates and endangers the young lovers, whose potential for happiness is linked to the liberation of the village and the restoration of peace and harmony. As with *Intolerance* (1916), both the thematic and melodramatic issues are effectively resolved by the last-minute rescues at the end, when first Bobby Harron saves Lillian Gish from the lecherous designs of the German officer Von Strohm (George Siegmann), then, soon afterward, when both of the principals, on the brink of committing suicide out of desperation—death before dishonor—are rescued by the attacking Allied armies.

Thus the two lovers, who once lived in innocence and harmony on the "Rue de la Paix," are safely reunited, Americans in France saved by Americans in France, though by and large this was not an American war. This happy conclusion is overseen by the smiling portrait of Woodrow Wilson, as Griffith gives his moral benediction to the eventual American commitment to the Allied cause. At the end, victorious troops march under the flags of France and the United States. The final montage concludes with a shot of the lovers, arm in arm, under a halo of light, a typical Griffith sentimental touch. The war may be over, but the melodrama lingers on.

"Viewed as a drama," Griffith remarked to journalists of the time, "the war is in some ways disappointing" (qtd. in Schickel 354). Schickel remarks that for Griffith "war had to be an enterprise of sweeping movement," though World War I was "singularly and tragically, exactly the opposite—a war of stalemate and attrition" (353). After firsthand inspection, Griffith concluded: "A modern war is neither romantic nor picturesque. . . . It's too colossal to be dramatic." On this point Schickel concludes that Griffith "was more acute than his film indicates" (354).

The film was well received by reviewers and a commercial success. Cinematographer Karl Brown believed, however, that Griffith "had botched his picture abominably" and criticized it as "a made-to-order, government-sponsored, paid-in-advance propaganda picture" (198), though Schickel claims that propaganda "was more or less what people expected" at the time (359).

What Price Glory?

Hearts of the World was too close to the war itself, conceived as propaganda and informed by Griffith's 19th-century sensibilities, soon to be outmoded by the posturings of "the lost generation" after the war. Raoul Walsh's *What Price Glory?* was made eight years later, in 1926, adapted from the stage treatment developed by Maxwell Anderson (1888-1959) and his journalist colleague Laurence Stallings (1894-1968). The Broadway version, first produced at the Plymouth Theatre (on September 3, 1924), was successful enough to generate interest in Hollywood. Anderson, the senior collaborator, was the son of a Baptist preacher and a pacifist during the war who had been dismissed from the English Department at Whittier College for that reason and later was also dismissed from his editorial position with the San Francisco *Bulletin.* No doubt because of his influence, the play was considered the "last word in pacifism," according to editor John Gassner, because it "described fighting as a grimy business, employed considerable irony, and refrained from attributing exalted sentiments to its warriors" (58).

Laurence Stallings, by contrast, born in Georgia, had seen combat first hand as a captain in the U.S. Marine Corps. His leg was amputated after he had been wounded. Thereafter, he returned home, took a Master's degree in science, turned to a career in journalism, and wrote an autobiographical war novel, *Plumes* (1924). After the success of *What Price Glory?* he became a motion-picture scenarist. Stallings provided the blood-and-thunder entertainment value for *What Price Glory?* His first scenario for King Vidor's *The Big Parade* (1925) also draws on his experiences during the war. His work set the popular standard for understanding the war during the 1920s.

Griffith and Stallings represent values that are worlds apart, as the sweet innocence of Griffith's "old-fashioned" story gives way to the new sophistication and worldliness of the postwar era. *What Price Glory?* therefore reflects a considerable difference in substance and tone, though both films certainly reflect the experience of the Great War and both are carried along by a melodramatic romantic plot. The Griffith film, however, is mainly "about" the boy, the girl, and the village. The Walsh film, on the other hand, is mainly "about" the Marine Corps; although the romantic element is present, and strongly so, it is always secondary to the rivalry between Captain Flagg (Victor McLaglen) and Sergeant Harry Quirt (Edmund Lowe). Both films present a dilemma of love and honor, but in *What Price Glory?* the emphasis is more squarely upon honor. At the end of the film, Flagg and Quirt march off into battle together, leaving behind the girl who loves them both. Quirt is under no formal obligation to go: he has been wounded in action and he has bested Flagg in their personal battle over Charmaine (Dolores Del Rio). Having finally made her choice and claimed him, Charmaine clearly wants Quirt to stay. But he has, the viewer is told, "a weakness for bugles"; he is driven by a strong sense of personal honor and *esprit de corps*. His very being resists inaction and domestication. The character is so well defined that he cannot stay, even though the film ends with Charmaine's dire prediction that neither comrade will return from a third tour at the front.

In *Hearts of the World* Griffith takes well over forty minutes to establish his characters and create an impression of village life during peacetime. Director Raoul Walsh (1887-1980) also opens his film with establishing "business," but what he wishes to establish is the intense rivalry between Flagg and Quirt, the one a "man's man," the other a "ladies' man." Walsh takes us into the brothels of Shanghai to show the two men fighting over a bar girl named Shanghai Mable. Thence to the Philippines, where, again, Quirt takes advantage of Flagg and steals his girl. Can there be any question, then, about what will happen with Charmaine when Quirt finally shows up in France? Even so, Walsh somehow creates the impression that Flagg is indeed capable of winning Charmaine's love, as well as her heart.

What Price Glory? is perhaps as lopsided in the macho world it presents, where men are men and women are used, as *Hearts of the World* was in the old-fashioned world of naive sentimentality, where women are honored, respected, and defended. *What Price Glory?* effectively mingles chivalry with compassion and comedy with tragedy. After the brusque comedy of the opening sequences set in Shanghai and the Philippines, Walsh quickly makes his transition to the war in Europe: "France, 1914. Aflame with War—civilization dedicated to destruction—fields of production drenched with blood," a portentous title announces as a symbolic Roman soldier, sword and shield in hand, marches toward the camera. "Then, in 1917," the subtitle continues, "America joined the Allies and the old Marines were in the biggest war of all." The comic tone of *What Price Glory?* is reestablished, however, whenever Flagg and Quirt leave the front lines and resume their rivalry over Charmaine. In Griffith's film, by contrast, the comedy is exclusively confined to the peaceful opening sequence.

What Price Glory? never questions the need to fight, but it does establish a sense of compassion for the youthful victims: "Cannon

fodder. Young and green replacements. Boys from every walk of life."
Their first entry into battle is dramatized, as Captain Flagg leads his raw
recruits into their baptism of fire. After the ordeal, one of them writes a
letter, dated June 16, 1918, recalling the trauma: "Back again after the
first terrible experience under fire. We lost all but eighty. The horror of it
haunts me—the stench of the dead—the blood—the maddening rumble
of the guns."

Beneath his rough exterior, Flagg proves to be a man of feeling,
truly in sympathy with the inexperienced recruits and outraged that they
must be sent into battle. "There's something rotten," he remarks, "about
a world that's got to be wet down every thirty years with the blood of
boys like these." Flagg resents the need to sacrifice "boys like these" but
takes for granted the obligations of professional soldiers like himself.
Though not exactly insensitive to the issue of war, *What Price Glory?* is
hardly an antiwar vehicle, despite the rhetorical title, and Raoul Walsh to
the contrary. Walsh considered *What Price Glory?* an antiwar play: "Its
message was that war is not only futile but a dirty, bungled mess," he
wrote. "There was no glory for the men in the rifle pits and the trenches.
They had to launch or repel an attack against the enemy because the generals and Congress said it was their duty. I would film it that way"
(Walsh 186). Even so, Walsh also noted, "The War Department
applauded the film, claiming that it was responsible for a substantial
increase in Marine Corps enlistments" (193).

What Price Glory? is far more realistic in its portrayal of characters
than is *Hearts of the World*, and there is a crude but compelling charm
about this movie realism. When Captain Flagg swears and curses in
anger, one can see the inappropriate words forming on his lips, words
that will not be heard or recorded by intertitles. The battle scenes, moreover, are more extensively dramatized, and Walsh spends much more
time on the battlefield than does Griffith. Dolores Del Rio's performance
as Charmaine is disarmingly natural and plausible in its own right, even
though her dramatic function is primarily that of a comic and sentimental sideshow. Certainly the stereotypical girl in Griffith's film is the more
contrived character, but the contrivance is so well concealed by Lillian
Gish's performance that it is hardly noticeable.

As a generic prototype *What Price Glory?* is surely the more significant film, equalled only in importance by King Vidor's *The Big Parade*.
Both films give a similar impression of the American soldier in France,
and both depend upon a romantic involvement with a French girl, doubtless because of the common influence of Laurence Stallings, though the
girl (played by Renée Adorée) in Vidor's film lacks the insouciant abandon of Charmaine, just as Gilbert's American suitor of Vidor's film is

rather less interesting than his more experienced countrymen in *What Price Glory?* There are clear lines of development, however, from both *What Price Glory?* and *The Big Parade* to such a later reworking of the genre as William Wellman's *Wings* (1927), which works variations on formulas introduced by Stallings and Vidor (the "average" American transformed by the war experience, for example, and the careful transition from civilian life to army life through the rigors of basic training) and Stallings and Walsh (the rivalry between Jack Powell [Charles "Buddy" Rogers] and David Armstrong [Richard Arlen] in *Wings* for Mary Preston, played by Clara Bow as a sassy equivalent to Charmaine).

None of these later films captures quite the same atmosphere as *Hearts of the World* because of that film's proximity to the event, but all of them involve a mythicizing of the war experience, as one would expect from a genre picture, and stock characters have begun to evolve. There are advances in psychological development and the enemy is treated with more dignity. In *Wings,* for example, the enemy assumes a kind of aristocratic nobility, as symbolized by Count Van Kellermann (Carl Von Hartmann), who refuses to take unfair advantage of David Armstrong when he realizes that the American pilot's machine gun has jammed. Though this may seem a romantic whimsy, William Wellman (1896-1975) had experienced the war in France, first in the ambulance corps in 1917, then in the French Foreign Legion, and, finally, as an aviator in the Lafayette Flying Corps. As the intertitle explains: "There was a chivalry among these knights of the air." By contrast, *Hearts of the World*, springing from the passions of the moment, characterizes the Germans as ignoble, barbaric Huns. But D. W. Griffith was not intentionally making a genre film, and he succeeded because he was reworking the materials—the characters, the melodramatic formula, and the techniques (such as parallel montage) he knew best.

For *The Big Parade* Stallings provided the title and the five-page initial treatment. By his own account, King Vidor (1894-1982) improvised much of the rest, but Vidor admitted that Stallings himself was the prototype for the John Gilbert character: "That's why I had Gilbert lose a leg in the picture," Vidor told Kevin Brownlow. "Stallings was the biggest source of information about the war," Vidor added, "not so much in writing as in talking. I had to sit with him and draw it out of him. The research that I did was more or less suggested by Stallings" (qtd. in Brownlow 186). Hence Laurence Stallings, working in tandem with Maxwell Anderson, King Vidor, and Raoul Walsh, should be considered the founder of the genre as it came to be known and understood.

Works Cited

Brown, Karl. *Adventures with D. W. Griffith.* New York: Farrar, 1973.

Brownlow, Kevin. *The War, the West, and the Wilderness.* New York: Knopf, 1979.

Everson, William K. *American Silent Film.* New York: Oxford, 1978.

Gassner, John, ed. *25 Best Plays of the Modern American Theatre: Early Series.* New York: Crown, 1949.

Henderson, Robert M. *D. W. Griffith: His Life and Work.* New York: Oxford, 1972.

Schickel, Richard. *D. W. Griffith: An American Life.* New York: Simon & Schuster, 1984.

Walsh, Raoul. *Each Man In His Time: The Life Story of a Director.* New York: Farrar, 1974.

3

The Great War Viewed from the Twenties:
The Big Parade

Michael T. Isenberg

The decade of the 1920s long has stood in the popular perspective as a unity, bounded by the ignoble brackets of war and economic crisis. The customary view of the period, kept alive by dozens of colorful book titles, is that the time was one of carefree hedonism and relentless materialism, in which American society unleashed the pent-up energies of the war years.[1]

The traditional vision sees the war not only as Woodrow Wilson's great crusade, but as the great watershed in modern American history. The war broadened the breakdown of the old moral code, particularly in relation to late Victorian concepts of femininity. It produced a universal social malaise that saw all gods dead, all heroes humbled, all causes exhausted. Americans responded to the Carthaginian peace of Versailles by withdrawing from world affairs and expressing a strong revulsion against war and militarism. The author of the League of Nations proposal died embittered and disowned by his own political party; Wilsonian idealism lay sacrificed on the altar of "normalcy" (Mowry 24-25, 35, 130-32.)

With the exception of the unfortunate Hoover and a few others, the decade was almost bereft of first-class political leaders at all levels. The economy, while it seemed to be booming right along, was disastrously uneven. By contrast, the nation's intellectual life flourished, particularly in areas of cultural criticism. The war produced a strong and antagonistic reaction from literature and the plastic arts. The postwar climate shaped by such authors as Ernest Hemingway, John Dos Passos, and e. e. cummings commonly is regarded as one of disillusionment.[2]

The traditional view is clear. A fatigued society, worn from patriotic exertion and with its almost hysterical idealism shattered, turned away from progressive reform and ran the gamut of self-indulgence. Only with the convulsive shock of the stock market crash and the sickening slide into economic depression did Americans begin to pay for their excesses.

Yet this traditional view of the war-spawned 1920s is drawn largely from the evidence provided by cultural elites dissatisfied with their society. The war itself was at least as much an accelerator as it was a cause of the postwar mood of dissatisfaction and rebellion.[3] Although many Americans doubtless took part in the war-induced climate of cynicism, historians have tended to overlook the continuities of the period. The flaming passions of the jazz age probably held more smoke than fire, for family and church life continued as the hub of social activity for millions. The progressive reform impulse still flickered; Robert La Follette was able to mount a strong third party movement on its base in 1924, and watchdogs like George Norris kept progressivism alive in Congress. Some old progressives were still around to praise the New Deal, although many became as intensely displeased with the second Roosevelt as they had been enchanted with the first.[4]

Especially overlooked has been the fact that in the minds of many Americans the war experience persisted as a legitimate theater for heroism and the display of national idealism. To be sure, this attitude was at a high pitch between 1917 and 1919, when government, organs of public opinion, motion pictures, and popular literature allowed almost no dissent from total and uncompromising support of the war effort.[5] But the public in the years following the war was probably as supportive of this alternative vision as of the pessimistic view that is historically far better known. With the nation in a conservative mood, the sacrifices of wartime met with approbation as well as disapproval. Veterans' organizations hawked their brand of patriotism. The Veterans of Foreign Wars, founded in 1899, gained new life and new blood from World War I, while AEF veterans developed the American Legion in 1919. These organizations had fond memories of the "Great War" and were assiduous in the cultivation of "Americanism" in textbooks and among teachers (Berthoff 440, 446).

While it is fair to say that most of the elitist literature and art was intensely critical of the war and of America's role in it, newspapers, popular magazines, cheap books, and motion pictures did not advance beyond the common sentimentality of daring heroism and noble sacrifice. This was particularly true of the motion picture industry, a young and growing business giant which during the decade advanced to the forefront of popular culture.[6] Americans became habitual moviegoers during these years when the silent film reached its artistic and financial peak. What once had been an inexpensive source of amusement for lower-class urban workers had blossomed into a major recreation for persons of every social and geographic background.

The evidence of the commercial film is useful because of its appeal to a mass audience. Common themes in films often reflect the fears, desires, ideas, attitudes, or beliefs of the mass audience to which they play. Producers depend on this relationship, for profit is maximized in the dead center of audience desires. Such evidence is indirect, but it must be noted that traditional forms of evidence are also indirect in this regard. Historians using novels, memoirs, and other literary productions often make assumptions of effect when they have no audience upon which to depend. The difference between using film and literature as historical evidence is one of degree, not of quality. If anything, film evidence may be more useful because of its wider audience. The American literary public for a Hemingway numbered in the thousands; the movie public for a Chaplin was in the millions.[7]

The motion picture industry generally had done well during the war years. Moviemakers dutifully had cranked out hundreds of one- and two-reel features with war plots, most of which had brought an average return of a few thousand dollars. Many of these films were of the trite heroic genre, although some moved far enough into the fantastic to be remembered today as examples of the extremism of the home front at war. *The Kaiser, The Beast of Berlin* (1918) might be regarded as the quintessence of the latter type. But with the armistice, the hate pictures quickly became ludicrous. All war pictures by November 1918 were falling off as profit makers. Caught with titles like *Red, White and Blue Blood* and *Break the News to Mother,* industry "flacks" hastened to assure distributors that these were not war stories. Movie pioneer Fred J. Balshofer remembered that on Armistice Day he completed final cutting on a "six-reel all-out anti-Kaiser picture." The market was dead, and he lost eighty thousand dollars (Balshofer and Miller 139).

The immediate postwar climate continued to treat the war film as a pariah. Very few pictures with a world war background were made between 1919 and 1925. Almost all sank at the box office. The one major exception, Metro's *Four Horsemen of the Apocalypse* (1921), succeeded largely on the strength of its exciting new leading man—Rudolph Valentino. In general, the industry rode the crest of the broadening wave of materialism, sexual freedom, and sensation.

Vidor, Mayer, Thalberg, and Stallings

Riding this crest with everyone else was a young director named King Vidor.[8] Vidor was born in Galveston in 1894, the descendant of a Hungarian grandfather who had emigrated to Texas at the close of the Civil War. By 1918, already a veteran maker of amateur newsreels, he had moved to Hollywood, the new golden land in which the motion picture industry had firmly seated itself during the second decade of the century.

In 1918 and 1919, Vidor did a series of feature films for the Brentwood Corporation, a group of doctors and dentists seeking profits in foreign fields. After a short stint with First National, he formed "Vidor Village," his own independent production company. As was common in those days, he inserted his "Creed and Pledge" in *Variety* in 1920. It was couched in the purplish prose and hyperidealism of a young man, and an inevitable recession from its extremes soon occurred. But throughout his life Vidor remained committed to film as an art and as a noble device of human expression. "I believe in the picture that will help humanity to free itself from the shackles of fear and suffering that have so long bound it with iron chains."[9]

In 1922 "Vidor Village" folded, and the young entrepreneur moved to the Metro lot. He then worked in "artistically respectable" productions for Louis B. Mayer, going as a staff director with Mayer to the newly formed Metro-Goldwyn-Mayer Studios in 1924.[10] By the age of thirty, Vidor had put a world of moviemaking experience behind him, a background not uncommon in an industry which was still congealing its organizational and bureaucratic patterns. Mayer regarded him as a reliable director of marketable films, and Vidor was entrusted with directing some of MGM's best talent, such as John Gilbert in *His Hour* (1924) and *Wife of the Centaur* (1925).

Irving Thalberg, Mayer's chief of production, was even younger than Vidor, having been born in modest middle-class comfort in Brooklyn in 1899 (Thomas). His father was a lace importer, but Thalberg broke away early from the world of trade and by 1919 was on the coast working for Carl Laemmle in the Universal Studios. For four years he learned about motion pictures from the front office. In February 1923 he amicably left Laemmle to join Mayer. The relationship worked out by the two men, which carried MGM to the leadership of the industry in less than a decade, was for Thalberg to concern himself with the production end and for Mayer to serve as administrator and link to the home office in New York. Thus Thalberg was the man the restless Vidor approached late in 1924 with an idea for a film which would tackle an important question. As a child of the Progressive Era, Vidor was concerned with the potential of a film on one of three major problem topics: war, wheat, or steel. Thalberg asked if he had a particular subject in mind; Vidor replied vaguely that this story would be about an average young American, neither patriot nor pacifist, caught up in war. Nothing was on paper, and the two men agreed to search for a good story centered on World War I (Vidor, *A Tree* 111-12). Both knew of the chilly box-office reception of war stories, yet each felt that a fresh and innovative treatment would find its audience. Thalberg, with production control, was the key to script approval.

Weeks later, Thalberg returned from a trip to New York accompanied by a writer named Laurence Stallings and a story, tentatively titled "The Big Parade," typed on five pages of onionskin paper. Unlike Thalberg or Vidor (who was his exact age), Stallings was an AEF veteran. As a Marine captain, he had lost his right leg in Belleau Wood. When Thalberg met him, the young veteran and Maxwell Anderson had one of the hottest plays of the 1924 season, *What Price Glory?*, running on Broadway.[11]

The ex-marine had recently completed a semiautobiographical novel, *Plumes,* about the painful rehabilitation of a wounded war veteran. Overwritten and consciously tendentious, *Plumes* was a weaker version of the postwar climate of disillusion more artfully limned by such writers as Hemingway and Dos Passos. For Stallings, the sound of the trumpets persisted among the carnage. Despite a shattered leg, his hero, Richard Plume, remained a patriot, albeit a troubled one.

Until his death in 1968 Stallings retained the love-hate relationship for the war that is so evident in *What Price Glory?* and much of his later work. The memory of his doughboy comrades was constantly with him. "Why write of them at this hour," he asked rhetorically in 1963. "Why open the door of a room sealed off in my mind for so many years?" In fact the door was never sealed; the stump of his right leg was a daily reminder. "I have my Idaho willow foot to remind me now." As in many aging veterans, romanticism battled horror for memory's hand and won. Stallings claimed in his final testament concerning the earth-shaking adventures of his young manhood that he wrote about the doughboy "conscious of being unable to summon him back in entirety, and heartsick of enduring the melancholy of trying to recover long-buried remembrances of the past" (Stallings, *Doughboys* 1, 6-7).

In 1924 Stallings's memory of the war was fresh and unencumbered by time. The theatrical realism of his brawling, cursing marines in *What Price Glory?* brought him to Thalberg's attention. The five pages were loosely based on *Plumes,* but what evolved bore little resemblance to the original. While *Plumes* was concerned with a veteran's postwar struggles, the onionskin treatment dealt mostly with the war itself. Both Thalberg and Vidor felt they had their story. Vidor and writer Harry Behn traveled back to New York with Stallings, stayed a week, and returned with the completed script of *The Big Parade.* The title was a product of Stallings's romantic image of the trans-Atlantic chain of doughboys fighting in defense of liberty (Vidor, *A Tree* 113-14; Stallings, *Doughboys* 7).

Producing *The Big Parade*

Casting the film presented little problem, since MGM had a growing roster of contract actors from which to choose. Robert Sherwood, one of Stallings's friends at the celebrated Algonquin Round Table, would later claim that Stallings was allowed to select the director and the leads. While Vidor and Thalberg were young, they were not inexperienced in the industry. This was Stallings's maiden voyage in the hazardous seas of film creation, and it is most unlikely that the casting process ever had his veto (Baxter 26).

The male lead of the average American boy was cast against type. Thalberg, with Vidor's concurrence, selected John Gilbert,[12] although Vidor supposedly had had difficulties with the actor on the set of *Wife of the Centaur.* Thalberg convinced Vidor that Gilbert, shorn of his mustache, would fit the role of Jim Apperson nicely. The actor had developed a sophisticated, romantic acting style which began to attract public notice after Thalberg offered him a five-year contract with MGM (Crowther 103-04).

The female lead, that of a French peasant girl, went to an unknown with the improbable name of Renée Adorée. The roles of Apperson's two doughboy buddies were filled by raw-boned Karl Dane, who had just stepped up from a job as studio carpenter, and Tom O'Brien, a stocky "Irish" actor (Vidor, *A Tree* 115).

The story line, a collaboration of Stallings, Vidor, Behn, and perhaps Thalberg, was often modified slightly during shooting by Vidor, a common practice in the silent film era. What emerged was a tale hackneyed by today's standards, but fresh and engaging to the audiences of 1925.

As the film opens, the three principal characters are seen in their civilian occupations: Slim (Dane) at work as a steelworker on a skyscraper; Bull, or Mike O'Hara (O'Brien), as a bartender; and James Apperson (Gilbert) as a rich wastrel—a departure from Vidor's notion of an average young American. Apperson is persuaded by his sight of a recruit parade to enlist, leaping from his luxury car to join the marching men.

A montage sequence follows the conversion of raw recruits into doughboys, tracing the developing friendship of the central trio. The unit is sent to France, billeted in a small village, and shortly begins to mingle with the local population. Apperson meets a pretty girl, Melisande (Adorée) in the first series of light romantic scenes. Rash youth that he is, Apperson's first attempt to kiss her meets with a slap in the face.

The budding romance is postponed by the movement of Apperson's unit to the front, a melee of scurrying soldiers, careening trucks, and hur-

Jim Apperson teaches Melisande how to chew Yankee gum.

Credit: The Film Archive

ried goodbyes. The sequence includes one of the most famous separation scenes in cinema, in which Melisande has to be pried apart from her lover by a sergeant. Distraught, she clings to Apperson's leg, then to chain dangling from the rear of his truck transport, finally collapsing in the dust of the road. Apperson throws her his dog tags, watch, and an extra boot as a remembrance. The fade out is on the peasant girl clutching the precious boot and gazing toward the front.

The battle sequences follow, most prominently a tense march through woods heavy with impending death. Slim ventures into no-man's land and is killed. The enraged Apperson engages in hand-to-hand combat, but holding a bayonet to a German soldier's throat, he cannot kill him. Instead, he lights a cigarette for the German, who then dies of other wounds. Apperson takes the cigarette and calmly smokes it himself.

A parade of trucks returning from the front disgorges Apperson, minus a leg (like Stallings). The village has been evacuated, and Melisande is nowhere to be found. Apperson is repatriated to America, where his family is shocked by his appearance and his brother is courting his fickle fiancée. Nothing is left but a postwar return to France; he and Melisande are reunited in an open field as the film ends.[13]

Location shooting was rare under the studio system, and the adventures of Apperson and his buddies were mostly recreated on back lots. Many of the sets had an authentic air, a tribute to the talents of an artist named Warren Newcombe. Many of the bombed upper stories of French farmhouses and the roof a cathedral used as a field hospital were expertly painted by Newcombe to match the action taking place in the lower half of the camera frame.

The technical skill behind the picture is not readily apparent today, because the film is usually seen without the original orchestration. The most admired aesthetic aspect was the welding of visual imagery to music. As a young man, Vidor had shot footage of Army maneuvers in Texas; some of these compositions helped him order the crowd shots of *The Big Parade*. In preparation for filming, the director screened almost a hundred reels of Signal Corps war footage. In the process, he was struck by the rhythmic cadence of the soldier images in combat—"the whole pattern spelled death." For the sequence of the doughboys advancing through the woods, filmed in Los Angeles's Griffith Park, Vidor used a metronome for pacing and had a bass drum keep the beat for the actors. In theaters, the orchestra stopped playing during this sequence and only a muffled bass drum kept cadence with the warily advancing soldiers on the screen, a highly evocative suspense mechanism (Vidor, *A Tree* 156-57).

Vidor and his assistants also created distinctive orchestral rhythms for the love scenes and the hurly-burly of the movement to the front. Most of the war footage was shot for the film, adhering rigidly to Vidor's visual conceptions gleaned from the Signal Corps material. The director sent an assistant down to Fort Sam Houston to get shots of trucks, planes, and men all moving in a straight line (the "big parade" to the front). While army personnel were most cooperative, they convinced the assistant that the actual conditions on the western front had not encouraged such geometry. Vidor was aware of this, but the convolutions in the resulting footage did not match his vision. Everything was reshot. Thus realism and aesthetic considerations were interwoven, although some of the scenes of trucks moving at night look like model work. The director also at times kept his camera running through three and four hundred feet of film without a cut. This was a considerable innovation at the time, since longer scenes were the later creation of the wider use of synchronized sound and of what Vidor called "panning and perambulating cameras" (Vidor, *A Tree* 120-21).

During the shooting, Thalberg had looked at the rushes and decided to promote the film into a big feature. Originally, the picture had been intended as a standard production, budgeted at $205,000. An exhibitor named J. J. McCarthy, whose release of *Ben-Hur* shortly gave MGM another box-office hit, viewed the finished print and offered to promote it if more battle scenes and romance were added. Under pressure, Vidor added the weak Apperson family sequences toward the end and created the subplot with Apperson's fiancée. Since Vidor was already involved with his next project, *La Boheme*, director George Hill filmed additional night battle scenes at a cost of $40,000. This tinkering did not enhance the film, but it gave rise to the legend that Thalberg overhauled *The Big Parade* to make it a major release. Vidor later claimed only about seventy feet of additional combat footage got into the final print (Baxter 21-24). Certainly the film is strongest in its recreation of combat and in the romantic bits Vidor dreamed up for Apperson and Melisande. The next-to-closing sequences are conventional domestic soap opera.

With the studio firmly behind the picture, its New York release was heavily promoted. Vidor arrived in the city with a print of 12,800 feet. This running time was a bit too long for the distributor, who claimed commuters in the audience would be put off their schedules by such length. The director was requested to pare 800 feet from his creation. Vidor was naturally averse to letting an editor hack away at the footage, so he took the print back to the coast with him. Each night, after a day with *La Boheme*, Vidor snipped three frames from the beginning and end of each scene, making a loss of six frames at every splice. Upon completion of this labor, he found himself still 165 feet short of the desired length. So he pruned one additional frame on each side of all splices. The total eliminated then came to exactly 800 feet. The whole process would have been impossible with a sound film (Vidor, *A Tree* 123-24).

The orchestral scores were written in New York City after the distributors received the truncated version. A full orchestra was in the pit at the Astor Theater, but Vidor's idea of the single bass drum accentuating the foreboding walk into the forest was not used until the film opened at Grauman's Egyptian Theater in Hollywood (Vidor, *King Vidor* 142).

The Big Parade was a money-maker from the beginning. At the Astor alone, the picture took in $1.5 million during a ninety-six-week run. By 1930 it had grossed over $15 million nationwide. In 1931 it was rereleased with a musical score to capitalize on the new sound technology, The final gross was in the neighborhood of $20 million (Vidor, *A Tree* 125). Vidor personally reaped little of this bonanza. Originally he had owned 20 percent interest in the film, but his own lawyer convinced him that a fixed directorial fee was safer than a box-office percentage. Later in life he sourly remarked, "I thus spared myself from becoming a millionaire instead of a struggling young director trying to do something interesting and better with a camera" (Vidor, *A Tree* 125).

Critics and Audiences Respond

Critics nationwide generally applauded the picture, which played well in urban and rural areas alike. Both Stallings and Vidor burned with the desire to show war realistically, and this realism was the most common point of admiration among the critics. Gilbert Seldes thought the war scenes were magnificent. Stallings's friend Robert Sherwood was amazed that the war scenes actually resembled war (Seldes, "Theatre" 169), while another admirer expostulated that "in every sense of the word, *it is the war*! (emphasis in original) (Finch 25). Military organizations also favored the film's vision; the fact that Vidor had used AEF veterans as technical advisors had been widely publicized.

The favorable critical reception reflected several themes infusing *The Big Parade* that were also congenial to Americans. The war was perceived not only as democracy's war, in a righteous sense, but also as an intrinsic leveler of class pretensions. Apperson quickly fuses interests with the steelworker and the bartender; in avenging Slim he is mourning a friend. His romance with the peasant girl furthers the democratization process, and his rejection of his former way of life assures a simpler, unostentatious existence.

The combat sequences did not part substantially from heroic, adventurous patterns. Several critics mistakenly praised the film as anti-

Romance behind the front lines—a democratizing process?

Credit: The Film Archive

war because of the shell-hole incident in which Apperson balks at killing. But Apperson, Bull, and Slim do their share. A publicity still for the picture had the primitive steelworker simultaneously bayoneting one German and decking another with his free hand. Virtually all of the war films of the era preached the litany of commitment-duty-heroism-sacrifice, and *The Big Parade* made no innovations in this regard. The heroics are individualized by dramatic convention. Apperson's war is an intensely personal one: "I came to fight—not to wait and rot in a lousy hole while they murder my pal." His sacrifice (which is double—in friendship and with his own body) is rewarded in the fade out.

In this context, *The Big Parade* offered a most admiring view of the American soldier and his war efforts. The doughboy is a committed civilian who, when aroused, becomes a dominant warrior, only to yearn for the blessings of peace. Here Vidor's humanitarianism, which infused the film, was unable to overshadow the ambiguities of Stallings's relationship to the war. Stallings and most of his comrades could never finally admit the possibility that the whole thing had been unnecessary, meaningless, disastrous. This would have made the loss of life and limb unbearable as well as tragic. So the war became a legitimate theater for the heroics of the democratic fighting man, the New World Cincinnatus.

The general critical tone indicated that the audience response was appreciation of an epic entertainment which was grounded in human emotion. While no one wanted to applaud the fact of the war itself, *The Big Parade* did not indict American war aims or practices nor those of any of the Allies. This statement by an industry reviewer unintentionally keyed the significant qualities of the picture: "It is the first production that I have ever seen that has caught *the spirit of national pride* that makes the United States Army the greatest fighting organization on earth—that subtle yearning to acquit themselves honorably in doing *that which the situation demands*, that brings heroes out of the slums and the mansions of wealth alike" (author's emphasis) (Finch 59).

The themes of nationalism, honor, duty, and heroism are all common to the war adventure genre. Plots threaded with them cannot make a coherent antiwar or pacifist statement, since the focus of such themes is individualistic rather than situational. When another member of the Algonquin Round Table, Alexander Woollcott, viewed *The Big Parade* he observed among his neighbors in the theater pity for dying doughboys and satisfaction in scenes of German deaths (40). The individualism of the film is sketched in the positive attributes of friendship and democratic solidarity. Transferred to the emotional level of the viewer, these became the admirable qualities of loyalty, devotion, and dedication to service. Here patriotic impulse overcame the horrors of war, not vice versa.

The mass audience that saw the film probably was unaware of the ambiguities actually underlying the plot. *The Big Parade*'s patina of realism was deemed to be significant comment in itself. Also, many in the audience doubtless shared these ambiguities without any intellectual tensions whatsoever. Thus "war" could be applauded and excoriated at the same time. Thalberg in particular was convinced that his production marked a significant departure from earlier war films:

The only difference between it and the other war pictures was the different viewpoint taken in the picture. We took a boy whose idea in entering the war was not patriotic. He was swept along by the war spirit around him and entered it but didn't like it. He met a French girl who was intriguing to him, but he wasn't really serious about her. The only time he was interested in fighting was when a friend, who was close to him, was killed. It was human appeal rather than patriotic appeal, and when he reached the German trenches and came face to face with the opportunity to kill, he couldn't do it. In other words, a new thought regarding the war was in the minds of most people, and that was the basis of its appeal. (qtd. in Thomas 129)

The producer offered a virtually complete list of mistaken reasons. The basic appeal of *The Big Parade* was adventure and romance. None of its ingredients was new, only packaged differently. The theme of war as a democratic leveler stretched back in movie time at least to Thomas Ince's *Civilization* (1915). Rich boys democratized by war had been prominent in such earlier films as Edison's *The Unbeliever* (1918) and McManus's *The Lost Battalion* (1919). Apperson reached romantic fulfillment with Melisande at war's end, in spite of being "not really serious about her." Finally, it is difficult to reconcile the audience partisanship observed by Woollcott and applauded by many reviewers with a "human" rather than a patriotic appeal.

The Big Parade was flawed as an antiwar statement by the very individualism Thalberg regarded as its primary virtue. Years later Budd Schulberg would for this reason succinctly call the film "second-rate perfection." While in Gilbert Seldes's terms Vidor gave American audiences the "spectacle of the war," he gave little else (Seldes, "Parades" 111-12). As long as individuals stood apart from the mass and were made *special* through devices of romance or action, the cinema could never come to grips with the nature of twentieth-century warfare. The protagonists of *The Big Parade* did not lay down their arms and refuse to fight, nor were they left numbed by the potential nihilism of their situation. They dwelt in a rational, if horrible, condition and responded to it in a necessary and rational way. *The Big Parade* was thus a prisoner of dramatic convention and, judging from its reception, so was its audience.

Although English and French viewers naturally tended to resent the film on chauvinistic grounds, its real difficulty lay in a fundamental misapprehension of the war itself. If international combat is conventionally seen as a process with winners and losers, the screen in the 1920s transmuted these into heroes and villains. *The Big Parade* marched in an intellectual arena heavily populated with the ghosts of nineteenth-century romanticism and the American cult of the individual. Here it tapped one of the deepest veins in the national character, and herein lay its success—not in any new conception of the war, for it had none. "No film dare show what [war] resembled," wrote critic Iris Barry. *The Big Parade* "wreathes machine-guns in roses" (946-47).

Vidor himself later admitted that his love for documentary realism had been dominated by conventional screen action and romance. He saw the picture as late as 1974: "I don't like it much . . . Today I don't encourage people to see the film. At the time I really believed it was an anti-war movie." Even the director conceded that the basic appeal of the film was not the "parade" of masses of young men towards the maelstrom of death, but the romantic bits developed for Apperson and Melisande (Baxter 21).

What remains is nevertheless an exceptional piece of screen storytelling. By the standards of its day, *The Big Parade*'s battle scenes were realistic. A few critics derided the forest sequence as militarily inaccurate, but Vidor claimed to have received a letter from the War Department praising precisely these scenes (Mitchell 180). The basic merit of the film was in Vidor's ability to maintain the action without interrupting overmuch with titles; in this sense the picture is a choice example of mimetic art.

MGM's box-office success inevitably keyed a war-adventure film cycle throughout the industry. The cycle lasted for five years—at least through the release of Howard Hughes's *Hell's Angels* (1930). *What Price Glory?* and its brawling marines appeared in 1926, and William Wellman's aviation epic *Wings* the next year, both spawned dozens of imitators. Vidor's original plot contributions became stale through reiteration, until Gilbert Seldes finally threw up his hands in surrender as he wrote in the *New Republic* of July 3, 1929: "In all American films since *The Big Parade*, if a regiment is marching away, or a thousand trucks roll by, the hero or heroine staggers through the lines, fighting off the men in the trucks, trying to make his or her way to the beloved and departing one" (179-80). Not until Universal gambled with a screen adaptation of Erich Maria Remarque's novel *All Quiet on the Western*

Front in 1930 did the American public see an American film truly anti-war in intent and execution. Even then, films depicting war as a worthy arena for heroic adventure and romance were not extinguished. The genre survived to fuel the build-up to new and greater war.

Stallings stayed with motion pictures, working as an editor of Fox Movie-Tone Newsreels and turning out journeyman film scripts, several for Vidor. Stallings's documentary film, *The First World War* (1934), was his harshest statement on the experience, but his bittersweet written history, *The Doughboys*, retained the essential ambiguities first developed in *Plumes*, *The Big Parade*, and *What Price Glory?* Thalberg continued his record of high-quality film production until his untimely death from lobar pneumonia in 1936. John Gilbert's career faded in the late 1920s. His deterioration and early death, which also occurred in 1936, comprise a case history often cited as a classic example of the decline and fall of a star.

Vidor went on to become, by any standards, one of the finest directors in Hollywood history. He tackled a wide variety of projects, from socialist symbolism (*Our Daily Bread*, 1934) to Western epic (*Duel in the Sun*, 1946), before finally closing the books with the routine biblical tale of *Solomon and Sheba* (1959). His original concerns—humanistic, idealistic, freighted with optimism—remained remarkably consistent throughout a career that spanned five decades.

Vidor, Stallings, and Thalberg, all of them thirty or under at the time, bear the essential creative responsibility for *The Big Parade*. The realistic vision of the war is that of Stallings; the aesthetic vision belongs to Vidor. Put another way, the picture was largely a story by Stallings, one which he felt intensely—but the storyteller was Vidor. Their product is symbolic of an American view of the great crusade as seen from the 1920s, a vision alternate from the traditional consensus.

Conclusions

Historian Otis L. Graham, Jr., in a succinct study of continuity and discontinuity in the Progressive reform impulse, has recently restated the traditional view. World War I was "the stimulus to private indulgence and social irresponsibility." To Graham and many others, the war caused the spirit of reaction so evident in many of the social conflicts of the decade (91, 109). This spirit suffused the debates over fundamentalism, rekindled nativist sentiment, and heightened the tension between urban and rural sectors of American life. Reaction, like almost all American social trends, had no distinctive class basis. Thus films like *The Big Parade* cannot be analyzed as mouthpieces of social thought, either from the left or the right.

Instead, *The Big Parade* is an indicator of a broad, classless climate of opinion, circa 1925, concerning the nature of the Great War. "Consensus" is too strong a word, implying as it does a reasoned decision based on choice.[14] Evidence from films such as this resolves a seeming paradox concerning the historical analysis of the 1920s, which may be stated: How can a decade usually classed as reactionary or conservative also be seen as one of intense antiwar sentiment? To be sure, conservatism and militarism do not always fit snugly, but the instinct for tradition and order implicit in the former camp usually finds a welcome home in the latter. There is sketchy evidence, for example, the empty pacifist idealism of the Kellogg-Briand Pact (1928), to indicate that hostility toward war could encompass reformers and conservatives alike. But such evidence is sparse and does not drive a lasting wedge between conservatism and militarism as patterns of thought and behavior.

The paradox vanishes when the elitist basis of traditional 1920s historiography is recognized. Our evidence of the antiwar and antimilitarist condition of the period is drawn largely from professional cultural critics: novelists, journalists, artists, and others whose business it is to criticize. This is hard evidence and convincing in its sphere; the mistake lies not in accepting it but in allowing this material to dominate the historiography of the decade.

The Big Parade, touching as it did a far wider audience than anything produced by cultural elites in the 1920s, departs from the common view. Its alternate vision, of course, does not stand alone—but neither should that of the antiwar elites. The foggy differentiation between art and entertainment, or high culture and popular culture, should not separate us from the fact that in relying on film evidence to test the nature of American thought concerning the war, we are using precisely the same method as historians utilizing written materials. Only the nature of the evidence is different.[15]

The popularity of the war adventure film of the 1920s strongly indicates that a considerable number of Americans retained an ambiguous relationship to the war experience. For many, the image of war persisted as that of a legitimate theater for heroism and nationalistic endeavor. America had confronted Europe with ancient European wrongs; having righted them on the battlefield (the patricentrism that enraged the English and French audiences of *The Big Parade*), the young giant of the West rejected involvement in the corrupt diplomacy of a decadent continent. Thus the feelings of frustration and disillusion strengthened the climate of isolation, which was indeed strong throughout the interwar period.

But isolationism is not antimilitarism. Intellectual elites might inveigh against the sword, but the qualities of patriotism, service, and social hierarchy implicit in a uniform remained positively symbolic of the essence of national idealism for many Americans. In this sense, the war was perceived as an unwelcome task that had to be done. The passionate excesses of the war years had dampened even before Wilson's debilitating stroke, but the conviction that the war was *necessary* survived in many quarters. The tragedy was thus not only one of lives destroyed and bodies shattered, but also of a task completed with an imperfect ending. Here there was no nation to forge, no sundered union to reunite, no defeated Mexicans or Spaniards waiting to drop vast acreages into the lap of Uncle Sam.

It had been a war fought, in the last analysis, for ideals of the highest order. Human imperfection can suffer this strain so long and no longer, and the resulting disillusionment is compounded by the strength of the original moral fervor. The motion picture theater, however, is the house of dreams. Here ideals may not only achieve perfection, but may endure in screen time forever. The steadily unwinding spools of celluloid may simultaneously reduce a world war to romance and enshrine it as a fit pantheon for heroes. American filmmakers were only beginning to learn the language of tortured ambiguity, and their audiences remained largely unreceptive to this language when it spoke of war.

So Vidor and the others failed, in a sense, to make their antiwar statement. Like all of us, they were culture-bound, working in a medium that relied on broad cultural acceptance for its livelihood. *The Big Parade* inspired no marches to the recruiting station, but neither did the film indict the war itself. An era rich in contradictions blandly ignored one of the most profound contradictions of all: the reconciliation of militancy and pacifism under the symbolic blanket of democratic idealism.

Notes

1. See in this regard Frederick Lewis Allen, *Only Yesterday: An Informal History of the 1920s* (New York: Harper, 1931); Mark Sullivan, *Our Times*, Vol. 6 (New York: Scribner, 1935); Preston Slosson, *The Great Crusade and After*, 1914-1928 (New York: Macmillan, 1930). Two excellent general studies of the period are John D. Hicks, *Republican Ascendancy*, 1921-1933 (New York: Harper 1960), and William E. Leuchtenburg, *The Perils of Prosperity*, 1914-1932 (Chicago: U of Chicago P, 1958). A shorter, more feisty approach is that of Paul A. Carter, *The Twenties in America* (2nd ed.) (New York: Crowell, 1975). Attempts to unify the 1920s under colorful conceptualizations include Lawrence Greene, *The Era of Wonderful Nonsense* (Indianapolis: Bobbs-Merrill, 1939); Isabel Leighton, ed., *The Aspirin Age* (New York: Simon and Schuster, 1949);

James Prothro, *Dollar Decade: Business Ideas in the 1920s* (Baton Rouge: Louisiana State UP, 1954); Charles Merz, *The Dry Decade* (New York: Doubleday, 1930); Robert Sklar, ed., *The Plastic Age*, 1917-1930 (New York: Braziller, 1970).

2. For material on 1920s political life, see Robert K. Murray, *The Harding Era: Warren G. Harding and His Administration* (Minneapolis: U of Minnesota P, 1969); William Allen White, *A Puritan in Babylon: The Story of Calvin Coolidge* (New York: Macmillan, 1938); Joan Hoff Wilson, *Herbert Hoover: Forgotten Progressive* (Boston: Little, Brown, 1975). For economic insight, George Soule, *Prosperity Decade: From War to Depression, 1917-1929* (New York: Rinehart, 1947) is excellent. Cultural trends are treated in Frederick J. Hoffman, *The 20s: American Writing in the Postwar Decade* (rev. ed.) (New York: Free Press, 1965). For varying interpretations concerning intellectual life, see Roderick Nash, *The Nervous Generation: American Thought, 1917-1941* (Chicago: Rand McNally, 1970); Robert H. Elias, *Entangling Alliances With None: An Essay on the Individual in the American Twenties* (New York: Norton, 1973). A perceptive contemporary assessment, clouded by pessimism, is that of Joseph Wood Krutch, *The Modern Temper, A Study and a Confession* (New York: Harcourt, 1929).

3. For evidence on this point, see Henry F. May, *The End of American Innocence: A Study of the First Years of Our Own Time, 1912-1917* (New York: Knopf, 1959).

4. See in particular Clark A. Chambers, *Seedtime of Reform: American Social Service and Social Action, 1918-1933* (Minneapolis: U of Minnesota P, 1963) and Otis L. Graham, Jr., *An Encore for Reform: The Old Progressives and the New Deal* (New York: Oxford UP, 1967).

5. For motion pictures in this regard, see Michael T. Isenberg, *War on Film: The American Cinema and World War I, 1914-1941* (Rutherford: Fairleigh-Dickenson UP, 1981); for popular literature, Charles V. Genthe, *American War Narratives, 1917-1918: A Study and Bibliography* (New York: Lewis, 1969).

6. General histories of American film include the still valuable work of Lewis Jacobs, *The Rise of the American Film: A Critical History* (New York: Harcourt, 1968); Robert Sklar, *Movie-Made America: A Cultural History of American Movies* (New York: Vintage, 1975); and Garth Jowett, *Film, the Democratic Art: A Social History of American Film* (Boston: Little, Brown, 1976). There is no competent history of film in the 1920s, although the final chapters of Terry Ramsaye, *A Million and One Nights: A History of the Motion Picture* (New York: Simon and Schuster, 1926) are still useful. David Robinson, *Hollywood in the Twenties* (New York: Barnes, 1968) is a sketchy overview. Many excellent insights on the period may be gleaned from Kevin Brownlow, *The Parade's Gone by . . .* (New York: Knopf, 1968), and Edward

Wagenknecht, *The Movies in the Age of Innocence* (Norman: U of Oklahoma P, 1962).

7. This is not to argue that historical impact is measured in numbers alone. The reasons for the mistrust of film evidence by the historical profession are analyzed in Michael T. Isenberg, "A Relationship of Constrained Anxiety: Historians and Film," *The History Teacher,* 6.4 (1973) 553-68.

8. The best material on Vidor is still his autobiography, *A Tree Is a Tree* (New York: Harcourt, 1953). See also King Vidor, *King Vidor on Film Making* (New York: McKay, 1972), and John Baxter, *King Vidor* (New York: Monarch, 1976). A briefer and highly aesthetic appreciation of Vidor's work is Raymond Durgnat, "King Vidor," *Film Comment,* 9.4 (1973) 10-49 and 9.5 (1973) 16-51. A bibliography on Vidor, largely of light articles, may be found in Mel Schuster, *Motion Picture Directors: A Bibliography of Magazine and Periodical Articles, 1900-1972* (Metuchen: Scarecrow, 1973) 375-77.

9. Vidor's "Creed and Pledge" is reproduced in Baxter, *King Vidor,* 10.

10. A readable history of the Metro-Goldwyn-Mayer Studios is Bosley Crowther, *The Lion's Share: The Story of an Entertainment Empire* (New York: Dutton, 1957). The creation is described on 79-81. For Mayer, see Bosley Crowther, *Hollywood Rajah: The Life and Times of Louis B. Mayer* (New York: Holt, 1960); for Marcus Loew, see Robert Sobel, *The Entrepreneurs: Explorations Within the American Business Tradition* (New York: Weybright, 1974) 247-88.

11. For the play *What Price Glory?,* see Maxwell Anderson and Laurence Stallings, *Three American Plays* (New York: Harcourt, 1926) 5-89.

12. A bibliography on Gilbert may be found in Mel Schuster, *Motion Picture Performers: A Bibliography of Magazine and Periodical Articles, 1900-1969* (Metuchen: Scarecrow, 1971) 277-78.

13. A convenient summary of the story line of *The Big Parade* may be found in Thomas, *Thalberg,* 332-35. A print of *The Big Parade* is in the Museum of Modern Art, New York City (hereafter cited as MOMA). Frederick James Smith, "Making *The Big Parade,*" *Motion Picture Classic,* 23.3 (1926) 26, 71, is a brief presentation of Vidor's comments shortly after the picture was released.

14. For favorable comment on the usefulness of climate-of-opinion historiography, see Robert Allen Skotheim, ed., *The Historian and the Climate of Opinion* (Reading: Addison-Wesley, 1969).

15. We leave in abeyance the question of causation, which is exceedingly difficult to resolve in the context of intellectual history. This difficulty holds regardless of the nature of the evidence. The contours of this question are examined in Michael T. Isenberg, "Toward an Historical Methodology for Film Scholarship," *The Rocky Mountain Social Science Journal,* 12.1 (1975) 45-57.

Works Cited

Balshofer, Fred J., and Arthur C. Miller. *One Reel a Week.* Berkeley: U of California P, 1967.

Barry, Iris. "The Cinema: The Big Parade." *The Spectator* 5 June 1926.

Baxter, John. *King Vidor.* New York: Monarch, 1976.

Berthoff, Rowland. *An Unsettled People: Social Order and Disorder in American History.* New York: Harper, 1971.

Crowther, Bosley. *The Lions Share: The Story of an Entertainment Empire.* New York: Dutton, 1957.

Finch, Robert M. "The Big Parade." *Motion Picture Director* Nov. 1925.

Graham, Otis L., Jr. *The Great Campaigns: Reform and War in America, 1900-1928.* Englewood Cliffs: Prentice-Hall. 1971.

Mitchell, G. J. "King Vidor." *Films in Review* 15.3 (1964).

Mowry, George E. *The Urban Nation, 1920-1960.* New York: Hill and Wang, 1965.

Seldes, Gilbert. "The Theatre." *Dial* Feb. 1926.

——. "The Two Parades." *New Republic* 16 Dec. 1925.

Stallings, Laurence. *The Doughboys: The Story of the AEF, 1917-1918.* New York: Harper, 1963.

——. *Plumes.* New York: Harcourt, 1924.

Thomas, Bob. *Thalberg: Life and Legend.* Garden City: Doubleday, 1969.

Vidor, King. *King Vidor on Film Making.* New York: McKay, 1972.

——. *A Tree Is a Tree.* New York: Harcourt, 1953.

Woollcott, Alexander. " 'The Big Parade' of British Anger." *Literary Digest* 12 June 1926.

4

The Dawn Patrol and the World War I Air Combat Film Genre: An Exploration of American Values

Dominick A. Pisano

Films about air combat in World War I make up a fraction of the total number of war films produced, but they are important for what they say about American perceptions of heroism and how Americans view men who master a complicated machine like the airplane, especially in wartime. Because the airplane has played a major cultural role in the twentieth century, films about combat in the air deserve to be given the same measure of scrutiny as the western, the gangster film, and other film genres. Since World War I, standardized aesthetic conventions have developed concerning air combat and the heroism of combat pilots, many of which persist in the public mind.

Clearly, Hollywood helped to influence the prevailing image of heroism in air combat in World War I through genre films like Howard Hawks's *The Dawn Patrol* (1930). The popularity of World War I air combat films suggests that the cultural values they espoused struck a responsive chord with their audiences. The archetypal patterns of heroic behavior established by *The Dawn Patrol* are similar to those in films in other genres like the professional western. These similarities suggest that World War I air combat genre films are not entirely discrete from other genres or even from air combat films of subsequent eras. In fact, generic elements in *The Dawn Patrol* are very much in evidence in later films like *Air Force* (1943) and *Top Gun* (1986).

The Development of the Air Combat Film Genre

In 1914, at the beginning of World War I, the Hollywood motion picture stood at the crossroads of a new era of recognition as an artistic and propagandistic medium. The film industry responded to the European war with caution in the years of American neutrality, but—even before the United States entered the war in 1917—motion pictures were beginning to shape public opinion in favor of involvement. The first of the prowar films to appear was J. Stuart Blackton's *The Battle Cry of Peace* (1915), which told of the invasion of New York by a foreign enemy. Blackton later admitted that the film was intended as "a call to arms . . . propaganda for the United States to enter the war . . . made deliberately for that purpose" (Spears 15). Subsequent films like C. B. DeMille's *The Little American* (1917) and D. W. Griffith's *Hearts of the World* (1918) continued propagandizing and were virulently anti-German (Soderbergh 511).

After the Armistice, public weariness with propaganda films about war made such productions unmarketable. Hollywood believed that most Americans shared the disillusion with war sentiments of such lost generation writers as F. Scott Fitzgerald, Ernest Hemingway, and John Dos Passos. The industry, unwilling to risk losses from films about unpopular subjects, initially shied away. In 1925, however, King Vidor, a director from the Goldwyn Company, and Irving Thalberg, the brilliant young production assistant to Louis B. Mayer at the newly formed MGM Studios, decided that the time was right. The result was *The Big Parade*, the financially successful progenitor of the war film genre, which made $10 million for MGM. As Peter Soderbergh observes, *The Big Parade*, "gave the public what it wanted . . . a kind of perfect neutrality which fit comfortably between embarrassing flagwaving and noxious despair" (518).

The Big Parade was followed by *What Price Glory?* (1926), adapted from a long-running, successful Broadway play coauthored by Laurence Stallings and Maxwell Anderson. Other films like *All Quiet on the Western Front* (1930), based on Erich Maria Remarque's novel, *Journey's End* (1930), *The Road to Glory* (1936), *The Road Back* (1937), *Three Comrades* (1938) and many others ensued, and the genre stretched well into the late 1930s. Historian Michael T. Isenberg believes that for the most part, these films are romantic adventures that reflect American attitudes toward World War I. Whereas Europeans saw the Great War as "nothing less than a political, economic, social, intellectual, and moral holocaust," Isenberg writes, "the tale of the film conveys the feeling that many Americans continued to view it as the supreme adventure of the democratic conscience" (218).[1]

If Isenberg is correct, it is no surprise that in the hope of repeating the financial success of *The Big Parade* and *What Price Glory?* Hollywood turned to the air. *Wings* (1927), *Hell's Angels* (1930) and *The Dawn Patrol* (1930, remade in 1938), *Ace of Aces* (1933), *The Eagle and the Hawk* (1933), *Today We Live* (1934), *Suzy* (1936), and *The Woman I Love* (1937) were only a few of the films that capitalized on the appeal of aviation in World War I. The motion picture industry realized that while films about the war in the trenches had some attraction, they were often static and depressing; the war in the air, at least in popular conceptions of it, was distinctly romantic. The disparity was striking. While soldiers burrowed deep into the ground or dragged themselves across the mud and barbed wire of no man's land, courtly young "knights of the air" battled heroically in the sky. The public, wildly enthusiastic about aviation after Lindbergh's transatlantic flight in May 1927, needed no convincing.

The first full-scale aviation epic—and the first in a long series of films that explored the war in the air—was *Wings*. In its pioneering cinematic techniques and portrayal of aerial action, *Wings* was like no other film produced up to that time. The film was adapted from a story by John Monk Saunders and directed by William Wellman, a veteran of the Lafayette Flying Corps. Saunders, a screenwriter who had been an instructor in the Air Service during the war, helped convince Jesse L. Lasky, head of production at Paramount Studios, to make a film based on aviation in World War I. Saunders argued that such a film would rival the success of MGM's *The Big Parade* and Fox's *What Price Glory?* The War Department agreed to provide a labor force, equipment, shooting sites, and logistical and engineering support for what was to become a tremendous undertaking.[2] Production, which began in 1926, took an entire year and cost $2 million (Suid 25-33).

Wings premiered in August 1927 at the Criterion Theater in New York City and played there for more than a year. The film was financially successful and critically acclaimed. *Literary Digest*, for example, gushed:

Eagles strike and are stricken. The vanquished, blazing into meteors, topple, plunge and write their own epitaphs down the sky in serpentine trails of fire and smoke. Spiralling drunkenly earthward, they are dogged at each turn by relentlessly inquisitive cameras—now above, now below, now happily on the same level—intent on not missing the smallest pirouette of the dance of death. Peaceful audiences, digesting their comfortable dinners in plush covered seats, find a sharp, emotional "kick" rivalling that of a first-class prize-fight in seeing with their own eyes, as by a visual throwback of history, some of the incredible air duels of a decade ago, which the whole world used to read about with bated breath in the war dispatches from the Western Front. (qtd. in DeBauche 5)

The *New York Times* was equally effusive. Its reviewer Mordaunt Hall wrote:

This feature gives one an unforgettable idea of the existence of these daring fighters—how they are called upon at all hours of the day and night to soar into the skies and give battle to enemy planes: their lighthearted eagerness to enter the fray and also their reckless conduct once they set foot on earth for a time in the dazzling life of the French capital. (Hall 10.4)

The striking thing about these reviews is how insistent they are that what they have seen on screen is realistic, that these events took place in a historical sense.

The realism of *Wings* and the air combat films that followed it would be an important consideration in how they were received by audiences. Aside from its verisimilitude, *Wings* was significant as the first film of the World War I air combat film genre. The generic elements in *Wings* would be repeated and reworked in many films made during the 1930s. The verisimilitude of the films—combined with their generic elements—tell us something about the values of the culture in which they were produced and suggest how air combat in World War I was mythologized on the movie screen.[3]

The Dawn Patrol: Genre, Verisimilitude, and American Values

Howard Hawks's *The Dawn Patrol* (1930) blended the realism of *Wings* with more fully developed generic elements. More than any other World War I air combat film, *The Dawn Patrol* was responsible for redefining the genre, and moving it beyond its iconographic elements of setting and staging. *The Dawn Patrol* differs from its predecessors in that it begins to interpret the genre and stretches its boundaries by exploring the psychological pressures and stresses of wartime flying. These tensions are characterized by situations in which fighter pilots must come face to face with their imminent death and the death of their comrades, and by the emotional difficulties faced by squadron commanders who must send their young men out to die. Although Hawks was just beginning to establish his reputation as a director, *The Dawn Patrol* shows the incipient touches of what would become hallmarks of his directing style: terse and spare dialogue; a tendency to transform genre conventions by the sheer force of his personality and wit; a celebration of self-respect and instinctual behavior; an exploration of group dynamics and the primacy of responsibility within the group; comradeship among male characters.[4]

The Dawn Patrol was based on a story by John Monk Saunders titled "The Flight Commander."[5] The screenplay was written by Hawks, Dan Totheroh, and Seton I. Miller. The film chronicles the 59th Squadron of the Royal Flying Corps during 1915, when the RFC was suffering severe casualties at the hands of the German air force. Squadron Commander Brand (Neil Hamilton) faces the difficult task of sending young and inexperienced fliers to fight the Germans because so many of his veteran pilots have been killed. Flight Commander Courtney (Richard Barthelmess) accuses Brand of butchery, but finds himself in the same position when Brand is promoted and he becomes squadron commander. Nerves stretched to the breaking point by the pressures of command, Courtney finds that he must send the unseasoned younger brother of his best friend, Scott (Douglas Fairbanks, Jr.), into battle. Scott's brother is subsequently killed, and Courtney's relationship with Scott is damaged irreparably. Courtney himself takes on a suicidal mission that Scott had volunteered for and is killed. At the end of the film, Scott finds that he must assume the duties of command, re-initiating the deadly cycle.

Like *Wings, The Dawn Patrol* was praised for realism and the film's authenticity was publicized and partially responsible for its popularity. A newspaper account reported that Hawks's aim was to "reproduce with the utmost attainable authenticity the actual conditions of air warfare between the British and German flying services." The account also noted that

for many weeks before "The Dawn Patrol" went on location in the Pico Valley, near Newhall, Cal., an intensive search was being made for arms, uniforms and equipment dating from the early phases of the World War, with the result that many of the externals of the picture are ultra-realistic. . . . The uniform worn by [Richard] Barthelmess, for instance, belonged to a young English flier who was shot down behind the German lines after such a raid which carries the story of "The Dawn Patrol" to its climax. At least a dozen old war kits were bought or rented. Some of them were ripped and torn, some had bullet holes and mud-stains—and they are worn in the picture in just that condition, for by 1915 the fliers on both sides had ceased to bother about appearances when they were on active service.[6]

These realistic touches reinforced the film's iconography and added to its verisimilitude.

Reviews from around the country praised the film for its lifelike quality. The reviewer for the *Fresno Republican*, for example, declared that "for thrills, chills, terrors, triumphs and sweep of sheer reality it surpasses all other air pictures." The *Pittsburgh Post-Gazette* reviewer noted that "breath-taking stunts, dangerous excursions over the enemy lines, thrilling combat scenes and spectacular bombing expeditions all are presented with such startling fidelity that the present Barthelmess vehicle becomes a masterpiece of camera work in the clouds." The *Richmond Times-Dispatch* said there was "not a dull moment" in the film and that there were so many moments "so intensely thrilling that when the danger was over for the time being the whole house clapped." The *Times-Dispatch* reporter clapped so enthusiastically that he lost his pencil and "couldn't take any more notes."[7]

Another element of *The Dawn Patrol*'s authenticity is that it borrows from microcosmic and macrocosmic historical events and situations to tell its story.[8] In March 1915, for example, Royal Flying Corps Lt. W. B. Rhodes-Moorhouse flew a suicide mission similar to the fictional Courtney's in *The Dawn Patrol*. In the midst of intense ground fire, the pilot attacked the railroad station at Courtrai with a 100-pound bomb. Rhodes-Moorhouse was not killed immediately (as is Courtney); he managed to fly back to his aerodrome, but died of his injuries. He was awarded the RFC's first Victoria Cross (Morrow 113-14). British air strategy during the war is also illustrative of *The Dawn Patrol*'s verisimilitude. Hugh Trenchard, head of the Royal Flying Corps' First Wing, is reported to have "pressed his wing so hard that it suffered losses wholly disproportionate to any good that was achieved" (Collier 47).

In this regard, historian Malcolm Cooper has observed that British air doctrine was responsible for the RFC's extensive casualty list. As long as the RFC depended on a "strategy of attrition," it would certainly have to accept heavy losses. Nevertheless, Cooper says, the rigidity of the RFC's air tactics made losses much higher than necessary. (In a sense, Trenchard's Western Front air policy of "relentless and incessant offensive" mirrored that of Sir Douglas Haig, the British commander in France, against the controlling position of the German army.) Force applied to an "imperfectly perceived" objective brought about an unnecessarily high casualty rate (76).[9]

The authenticity of *The Dawn Patrol* is only one factor in its popularity, reception, and the values it espouses. Another has to do with its generic elements. By 1930, the World War I air combat film genre had been developing in *Wings* and its successors, *Lilac Time* (1928), *The Legion of the Condemned* (1928), and *Hell's Angels* (1930). Like other film genres, the World War I air combat film is characterized a pattern of conventions in which characters perform familiar actions that idealize accepted types. This generic patterning of the World War I air combat film is not accidental; Hollywood had been impressed with the financial success of *Wings*. Success for later films in the genre meant holding fast to this narrative formula, making adjustments whenever necessary to provide a semblance of uniqueness, but continuing to present similar storytelling patterns, attitudes, and stereotypes.

As each film appeared, the World War I air combat film genre became better defined, forming an intentional relationship between each new film and its predecessors, and making for a more powerful effect on audiences, who by now had grown accustomed to the narrative patterns and were expecting more of the same. More important in a cultural sense was what the film genre represented to its audience. The genre-audience interaction exemplified, as Thomas Schatz suggests, "a distinct manifestation of contemporary society's basic mythic impulse, its desire to confront elemental conflicts inherent in modern culture while at the same time participating in the projection of an idealized collective self-image" (qtd. in Grant 99). What are the elements that make *The Dawn Patrol* so important in the development of the World War I air combat film genre? The paradigm below outlines characteristics that are the most integral elements of the World War I air combat film genre as defined by *The Dawn Patrol*:

1. *Characters:* Like many of Hawks's male characters, the men of *The Dawn Patrol* are, as Joseph McBride has observed, "a tightly knit group of professionals trying to perform a difficult task together while upholding their own rigorously defined code of conduct" (1). Hawks's male characters are often pitted against hostile environments of one type or another and in *The Dawn Patrol* it is the air that represents uncertainty and death. Hawks's male characters in *The Dawn Patrol* (Brand, Courtney, and Scott) are in psychological torment over having to send innocent youths to their deaths. Finally, in most air combat genre films, women characters are present but unessential. (In *The Dawn Patrol*, Hawks has eliminated them altogether.)

2. *Values:* In *The Dawn Patrol*, the male characters unite into a fraternal organization with a code that stresses stoical adherence to professionalism, honor, and responsibility to oneself and the group. One of the pilots, the high-strung Hollister (Gardner James), deviates from the norm because he is overtly emotional and perceived to be weak. However, he manages to salvage respect among his colleagues when he sacrifices his life for a comrade. *The Dawn Patrol* emphasizes the values of the group, but it also recognizes the need for harmony between individual and community values. Hawks's men are fatalistic: they accept their fate, but not willingly. There is resentment in the tone of their response ("Right" or "It'll be done") to orders issued by the squadron commander.

3. *Actions:* Although part of a tightly knit group, the men of *The Dawn Patrol* are involved in individualistic combat with chivalric overtones set against a backdrop of impending doom. The characters feign a denial of death as when they adjourn to their "club" after the missions have been flown to drink and toast "the next man to die." Yet, they are tortured by a sense of guilt for having survived, which they temporarily assuage with alcohol (both Major Brand and Courtney keep a bottle

handy on their desk). This guilt is expiated by self-sacrifice, as when Courtney undertakes his suicidal mission to atone for sending Scott's younger brother to certain death.

4. *Iconography:* Much of the iconography of the air combat film originated in *Wings*. *The Dawn Patrol*, however, contains visual elements that became trademarks of the genre. Pilots are costumed in leather coats and helmets, and outfitted with goggles, scarves, and winged insignia. Aircraft are usually 1930s-vintage made up to look like World War I airplanes and often appear fragile—to give the impression of danger. The aircraft are outfitted with weapons, especially machine guns. Flight maneuvers, filmed by aerial cinematographers, include spectacular crashes, complete with smoke and flames. Sound effects are commonplace and consist of aircraft engines, machine guns, and sometimes a dramatic musical score. Often, there are ominous symbols like the skull and crossbones, villains dressed in dark flying garb, chalkboards with the names of dead fliers crossed out.

Thus, the generic elements of *The Dawn Patrol*—characters, values, actions, and iconography—combine with its verisimilitude to produce a set of dramatic elements that fit American notions of heroism. The war in the air, because it had little of the horror of the war on the ground and a great deal of heroic potential, was Hollywood's choice to convey its message. The message was that war in the air was heroic and chivalrous, that individualism and group loyalty were not mutually exclusive but able to be reconciled, and that it was a fighter pilot's war. As Robert Wohl has observed:

[I]t was not the pilots of reconnaissance planes, tactical aircraft, or bombers who captured the imagination of the public during and after the First World War. It was the ace who (regardless of the formation flying practiced in 1917-18) was portrayed as fighting and triumphing alone. Few were aware that the aces built up their scores by attacking inexperienced pilots, who were often flying slow and relatively defenseless reconnaissance aircraft. Aces seldom bothered to point out that the most successful combat pilots were those who avoided battle when the odds were even or against them. Why not give the public what they wanted? For years after the Armistice, Rickenbacker and other aviators supplemented their income with popularizations of their adventures during the war that had little to do with what had actually happened. (249)

By constructing, formalizing, and mythologizing the actions and attitudes of fighter pilots, especially aces, the expert ones who had shot down many aircraft, the World War I air combat films like *The Dawn Patrol* constructed a mythical reality more real than history itself.

Yet if there is an illusion of "truth" in *The Dawn Patrol*, there is also the "falsity" inherent in the film medium. Siegfried Kracauer has commented on film's remarkable capacity to record and reveal physical reality. Like photography, its predecessor, film shows "a marked affinity for the visual world around us." Kracauer admits that "films cling to the surface of things," but they also "evoke a reality more inclusive than the one they actually picture . . . they suggest a reality which may fittingly be called 'life'" (qtd. in Hughes 42-53). In truth, however, feature films and documentary films (i.e., those that claim to portray historical reality) are the product of subtle manipulations; a film is shaped and reshaped by editing to suit a particular need or illustrate a particular point of view. Naive viewers see what has been presented in the film medium and form impressions about its historical truth and falsity. These impressions are so lasting and difficult to efface that reviewers (and audiences) were often convinced that the reality portrayed in *The Dawn Patrol* and other World War I air combat films was historical. As Graeme Turner suggests, realist film efficiently disguises "the constructed as 'the natural'" and is powerful "in its ability to appear to be an unmediated view of reality" (155).

Because films thrive on melodrama, they tend to exaggerate or highlight elements of truth. In the World War I air combat film, the complexity of aerial warfare is reduced to its most dramatic elements, diminishing the intricacies of war itself, but providing a semblance of historical truth. History is complex and ambiguous; genre films, on the other hand, resolve apparent contradictions. This is part of the nature of genre films, which, Thomas Schatz says, "both criticize and reinforce the values, beliefs, and ideals of our culture within the same narrative context" (35).

The result is that *The Dawn Patrol* and subsequent films in the World War I air combat film genre resolve opposing and often contradictory modes of behavior and ideology. While Courtney's psychological struggle may be intense and real, it never confronts the existential terror of the war nor challenges the society that produced it. Courtney's adoption of a private code of honor (i.e., a romanticized notion of individualistic heroics, a pretense of denial of death, a refusal to face the horrors of combat, a slavish devotion to duty), tends to mitigate his struggle. The irony is that the code ultimately results in capitulation to, and reinforcement of, the ideals and values of a society that allows war to happen. The audience can empathize with the hero's psychological struggle, criticize the values of a society that would allow young men to be sacrificed, but finally concede that the hero's private code—despite its acquiescence to societal values—is worthy and admirable.

While the portrayal of air combat in *The Dawn Patrol* professes to be authentic and does contain more than a kernel of truth, it is an inaccurate representation. The film asserts that fighter pilots were the most courageous combat pilots, that *mano a mano* combat and chivalry among pilots were the norm, and that the air war helped to win the struggle. These ideas, which have been advanced by "experts" in the field for years, have gone unchallenged until recently. In the 1990s, a new group of scholars such as Lee Kennett, John Morrow, and Robert Wohl began to explore the historical complexities of air combat in World War I and reached quite different conclusions. Kennett, for example, argues that "the whole subject of the first air war is like some imperfectly explored country: there are areas that have been crisscrossed by several generations of historians; there are regions where only writers of dissertations and abstruse monographs have ventured, and others yet that remain *terra incognita*" (ix). He concludes that while many assumptions and judgments about air combat in World War I "are solidly anchored in fact; others have seemed . . . simplistic, and still others grounded in little more than myth and wishful thinking" (ix).

The creation of the perceptual conventions of air combat began during the war itself. Early in the conflict, champions of aviation in Britain, France, and Germany began calling for identification of aerial combatants. With identification came government recognition. In Great Britain, for example, H. G. Wells advocated "a knighthood" to the aviator "or the prompt payment of a generous life assurance policy" to his survivors for feats of aerial fighting (qtd. in Kennett 152-53). In France and Italy, André Michelin and Giovanni Pirelli created huge funds to compensate pilots who distinguished themselves. In Germany, the Pour le Mérite, (or "Blue Max"), which had previously been awarded only for extraordinary gallantry in fighting on the ground, became emblematic of aviators' high status (Kennett 152-53).

Soon, governments became aware that in the anonymous killing ground of the Western Front, soldiers were hard to dramatize as heroes, and they turned to pilots as a means of recruitment and to garner support for the war. All of the attention, however, focused on the "aces," a distinction given (except in Great Britain) to Allied and Central Forces pilots who had shot down five aircraft or more. Later, memoirs by aviators further lionized the deeds of pilots. In the late 1920s, after Lindbergh's transatlantic flight had created an atmosphere of favorable publicity for aviation, articles and stories in pulp magazines often exaggerated the nature and importance of air combat in World War I. Gradually, the true nature of aerial warfare was obscured; Hollywood was primarily responsible for fashioning the legend. In *The Dawn Patrol* and films like it, idealized images of young pilot-heroes clad in leather coat and helmet, with long silk scarves flowing from their necks as they peer out of the open cockpits of their fragile biplane aircraft, reinforced the myths.

John Morrow, a prominent scholar of aviation in World War I, aptly describes the Hollywood stereotype:

Darting about the heavens in their lightly armed and unarmored planes and pouncing on one another in individual combat, they fight tenaciously, win gallantly, die heroically, their flaming craft plunging to earth like meteoric funeral pyres, extinguishing their equally meteoric careers with scorching finality. Their names—Boelcke, Ball, Richthofen, Guynemer, Mannock—are legend; their lives, terribly short; their exploits, the material of myth. (xiv)

This concentration on the knights of the air, Morrow goes on,

stems from a natural tendency to emphasize the heroic. The very circumstances of the conflict encouraged a mythologizing of the air war into a single image of individual combat, deadly but chivalrous. Mass slaughter on an unprecedented scale was rendering individuals insignificant. Aerial heroes provided a much-needed, though misleading, affirmation of the importance of the individual and of youth in a slaughter of both. (xv)

Yet, placing the dominant focus on the individual deeds and stereotypes of the fighter aces in World War I, Morrow says, gives short shrift to the air arms of the military forces and implies that they were merely primitive instruments in a complex technological-industrial war. This perspective detracts from air power's true military-industrial importance. In addition, placing undue emphasis on the individual deeds of a relative handful of aces in an anachronistic context of chivalric battle, clouds the technologically innovative nature of the air war, which although executed crudely, epitomized a modern way of fighting. This new mode of combat assumed that military, civilian, political, technological and industrial aspects were interrelated. Moreover, the fighter aces were merely a much publicized manifestation of various, less heralded, aircraft roles—bombing, photo reconnaissance, artillery spotting, ground attack, among others (xv).

Nevertheless, *The Dawn Patrol* struck a significant chord with audiences. The film had a long, popular run at the Winter Garden Theater in New York City. The doors of the theater opened every day at 10:00 A.M. and showings went on continuously until 2:30 A.M. the next morning. One reviewer reported that the film was "daily attracting capacity audiences in a season when many other films along Broadway are finding it difficult to roll up even moderately satisfactory box-office figures." At a performance the reviewer recently attended, "only standing room was available. Standees were grouped behind the orchestra seats in formations four and five rows deep, and most of them were willing to remain corralled inside the white tape lines in spite of the fact that the Winter Garden's polite ushers held out no promise of seats for an hour or more." During the first four days of its engagement at the Winter Garden Theater, the film grossed $31,400, and the weekend crowd was the largest in the history of the theater. The crowds and popularity were repeated at openings in other major cities. First-night crowds in San Francisco stormed the entrance and stampeded their way into the theater. In Philadelphia, "police had to send a call for reserves, who arrived just in time to save three badly harassed doormen."[10]

The Dawn Patrol's thematic material, especially its focus on the psychological pressures of air combat and atonement, and its popularity strongly influenced other films in the genre. *The Eagle and the Hawk* (1933), for example, portrays the mental deterioration of Jerry Young (Fredric March), an American in the Royal Flying Corps. Proclaimed a hero for his aerial exploits, Young finds that he cannot bear to see his comrades dying in combat and eventually commits suicide after an impassioned and bitter antiwar speech. Ideologically, however, Young's character must find heroic redemption. The plot contrives to have his gunner-observer, Henry Crocker (Cary Grant), make everyone believe that Young had been killed in battle, thus perpetuating the image of the traditional hero. In *Ace of Aces* (1933), Rex Thorn (Richard Dix), a sculptor, abandons his art and his idealistic antiwar notions when his fiancée accuses him of cowardice. He enlists in the Air Service and, once he gets a taste of killing, becomes the "ace of aces," with more than forty "victories" to his credit. After he shoots down an unarmed cadet who has dropped a message on his airfield, Thorn suffers pangs of guilt and seeks redemption.

The cultural reasons for the popularity of *The Dawn Patrol* and of the World War I air combat genre are varied. Perhaps, as British historian J. M. Winter suggests, in the three quarters of a century since the Armistice, film has "reached a wider audience" and "had a much greater effect on the way the war has been imagined." Too, Winter argues, films about World War I have one thing in common: "the capacity to mythologize the war, to recreate it in a form which was much more palatable to live with than was the event itself. Hence many war films, in particular those of the interwar years, served (and still serve) an essential purpose: to bury the past and help people recreate it in a form they can accept" (238). George Mosse calls this phenomenon the "myth of the war experience," and says that it "made good use of visual materials to sanitize, dramatize, and romanticize war" (50, 59).

Another reason for the popularity of *The Dawn Patrol* may have to do with the time in which it was made. *The Dawn Patrol* appeared in August 1930, during the first year of the Great Depression.[11] This was a time when movies were extremely popular in the United States: in the early 1930s, for example, an average of 60 to 75 million movie theater tickets were purchased each week; some estimate these figures are higher; i.e., 80 to 90 million film goers per week (Belton 3). Many of these tickets were bought by customers who went to the movies repeatedly, but the number of tickets sold represents attendance by some 60 percent of the population (as opposed to 10 percent in the 1990s (McElvaine 208).[12] Thus, the films of the 1930s, especially genre films designed to attract return audiences to similar kinds of film, reflected (or reflected on) themes that were of concern to ordinary American citizens. During the 1930s, economic hardship was on everyone's mind. Intentionally or unintentionally, the themes of wartime courage and group solidarity could easily be adapted to times of economic despair.[13]

The Dawn Patrol could thus be seen as celebrating values of teamwork, of "sticking together," of community and sharing—values seen by many as contrary to the values of acquisitive individualism inherent in modern industrial capitalism. While individualistic acts take place in *The Dawn Patrol* (Courtney and Scott's attack on the German aerodrome; Courtney's suicide mission at the end), they are done for the good of the group. The voiceless, faceless "headquarters," which seems to give orders without concern for the lives of inexperienced pilots, could represent the anonymity of the unfeeling capitalist system. *The Dawn Patrol*'s denial that anything was wrong with the system, and that the job must be done in spite of what the pilots think about headquarters, is similar to the prevailing attitude that the Depression was a temporary aberration rather than a symptom of more essential flaws in the economic system (McElvaine 196-223). In this context, the thematic thrust of *The Dawn Patrol* also reflects American concerns, despite its setting in a Royal Flying Corps squadron in World War I.

Remaking *The Dawn Patrol* and Subsequent Genre Development

In 1938 Warner Bros. produced a remake of *The Dawn Patrol*, directed by Edmund Goulding and starring Errol Flynn as Courtney, Basil Rathbone as Brand, and David Niven as Scott.[14] The updated version maintained the generic characteristics of its predecessor and was faithful to Howard Hawks's original conception, even using aerial footage from the original. The film appeared, however, at a time when the World War I air combat genre had run its course. In addition, there was a new war on the horizon, and the updated version of *The Dawn Patrol* reflected concern over the impending conflict in Europe.

Goulding's *Dawn Patrol* premiered at the Warner Bros. Hollywood Theater on December 12, 1938. It came at the end of a momentous year in which the Nazis first took Austria in March and then occupied the Sudetenland in October, virtually guaranteeing the fall of Czechoslovakia. In November, the Nazis launched a terrible campaign marked by *Kristallnacht*, during which Jewish shops were wrecked, Jews were killed and arrested, and synagogues pillaged. The Warner brothers were conscious of the European situation in terms of a potentially shrinking market for its films (overseas markets represented 40 percent of film industry revenues). The studio was equally conscious of how important the British market was to the profitability of the studio. Sensing the mood of the European situation, Hal Wallis, executive producer at Warner Bros., wrote to Jack Warner on April 30, 1938, that in reissuing the original 1930 film, the British "must consider the subject matter very timely" (qtd. in Behlmer 73). Wallis was convinced that in remaking *The Dawn Patrol*, Warners "could knock out a very great picture in a very short time, and one that I think would bring us a fortune now when the whole world is talking and thinking war and re-armament" (qtd. in Behlmer 73).

Warner Bros. publicists reinforced Wallis's thinking. A promotional blurb for the 1938 version makes a strong plea for unity in the face of oppression in Europe and connects it with World War I:

The bloody horror of the last great war could have been averted—had the people of the world a clear vision of what was to come, before the fateful August of 1914. Today, in 1938, you are faced with the imminence of another such catastrophe. . . . This time its possibilities of ghastliness are unthinkable. The warning glare of munitions plants redden the sky unceasingly. . . . At any moment your streets can be strewn with your dead. . . . At any moment your boys can be rounded up for slaughter. . . . The war-mad maniacs are on the march again. . . . Only a World—rising as one man—can stop them! Fight now . . . for peace!"[15]

To create a new mythos for impending war, the studio turned to the World War I air combat genre for themes of duty, cooperation, and courage.

In various ways, the two versions of *The Dawn Patrol* point the way to the World War II air combat film genre. Jeanine Basinger believes that "in a sense, it is probably *The Dawn Patrol* that the World War II film is working against when it appears" (96). Robert Ray contends that the development of the entire World War II combat film genre begins with Howard Hawks's 1939 *Only Angels Have Wings*, a defining film in the aviation film genre. This film, Ray argues, had the five basic motifs essential to the World War II combat film genre: "an isolated male group involved in a life-and-death task"; "the group, composed of distinct types, that relies on both teamwork and individual exploits"; "professionalism and stoicism in the face of danger and death"; "outsiders enter the group and become threats to it"; "outsiders must win admission to the group" (115-18).

By Ray's standards, Hawks's *Dawn Patrol* arguably could be the progenitor of the World War II era combat film because it, too, contains these five elements, and, curiously, it appeared nine years before *Only Angels Have Wings*. The first three of Ray's criteria—male struggle; teamwork and individualism; and stoicism in the face of death—are central to *The Dawn Patrol*. The last two are problematic, but not overly so. One interpretation could be that these last two elements were developments that appear later in the genre. Another is that headquarters is the "outsider" in *The Dawn Patrol* because it is faceless and concerned only with giving orders, orders that are literally threats to the well-being of the pilots. Yet another is that Major Brand is an "outsider," who, while he is the nominal leader of the squadron, always clashes with the "true" or spiritual leader Courtney. When Courtney becomes squadron commander, he becomes the outsider, and he must contend with the true leader, who is now Scott. Thus, as one reviewer observes, *The Dawn Patrol*'s "story would be adaptable to any wartime setting" because "it relates a pattern of action and reaction, perceived by the film to be so unchanging and unresolvable that it becomes a cycle which can only be endlessly repeated" (Lucas 578).

Hawks's working out of this pattern (male group characterized by teamwork and individual exploits, professionalism and stoicism in the face of death, and the threat by outsiders) begins with *The Dawn Patrol*, and proceeds through *Only Angels Have Wings* to its logical conclusion in *Air Force* (1943). Thomas Doherty has observed that "in Hawks, auteurist sensibility matched wartime necessity. A loving celebrant of men in groups and machines in flight, his personal vision saw eye to eye with the needs of the Army Air Force" (110). *Air Force* contains all the familiar elements of the propagandizing World War II combat film. These consist of a tightly knit group of ethnically diverse Americans, led by an Anglo-American, who possess interrelated skills and are molded into an effective combat unit. Another characteristic is that the evolving narrative focus moves away from personal concerns toward the mission. Thus, *Air Force* presents an idealized portrait of democracy in action poised to win a difficult struggle.

After World War II, the notion that individualized heroism and group loyalty are not mutually exclusive (which begins with Courtney's suicide mission in *The Dawn Patrol* and moves forward through Sergeant Winocki's saving of the bomber *Mary Ann* after its crew has bailed out) starts to break down. In the postwar context, heroism can only be achieved by being a member of the group, and individual heroics are prohibited—even punished. The reason for this change, Peter Biskind argues, is that "war films could help create a cultural climate hospitable to cold-war objectives" by stressing the cooperative nature of modern war and its applicability to withstanding the Soviet threat (57).

In *Twelve O'Clock High* (1949), for example, General Savage (Gregory Peck), a strict disciplinarian, forbids individual heroics within his bomber wing in the interest of group cohesion, morale, and survival. He breaks his own rule, however, when he refuses to turn back from a bombing mission that has been recalled by his commanding officer, General Pritchard (Millard Mitchell). Savage thinks his decision is for the benefit of the group, but Pritchard tells him, "You're swinging after the bell." While Courtney's heroism is unambiguous, Savage's is cloudy. Unlike Courtney, whose death is literal, Savage's "death" is symbolic in that he becomes psychologically and physically paralyzed by the burdens of command. Unlike Courtney, whose sacrifice ends in a heroic death, Savage falls into a catatonic state after pushing himself beyond human endurance. Savage's end is more in keeping with the tenor of early Cold War films in which psychosis (representative of death-in-life) becomes more fearful than death itself. Nevertheless, the conventions established in *Dawn Patrol*—regarding the tensions between individual and group and the pressures of command—are reworked to suit a post–World War II formula in *Twelve O'Clock High*.

The Hawksian archetype can also be seen in what has been termed the "professional western"; films such as Hawks's own *Rio Bravo* (1959), and others such as *The Professionals* (1966), *True Grit* (1969), *The Wild Bunch* (1969), and *Butch Cassidy and the Sundance Kid* (1969). In these films, professional outlaw-heroes, each with his own specialty—yet respectful of and loyal to the group—band together to defeat powerful villains. The group ends up staying together or sacrificing itself in a heroic death that confirms its personal code of honor (Wright 85-123). In this way, the World War I air combat film is related to the films of other genres. It is also, as Robin Wood suggests, evidence that film genres are not so discrete, but merely offer "different strategies for dealing with the same ideological tensions" (qtd. in Grant 62).

The conventions of the World War I air combat film genre, as represented by Hawks's *The Dawn Patrol*, evolved into the conventions of the World War II air combat film and extended beyond it. Eventually, however, the air combat genre began to stagnate. The western and the combat film genres underwent significant changes during the Cold War, and especially after the Vietnam War, often questioning—and sometimes abandoning—the traditional values they had championed earlier. This evolution simply did not happen in the air combat genre, which for the most part maintained its traditional attitudes and values. Thus, an immensely popular film like the Reagan era's *Top Gun* (1986)—made just a few years before the demise of the Soviet Union—espoused essentially the same values as *The Dawn Patrol*, without much consciousness of change. In *Top Gun*, air combat is mostly simulated, except for the beginning and end of the film, where the American pilots battle Soviet aggressors. Nevertheless, there is the same tension between individual heroics and loyalty to the group, the same conflicts between headstrong, instinctual pilots and "headquarters," the same psychological struggles with guilt over the death of comrades, the same iconography of aerial combat (with more modern aircraft and weapons).

The Dawn Patrol represents the turning point in the World War I air combat film genre, shifting the emphasis away from spectacle to the psychological examination of characters' motivations and emotions. In the tradition of genre films, it defines the role of a pilot-hero tested in combat and reconciles seemingly irreconcilable conflicts in American culture, especially those that have to do with war and the function of the individual versus the group in war. Its historical verisimilitude gives it a great deal of audience appeal but clouds the complex reality of the air war it supposedly depicted. *The Dawn Patrol*'s attraction seems rooted in its own contemporary scene, striking a sympathetic chord with viewers during the first painful year of the Depression, but the film's influence goes beyond the era in which it was produced by establishing its relationship to narrative conventions of other film genres.

Notes

1. Isenberg, *War on Film*, contains an excellent analysis of combat films that relate to World War I.

2. For details of the production of *Wings*, see Farmer, 29-41.

3. Some might argue that air combat movies belong to the war film genre, but a convincing argument can be made that they form a genre in themselves, distinct from—but related to—the war film genre. I am indebted to Schatz, *Hollywood Genres*, for his cogent discussion of genre.

4. Wood, *Howard Hawks*, uses these stylistic elements to make a detailed analysis of some of Hawks' most famous films. I am indebted to him for ideas concerning *The Dawn Patrol*.

5. Saunders, who had written the original story for *Wings*, was by 1930 a prominent aviation screenwriter; he won an Academy Award for *The Dawn Patrol* in the best original story category.

6. Richard Barthelmess Collection, Scrapbook #37 *The Dawn Patrol*, 14: newspaper clipping, "'Dawn Patrol' Authentic/Planes and Equipment Even to Uniforms, Used in War During 1915, 16, *Telegraph*, April 18, 1930, Academy of Motion Picture Arts and Sciences Archives, Los Angeles, California.

7. Richard Barthelmess Collection, Scrapbook #37 *The Dawn Patrol*, 101: newspaper clipping, *The Fresno Republican*, July 27, 1930; 121: newspaper clipping, *Pittsburgh Post-Gazette*, August 1, 1930; 111: newspaper clipping, *Richmond Times-Dispatch*, September 23, 1930, Academy of Motion Picture Arts and Sciences Archives, Los Angeles, California.

8. In a deposition made in August 1930, John Monk Saunders stated that during his time as a Rhodes scholar at Oxford University, he "met flyers from the Canadian, British, and French Air Corps and during [his] two years' residence at Oxford discussed with them frequently and in detail their own experiences and fears and hopes, adventures and activities while flying at the front during the war, and heard from them many recitals of the experiences and activities of other pilots" (qtd. in Behlmer 338). These incidents, Saunders contended, were the inspiration for his story "The Flight Commander."

9. Cooper, 71-81, contains an excellent analysis of Trenchard's "policy of relentless and incessant offensive."

10. Richard Barthelmess Collection, Scrapbook #37 *The Dawn Patrol*, 6: Norbert Lusk, "The Dawn Patrol Packs Theater/Barthelmess Air Film Best Seen in East," newspaper clipping, no source or date; 19: Martin Dickstein, "'The Dawn Patrol,' in Spite of Its Deficiencies, Is Breaking Records at the Winter Garden," *Brooklyn Eagle*, July 20, 1930; 29: "The Dawn Patrol at Winter Garden Theatre Breaking All Records," newspaper clipping, no source, August 30, 1930, Academy of Motion Picture Arts and Sciences Archives, Los Angeles, California.

11. If the case made for *The Dawn Patrol* and the Depression is true, how do we account for the popularity of *All Quiet on the Western Front*? One explanation is that no era in American history is entirely homogeneous in its cultural thought. *All Quiet* may have resonated with the widespread isolationist sentiments of the interwar years, and as Isenberg points out, "the onset of the

Depression, which brought with it films of despair and bitterness, may have made the anti-war film more acceptable" (128).

12. Information on film attendance in the 1990s was extracted from Barry Monush, ed., *International Motion Picture Almanac*, 66th ed. (New York: Quigley, 1995) 15A-18A.

13. I am indebted to McElvaine, chap. 9, "Moral Economics: American Values and Culture in the Great Depression," 196-223, and Roddick, chap. 4, "The Crash to Pearl Harbor," 64-70, for ideas about what films made during the Depression reveal about American culture.

14. When the 1938 version of *The Dawn Patrol* appeared, Hawks's original film was retitled *The Flight Commander*, after John Monk Saunders's script story title.

15. Publicity copy for *The Dawn Patrol*, 1938. Dawn Patrol Folder. Warner Brothers Archives, U of Southern California.

Works Cited

Basinger, Jeanine. *The World War II Combat Film: Anatomy of a Genre*. New York: Columbia UP, 1986.

Behlmer, Rudy. *Inside Warner Bros. (1935-1951)*. New York: Viking, 1985.

Belton, John. *American Cinema/American Culture*. New York: McGraw-Hill, 1994.

Biskind, Peter. *Seeing Is Believing: How Hollywood Taught Us to Stop Worrying and Love the Fifties*. New York: Pantheon, 1983.

Collier, Basil. *Heavenly Adventurer: Sefton Brancker and the Dawn of British Aviation*. London: Secker & Warburg, 1959.

Cooper, Malcolm. *The Birth of Independent Air Power: British Air Policy in the First World War*. London: Allen & Unwin, 1986.

DeBauche, Leslie Midkiff. "The Case of *Wings*: Film Distribution 'In Tune with These Changing Times.'" Unpub. paper presented at the Society for Cinema Studies Conference, 1988.

Doherty, Thomas. *Projections of War: Hollywood, American Culture, and World War II*. New York: Columbia UP, 1993.

Farmer, James H. *Celluloid Wings*. Blue Ridge Summit: TAB Books, 1984.

Grant, Barry Keith, ed. *Film Genre Reader*. Austin: U of Texas P, 1990.

Hall, Mordaunt. Rev. of *Wings*. *New York Times* 13 Aug. 1927: 10.4.

Hughes, William. "The Evaluation of Film as Evidence." *The Historian and Film*. Ed. Paul Smith. Cambridge: Cambridge UP, 1978. 52-53.

Isenberg, Michael T. *War on Film: The American Cinema and World War I, 1914-1941*. East Brunswick: Associated UP, 1981.

Kennett, Lee. *The First Air War, 1914-1918*. New York: Free Press, 1991.

Lucas, Blake. "The Dawn Patrol." *Magill's Survey of Cinema.* English Language Films, Second Series. Vol. 2. Ed. Frank N. Magill. Englewood Cliffs: Salem, 1981. 578-82.

McBride, Joseph. *Hawks on Hawks.* Berkeley: U of California P, 1982.

McElvaine, Robert S. *The Great Depression: America, 1929-1941.* New York: Times, 1984.

Morrow, John. *The Great War in the Air: Military Aviation from 1909 to 1921.* Washington, D.C.: Smithsonian Institution P, 1993.

Mosse, George. *Fallen Soldiers: Reshaping the Memory of the World Wars.* New York: Oxford UP, 1990.

Ray, Robert B. *A Certain Tendency of the Hollywood Cinema, 1930-1980.* Princeton: Princeton UP, 1985.

Roddick, Nick. *A New Deal in Entertainment: Warner Brothers in the 1930s.* London: BFI, 1983.

Schatz, Thomas. *Hollywood Genres: Formulas, Filmmaking, and the Studio System.* New York: McGraw-Hill, 1981.

——. "The Structural Influence: New Directions in Film Genre." *Film Genre Reader.* Ed. Barry Keith Grant. Austin: U of Texas P, 1990. 91-101.

Soderbergh, Peter A. "*Aux Armes!*: The Rise of the Hollywood War Film, 1916-1930." *South Atlantic Quarterly* 65 (1966): 509-22.

Spears, Jack. *Hollywood: The Golden Era.* New York: Castle, 1977.

Suid, Lawrence H. *Guts and Glory: Great American War Movies.* Reading: Addison-Wesley, 1978.

Turner, Graeme. *Film As Social Practice.* London: Routledge, 1991.

Winter, J. M. *The Experience of World War I.* New York: Oxford UP, 1989.

Wohl, Robert. *A Passion for Wings: Aviation and the Western Imagination, 1908-1918.* New Haven: Yale UP, 1994.

Wood, Robin. *Howard Hawks.* Hertford: BFI, 1983.

——. "Ideology, Genre, Auteur." *Film Genre Reader.* Ed. Barry Keith Grant. Austin: U of Texas P, 1990. 59-73.

Wright, Will. *Six Guns and Society: A Structural Study of the Western.* Berkeley: U of California P, 1975.

5

Hell's Angels above *The Western Front*

Robert Baird

One should not fault Hollywood too quickly for presenting two contradictory treatments of the First World War. The war itself divided easily (in the mind) between a realism of trench warfare on and in the ground and a romantic celebration of Promethean exploits above the clouds. This bifurcated vision was most evident in 1930, when Hollywood successfully released two entirely contradictory visions of war. The eventual Oscar winner for best picture, *All Quiet on the Western Front* (hereafter *All Quiet*), was described by a *Variety* reviewer as, "A harrowing, gruesome, morbid tale of war, so compelling in its realism, bigness and repulsiveness that Universal's 'Western Front' becomes at once a money picture. For this is war and what Sherman said goes double here" (May 7, 1930). Striking a far different chord with the public was Howard Hughes's long awaited *Hell's Angels* whose spectacular opening and public response Hughes's biographer John Keats describes:

The next morning, the telegrams began to arrive. THE ZEPPELIN SEQUENCE IS THE MOST DRAMATIC EPISODE I'VE EVER SEEN, Charles Chaplin wired. One Hollywood critic said the film contained "the most beautiful shots and thrilling action the movies had yet conceived." Another wrote, "Beside its sheer magnificence, all stage spectacles and colossal circuses become puny." Attendance records toppled at Grauman's Chinese Theater where it ran for nineteen weeks to capacity houses. *Hell's Angels* became the first picture to open simultaneously at two New York theaters. (43)

What conditions contributed to the concurrent release of two such disparate visions of World War I? The answers derive from many factors— in actual differences between air and ground combat in World War I, in the dominating sensibilities behind both films, and in this century's ambivalent response to warfare, a fluctuating tension between romantic heroism and realist pathos, celebration and condemnation, solemnity and mockery, "prowar" and "antiwar" stance. True to the logic of a dialectic,

79

analysis of *Angels* and *All Quiet* reveals that neither film is wholly dominated by a single mode; neither film fully represses the opposite sentiment. First, then, something about the romantic who made *Hell's Angels*.

Origin of the Ambivalent Visions

On May 27, 1930, planes buzzed Hollywood Boulevard as search-
lights scanned the sky and parachutists floated to earth. A wild hoard had
besieged Graumann's Chinese Theater. With ersatz illuminated airplanes
lining Hollywood Boulevard in front of an ersatz Chinese palace as real
planes buzzed the masses in ersatz strafing, the very real Depression
threatening America was forgotten, for the moment. The show was being
paid for by millionaire playboy Howard Hughes, who, orphaned in his
early twenties, had control of the steady and substantial profits of the
Hughes Tool Company. Looking beyond his late father's drill-bit business, Hughes made aviation and Hollywood his workshops. *Hell's
Angels* and its premiere highlighted Hughes's promotional extrava-
gances, his passion for aviation, and his bottomless bank account. After
four years of production (the longest major production in Hollywood
history and nearly as long as World War I itself) millionaire playboy
Howard Hughes had dovetailed three of his favorite subjects (women,
aviation, and movies) into one project. The *Hell's Angels* that premiered
that May night in Hollywood sported a production history as legendary
and eccentric as its director, a production history that reveals Hughes's
romantic obsessiveness and his showman's love of spectacle.

Hell's Angels was really the third version. Hughes, possessing
ample resources, simply scrapped two early rough cuts of the film. The
first "lost" *Angels* was a silent. When the *Angels'* production continued
into the sound era it was decided to make the film an "all talking picture," forcing the refilming of many scenes involving Norwegian actress
Greta Nissen, whose thick accent made her role as a British ingenue
impossible. The need for a new female lead eventually brought Jean
Harlow before the public in her first substantial role. The second lost
Angels was a film with plenty of good aerial work, in the can, and rough
cut, but lacking the necessary cloud cover, which Hughes had determined was essential for dramatic effect. The final *Angels*, deemed
worthy of release by Hughes, never fully integrated Harlow's melodramatic sequences with the spectacular air battle sequences, but this did
not seem to bother critics or viewers, who appreciated Harlow and the
aerial footage as distinct filmic spectacles. The excitement of the *Hell's
Angels* premiere was not lessened by the widespread belief that the film
had topped *Ben-Hur* as the most expensive motion picture ever produced. *Hell's Angels* had a successful theatrical run, including patriotic

reviews in England (the film's heroes being American actors playing Royal Flying Corp. aviators). To later generations the film became, along with *Wings* (1927) and *The Dawn Patrol* (1930), one of the best World War I air pictures.

In contrast with the hoopla and spectacle of *Angels'* release, *All Quiet* was, for the most part, respectfully lauded in America. In Europe, however, *All Quiet* was banned and censored, most notably in Germany, where Joseph Goebbels rallied storm troopers in street riots against the "pacifist," "Jewish" film. Under duress, novelist Erich Maria Remarque left Germany in 1932. It was, poetically, a German émigré Jew and his son, head of Universal Studios Carl Laemmle and Laemmle Jr., who bought the rights to Remarque's novel and lavished great expense on it, including turning a sizable portion of the Universal lot into a World War I battlefield.

But neither *Angels* nor *All Quiet* sprang newly formed from Hollywood's brow. Both were modeled on earlier, successful films: *Angels* built on *Wings* (1927) and *All Quiet*, although much more of an original, built on *The Big Parade* (1925). *Wings*, described as "a whopping air spectacle dominated by its remarkable action and aerial scenes," apparently "overwhelmed" its audience, in part because:

Paramount staged it grandly. On opening roadshow engagements, half of the picture was exhibited in *Magnascope*, a forerunner of the wide screen. Backstage effects were used to simulate the whine of plane motors and some of the battle scenes were in color. This was pioneer color, with sky and clouds tinted blue and flashes of red used to show spouts of fire shooting from planes. It was all new excitement for audiences of the day. No studio process photography was used in the action scenes, and it was the first major air show committed to film. It was also grand, red-blooded movie-making; the kind of visual entertainment with which the motion picture industry found its mass audience and support. (Osborne 11)[1]

It was *Wings* that initiated the air picture subgenre. Not least of those influenced by *Wings* was the young Howard Hughes, who saw in the film a spectacular template he aimed to surpass (Pendo 84). The melodramatic love triangle of *Wings* (Buddy Rogers, Jobyna Ralson, and Richard Arlen) is replicated in *Hell's Angels* (Ben Lyon, Jean Harlow, and James Hall). The color tinting of *Wings* is continued in *Angels* in a dueling scene, the famous zeppelin sequence, and in a long ballroom scene shot in two-color Technicolor. Similarly, many of the Hollywood stunt flyers and aerial cinematographers who worked on *Wings* were later hired by Hughes for *Angels*, including director of photography

Harry F. Perry and international airplane procurer Frank Tomick (Thomas 45; Pendo 87). King Vidor's *The Big Parade* had shown, too, that gritty depictions of trench warfare would not scare off American filmgoers or cost more in production than theatrical profits could bear.

Mythic Tensions: Irony and Empathy

In his acclaimed analysis of the effect of World War I on collective psychology and culture, Paul Fussell argues that the "static" and "stable" nineteenth-century worldview that helped launch World War I faltered under the deadly success of mechanized warfare. Replacing this stable old-world system was a vision born of no man's land: "one dominating form of modern understanding . . . essentially ironic" (35). For many of the literary generation who found themselves in the "Troglodyte world" of the trenches, old classics and nineteenth-century values were tested and found wanting. Veteran artists of World War I fell back to the only artistic position available: the brittle aesthetic and thin smile of modern irony. Siegfried Sassoon, Wilfred Owen, and Ernest Hemingway were only a few of the most successful artists of the lost generation who sharpened irony to a fine, bitter point. Fussell observes that long before our twentieth-century-long crisis of meaning,

Everyone knew what Glory was, and what Honor meant. It was not until eleven years after the war that Hemingway could declare in *A Farewell to Arms* that "abstract words such as glory, honor, courage, or hallow were obscene beside the concrete names of villages, the numbers of roads, the names of rivers, the numbers of regiments and the dates." In the summer of 1914 no one would have understood what on earth he was talking about. (21)

What the lost generation found was an attitude, bitterly ironic. Although Fussell is certainly correct in his assertion that World War I helped undermine a progressive modernism, it is much less obvious that the war's horrors and the accompanying ironic response displaced romance as a general modality of the mind and culture. Fussell himself devotes a chapter of *The Great War in Modern Memory* to the "Myth, Ritual, and Romance" of World War I, finding that the "general human impulse to make fictions had been dramatically unleashed by the novelty, immensity, and grotesqueness of the proceedings" (115). The romantic response to the war was not reserved for Hollywood, propagandists, and civilians. Eric J. Leed and George L. Mosse have each shown how participants of the war sought to "make sense" of the war through religion, ritual, myth, legend, rumor, and traditional notions of valor. Having combat experience or lacking it does not seem to have determined one's general "sense making" attitude toward the war, whether that attitude was dominated by romantic, realist, or ironic tendencies. Fussell's claim for the historical birth of "one dominating form of modern understanding . . . essentially ironic" from the experience of the Great War must be balanced with this later passage from his book:

Such leanings towards ritual, such needs for significant journeys and divisions and returns and sacramental moments, must make us skeptical of Bernard Bergonzi's conclusion: "The dominant movement in the literature of the Great War was . . . from a myth-dominated to a demythologized world." No: almost the opposite. In one sense the movement was towards myth, towards a revival of the cultic, the mystical, the sacrificial, the prophetic, the sacramental, and the universally significant. In short, towards fiction. (131)

It is this apparent contradiction (expressed in many texts of World War I) between mythicizing and demythicizing the war that *Hell's Angels* and *All Quiet* so readily betray. It is my argument that realism and romance are complimentary psychological attitudes that art and literature present in dialectical tension. It is this very conflict between real death (antimeaning) and romantic death (transcendence) that forms the tension in most intellectual responses to World War I. Apparently art and mind of this century rely on a strange symbiosis of both.

This dialectic tension is apparent in *Legend, Memory and the Great War in the Air*, a publication of the National Air and Space Museum, Smithsonian Institution, issued to accompany a November 1991 exhibit of the Smithsonian's World War I aviation material. The book is beautifully arranged with images from planes, war material, photographs, and posters, and is accompanied with eight intelligent and well-documented essays. Martin Harwit, director of the museum, writes assuredly in the preface that *Legend* "provides an accurate portrayal of aviation's role in the war, contrasting the romantic image of gallant combat in the sky with the grim reality faced by the aviators who fought and died in conflict." The task of undercutting romance with grim reality continues in *Legend*'s introduction by Dominick A. Pisano, entitled "Constructing the Memory of Aerial Combat in World War I." Pisano's epigraph quickly hints at his own view of romance: "War has nothing to do with chivalry anymore . . . the higher civilization rises, the viler man becomes" (qtd. in Robbins 88). Pisano then devotes his first paragraph to a summary of George L. Mosse's *Fallen Soldiers: Reshaping the Memory of the World War*, a work similar to Fussell's demythicizing *Modern Memory and the Great War:*

The memory of World War I was reconstructed as a "sacred experience," argues George L. Mosse. . . . The image makers . . . constructed a myth about the war that gave it a religious form and feeling, made saints of the war dead and shrines of their graves, and . . . provided a heritage that would be carried forward in wars to come. This myth, Mosse asserts, "would draw the sting from death in war and de-emphasize the meaningfulness of the fighting and sacrifice." The myth served to make acceptable what was intrinsically unacceptable, console the population, and assure the nation that the war had not been fought in vain. More insidious, but no less misleading was the trivialization of the experience of war "through its associations with objects of daily life, popular theater, or battlefield tourism." (11)

This is a fairly good summary of Mosse's book except for the emphasis on "image makers" bent on fabricating ideology for the duped masses. Mosse's work, although critical of this mythicizing and trivializing, stresses how the mythicizing of the war was a defensive psychological strategy used by nearly everyone to make sense of World War I—troops in the trenches as well as propagandists back home:

[T]he urge to find a higher meaning in the war experience, and to obtain some justification for the sacrifice and loss, was widespread. This need was greatest among veterans. They were often torn between their memory of the horror of war and its glory: it had been a time when their lives had taken on new meaning as they performed the sacred task of defending the nation. (6)

and:

The Myth of the War Experience was not entirely fictitious. After all, it appealed to men who had seen the reality of war and sought to transform and at the same time perpetuate the memory of this reality. These were often men who had felt enough enthusiasm to volunteer at the outbreak of the war. (7-8)

Pisano's piece marks a clear demarcation between reality and romance: "The pattern of distorting the reality of the war experience in the popular memory and record . . . can also be seen in the history of aviation in the World War I, especially in the minds of the American public" (11). Pisano calls the ground war the "primal reality" of World War I, "Yet, what is often remembered best are the heroic struggles of the pilots who fought above the carnage. These efforts, although heroic, have been exaggerated out of all proportion to their importance in the total war" (11). Pisano leaves a tiny gap for recognition of air war heroism with the inserted phrase "although heroic." In answering his own rhetorical question—"Why is the history of air combat in World War I so distorted and detached from the reality of the combat on the ground?"—Pisano replies that "historical accounts have too often emphasized the fantasy and adventure that are the intrinsic elements of aerial combat in World War I" (12). Again the "intrinsic" romance of the air beckons.[2]

Regarding American popular culture, Pisano feels that it was largely film that "helped form persistent opinions about the chivalry and gallantry of the air war" (12). But, again, even for Pisano, a thin wedge of romance remains:

To some extent, the cinematic stereotype depicted by *Wings* and its successors was true. Such aerial "aces" (pilots with considerable victories over enemy aircraft) as Britain's Albert Ball, Canada's William A. "Billy" Bishop, Germany's Manfred von Richthofen, France's Georges Guynemer, and the United States' Edward V. "Eddie" Rickenbacker accounted for an astonishing number of aerial kills and were legitimately lionized as combat heroes. (12)

The point I am making is that World War I air combat *historically* supported a romantic modality, and that this romantic modality was a naturally occurring psychological response to the idea of human flight during the tenuous birth of aviation; World War I air combat only raised the stakes of this romance with aviation. And Hollywood dramatized, embellished, and exploited this aerial romance.

In *Beyond Formula: American Film Genres*, Stanley J. Solomon adopts a strategy used by many to make sense of war films. He categorizes the genre through an analysis of subgenres, including the two most germane here: the "antiwar film" and "films of aerial warfare." The antiwar film takes as its goal the task of proving that, "Notwithstanding romantic illusions about valor, liberty, and righteousness, the ultimate realities of war are death and desolation" (250). The antiwar film, then, presents "ultimate realities" which are the "complementary alternative" to the "glamorized war film" (251). "Alternatives" because:

The major tradition of the antiwar film operates mainly in a realistic mode that serves to deglamorize the romantic elements associated with fighting for a cause, for freedom, or for the attainment of noble or heroic ends. A second prevalent tradition of the antiwar film employs an iconoclastic approach to debunk heroic warfare. (252)

The "glamorized war film" is best exemplified by the war film subgenre of the American air war picture:

Since in American films the profession of flying demands both courage and fatalism, we can only expect that the pilot will be a romantic. His romanticism manifests itself in his devotion to his duty, his tendency to immerse himself in the life of his squadron (much emphasis is placed on camaraderie), and his taking upon himself the responsibility for the lives of others. Thus, the hero must risk his own life before those of any of his fellow pilots, and the death of another will create guilt. (255)

As a romantic, the air war protagonist often becomes, in the no-win situation of the World War I context, a tragic hero. Also, "the original nature of air warfare emphasizes a potential for personal heroism not granted to ground troops in most situations" (254). Solomon notes that romantic air war films will often develop a "rotten war" theme, which has, however,

no particular social effect; it functions primarily to reinforce our sense of the pilot's courageous romanticism, a willingness to sacrifice themselves not so much for a country or a cause but for a romantic ideal of service—perhaps a realization that though life itself is "rotten" their deeds, at least, overcome its inherent deficiencies by their avowal of a glamorous fatalism. (256)

The juxtaposition of the antiwar film's sentiment that "war is hell" and the air war film's "rotten war" theme exposes a common thread behind the romantic/realist dialectic. Another link: although fear in combat may be presented as "natural" to all men in the antiwar film, the antiwar film protagonist is never a "coward." Thus, the antiwar film never fully renounces or "demythicizes" courage within the context of war.

Finally, in an amazing contradiction, Solomon groups *Hell's Angels* and *The Dawn Patrol* (his previous example of the glamorous air war film) with *All Quiet on the Western Front* as the three "classic antiwar films released in the same year" (267). How can *Hell's Angels* and *The Dawn Patrol* be both glamorous and antiwar? This is no simple contradiction. The "complementary" relationship of romance and realism in the war film suggests a paradox of psychological modalities, each of which is dependent on the other. In short, what is always beneath the romance of the air in World War I texts is the realism of the trenches: a common sense of self-preservation. And in no man's land, the realm of the ultimate realities of death and desolation, the poetic sentiment struggles to find meaning and fixes upon a spectacle in the sky.

There are, though, real narrative differences between a film dominated by romanticism and one dominated by realism. Romantic spectacles like *Hell's Angels* celebrate the individual as causal agent of history,

The struggle for survival in a Troglodyte world.

Credit: The Film Archive

generating Great Man narratives. Realist films like *All Quiet on the Western Front* present individuals as effects of history, objects buffeted by their environment. The power and agency of fictional characters can define a work's overall tone or even genre. In the final chapter of *The Great War and Modern Memory*, Fussell uses Northrop Frye's tripartite system of classifying fiction based on a "hero's power of action, which may be greater than ours, less, or roughly the same" (311; 33-42). Myth, romance, and the "high mimetic" traditions of tragedy and the epic utilize heroes with power greater than the ordinary reader's. The "low mimetic" of the novel utilizes heroes with power equal to the reader's; and the ironic mode utilizes a hero with less power than the ordinary reader's. For Frye, these modes work in cycles, and Fussell follows this system when he marks the rise of the ironic mode in literature as a response to World War I. After the war one begins to see "a standard character . . . the man whom things are done to. He is Prufrock, Jake Barnes, Malone, Charlie Chaplin" (313). Fussell's Hollywood character—Chaplin—neglects the great majority of matinee idols and air picture players, all of which possessed equal or greater power than the typical viewer. And this is my point: Fussell's contention that the ironic mode came to dominate memory of World War I neglects the culturally significant Hollywood film, where the war was remembered dialectically, peopled as often with romantic heroes as with realist victims.

The treatment of combat death and injury signals a war film's ideological stance. As a war romance, *Angels* stages death and injury within a context of purpose (sacrifice for a greater good). As a realist war film, *All Quiet* stages death and injury as exemplars of exploitation (war orchestrated by a political class), as expressions of negative meaning (insanity, revenge, blood lust), or as meaningless behavior (random, accidental, mechanistic). The few times that a war romance will present combat as exploitive, negative, or meaningless are when it presents the activity of the enemy, whose conduct both condemns and justifies war. In the most bitterly antiwar film, the only causally forceful human agents are those officers and enlisted men who actively undermine or exploit their own military for selfish or sadistic goals. In Stanley Kubrick's *Paths of Glory*, a French officer orders French artillery to fire on French troops, who refuse to advance under impossible conditions; he later settles for a symbolic execution of four randomly selected soldiers from the offending troops. The possibility that combat performance, killing and being killed, injuring and being injured, can influence tactical/strategic outcome is what ultimately separates the war romance like *Hell's Angels* from the antiwar realist *All Quiet on the Western Front*. By presenting protagonists who can positively (or negatively) influence tactical/strategic outcome, the war romance works as an action film, where the ebb and flow of battle *matter*. By presenting protagonists who are only victims of training/battle/war, the antiwar film adopts a knowledge-quest formula, where a young innocent experiences war as hell, and survives long enough to speak this lesson; this knowledge-quest formula marks the antiwar film as the "lesson film," a condition which led a *Variety* reviewer of *All Quiet* to advise, "Every male in the world, from 14 years, up, should see this picture" (May 7, 1930). *Variety's* reviewer of *Hell's Angels*, however, noted that "as an air film it's a pip," and went on to celebrate the spectacle of the zeppelin downing: "The way this final destruction is pictured will get a gasp from any audience. No film has yet had anything like it" (June 4, 1930).

A detailed comparison of key scenes in *Angels* and *All Quiet* will further expose the distinction between the war romance of spectacle, purpose, strategic-agency, military justification and "action" and the realist war film of the prosaic, negative, meaningless, nonstrategic, antiwar "lesson." A great contrast obtains by comparing *Hell's Angels'* most spectacular depiction of warfare (the zeppelin sequence) with *All Quiet's* most prosaic depiction of warfare (the death of Kat).

Critical Scene #1: Saving the Zeppelin

Nearly every commentator and reviewer of *Hell's Angels* praises what is generically called "the zeppelin sequence" (the same that Chaplin lauded). The symbolic usefulness and spectacular appeal of Count Ferdinand von Zeppelin's flying airships was not a discovery of postwar Hollywood filmmakers. Indeed, the massive dirigibles were immensely symbolic and spectacular before a single trench had been dug, and long after. Before the war, the German "press and popular scientific literature had represented the zeppelin as a symbol of German inventive spirit and greatness, a peerless wonder weapon" (Morrow 17). When zeppelin raids began in actuality, needed British men and resources were diverted to the defense of the homeland (177). But the fear and outrage of the successful zeppelin attacks far exceeded the actual military and industrial damage the lumbering and vulnerable weapons caused. The zeppelin became (or always was) for British, French, and German leaders, primarily a psychological weapon, which could, just as quickly, become a symbol of German failure when shot down or accidentally destroyed.

As he planned for *Hell's Angels*, Hughes embraced the visual spectacle of the zeppelin and spent $460,000 producing a number of large (thirty-foot) models of a zeppelin under the guidance of Dr. K. Arstein, who helped engineer the airships in Germany during the war. Filmed in a balloon hanger near Arcadia, California, the zeppelin sequence was recognized at the time as state-of-the-art miniature and special effects work. Hughes even approached the owners of the *Graf Zeppelin* about a promotional flyover of Manhattan for the *Hell's Angels'* East Coast premiere, and was shocked when they turned down his offer of $100,000 (Barlett and Steele 68). The zeppelin's owners probably did not feel the need for more publicity; in August 1930 over one million Canadians and Americans had come to see *Zeppelin R100* while it was tethered in Montreal for thirteen days (Botting 124). But Hughes's zeppelin sequence represents more than the successful application of Hollywood technical craft toward the creation of an exemplary action sequence. The zeppelin sequence is, in a very uneven and often melodramatic film, a work of expressive and symbolic art as good as anything in *All Quiet, The Big Parade*, or any other respected World War I film. Part of the sequence's power lies in the zeppelin itself.³

The zeppelin sequence of *Hell's Angels* derives much of its power from sheer imagery. The entire sequence takes place at night, over London, the scene bathed in a dream-like blue. Except for the intercutting of a few black-and-white scenes of zeppelin defenses in London, the zeppelin sequence's blue tinting serves to poeticize a highly realistic *mise en scene* (the interiors of the dirigible are highly detailed, and the sequence was praised for using subtitles under the zeppelin crew's German dialogue). With everything awash in blue, including the "white," billowing clouds and the actors, the sequence develops a surreal quality that serves the action well. What ultimately makes the zeppelin sequence more than spectacle-for-spectacle's sake is its terrible visualization of the simple plot conceit that a number of German airshipmen are asked to jump to their deaths in order to lighten the airship as it attempts to elude British biplanes. Only *The Deer Hunter,* with its notorious Russian roulette scenes, has presented a filmic metaphor for death in war with such expressive power and visual force. Although analysis shows how the scene can easily be read as a romantic, strategic, action-based war scene, the surreal tinting, the suicidal jumps of the German airship men, the sequence's lack of music, and the zeppelin's eventual apocalyptic destruction work powerfully toward a haunting evocation of combat.

The zeppelin sequence borrows upon *Hell's Angels'* narrative investment in Karl Arnstedt (John Darrow), who is presented in the film's first scene: "Germany before the War." The handsome and gentlemanly Karl is a college friend of the English brothers Monte (Ben Lyon) and Roy Rutledge (James Hall). The three young men enjoy themselves in a German beer hall, where gaiety, drinking, singing, and the good German folk poignantly contrast with the drunkenness, violence, and nationalism that come with the outbreak of war. Later, back in England, Karl's draft notice is delivered to the Oxford apartment Karl shares with Monty and Roy. The foundations of inner conflict are being laid for Karl's eventual quandary as a zeppelin bombardier returned to bomb his former school ground. Karl's gentle personality and English schooling help motivate his decision to guide the zeppelin's bombs harmlessly into a London lake, instead of Trafalgar Square—this heroic pacifism goes unknown to the zeppelin's crew because Karl's observation car is suspended below the clouds, the zeppelin above them. Karl's suspension in his tiny pod in the heavens does not fail to impress with its stark symbolism. After having saved London with his courageous pacifism (a pacifism more easily allowed, in this film, in the enemy), Karl is slowly being winched upward into the belly of the zeppelin. With the RFC flyers in pursuit, the zeppelin captain (saber scar on cheek beside a pointed goatee) orders all water ballast released in order to lighten the airship. With the RFC still gaining, the captain is told that the wind resistance of Karl's "sub-cloud" car is reducing the zeppelin's potential speed. The captain asks a crew member to cut the tether. The crew member returns with a pair of massive wire cutters, which the camera ominously reveals in a slow tilt down the crew member's arm. With the winch no longer pulling him up, Karl asks impatiently over a telephone for the captain. The crew member places the wire cutters on the cable and slowly begins squeezing the cutters; insert of an extreme close-up of the cutter blades as they begin to depress—but the crew member cannot cut the cable. The captain places his hands over the extended handles of the cutters and says, "Für Gott und Vaterland!" The cable is cut—a medium long shot of the observer's car as it falls, silently, its cable flapping awkwardly. Melodramatic? Yes, but the sub-cloud car was actually used in a number of German Army zeppelins (Botting 60-61). Moreover, although cutting a sub-cloud car is probably a bit of Hollywood contrivance, the inherent psychological position of being in such a car—described by an actual crew member as a "disembodied spirit floating in space" (Botting 61)—is poetically exploited by Hughes. Sounding contrived in print, the zeppelin sequence plays with real force in the film, perhaps due to the lack of music, the eerie aptness of the cloud effects, and the intercutting of Karl suspended below—ignorant of his fate.

If Karl's sacrifice to German military professionalism and nationalism were not enough, the zeppelin sequence continues toward one of the most haunting war-as-suicide scenes in film. In spite of Karl's being cut loose from the zeppelin, and all loose equipment being tossed out, the English planes continue to close. In desperation, the captain asks various crew members to sacrifice themselves—"Für Gott und Vaterland." In all, nine crew members jump to their deaths. Some of the jumps are shown from an overhead camera, which emphasizes the gaping opening in the belly of the airship. A few shots rely on a simple medium close-up of a crew member, who simply falls out of frame, offscreen space becoming, in the viewer's imagination, a deadly void. The scene is played without music, with only the steady drone of the zeppelin's engines. A few cutaways go to exterior overhead shots of crew members falling silently through the blue-tinted clouds; one airman's cap falls off and flips oddly through the air, falling slower than its owner. Although the zeppelin's captain could have as easily played his role on the vaudeville circuit, Karl and his fellow crew members are more humanized, more like *All Quiet's* clean-scrubbed, serious youth. In the end, the zeppelin sequence is, as has been said many times, one of the best "action spectacles" ever filmed of the air war. Praising or dismissing the zeppelin sequence merely for its effects and action, though, overlooks one of the more haunting moments of the war film. As well, those silent steps into oblivion give the lie to the reductive critique that the war romance always denies death through a form of transcendence. Thus, the romance of *Hell's Angels* dominates but does not obliterate the realist emptiness and irony that can arise in the mind of a viewer who is watching young men step into the void "Für Gott und Vaterland."

Critical Scene #2: No Man's Land

All Quiet, a more consistently artful and fully integrated work than *Angels*, has its own spectacular scene of large-scale warfare. Although the great bulk of injuries and deaths in *All Quiet* are staged as prosaic and nonstrategic, the middle section of *All Quiet* portrays a massive British assault and German counterassault, following a grueling five-day bombardment. Forced to deal with spectacle (the historical reality of war's size and fury) and the possibility of exciting a film audience with scenes of large-scale battle, director Lewis Milestone uses a number of alienating strategies to undercut his own action sequences. His first and most consistent strategy is to undermine, through staging and editing, the strategic omniscience of a viewer. Unlike the battle scenes of the war romance, where a clear cause-and-effect chain of attack, retreat, action, and reaction will be intertwined with the principal characters, Milestone evokes the chaos of battle by overwhelming the frame with teeming soldiers and incessant shelling, by rapid editing, and by rapid presentation of the action. In other words, unlike the romantic battle scene, which coherently stages principal characters amid a chaotic background of combat, *All Quiet* loses its principal characters amid battle confusion. Denying the viewer a strategic visual perspective (bird's-eye-view, for example) or strategic verbal description (officers' commentary) of a battle restricts the film's narration to the foot soldier's view. The soldier "extras" are also presented in such a way that any personal cause and effect sequence is undermined. By this I mean that Milestone often cuts away from action as it is occurring, where a war romance might often isolate individual combatants and their actions amidst the confusion of battle.

A second alienating strategy used by Milestone is one of the most noted formal effects of *All Quiet*—the famous machine-gun pans, tracking shots taken from behind machine-gun positions as the weapon sweeps down rows of attacking infantrymen. The power of this formal presentation of combat is comparable to that of *Angels'* zeppelin suicides, for here, too, a filmmaker has joined camera movement, staging, and narrative to create a visual expression of World War I combat that evokes a powerful intuitive response. Milestone joins the clackety mechanization of cinema (camera/projector) to the mechanization of the machine gun, the success of mechanical camera panning/projecting ironically critiquing the ease of machine-gun panning—a horrible harmony of form with content. Further, the speed of the tracking camera/machine gun, and that the victims are passed over before they are given time to fall, reflects back on the nonstrategic staging of the entire battle. The shift in worldview is from the God who notices a sparrow's fall to the camera/machine gun that does not dally on a dying soldier's fall. Milestone further undercuts the possibility that the first "machine-gun tracking shot" against the attacking British troops can be read as the prowess of German soldiery and technology (the taking of sides that most war romances indulge in); he does this brilliantly by giving the British defenders the same "machine-gun" tracking shot, but reversed, now right to left, as the Germans counterattack. With such a (camera) move, Milestone visually and formally marks World War I ground combat as a mechanized and impersonal mass murder.

Milestone's last alienating effect is a bit of shock editing worthy of the Grand Guignol. In an image lasting only an instant, a British soldier lunges into the German barbed wire just as a shell detonates near him. Horrifically, the soldier's hands are left dangling, grasping the barbed wire the soldier never scaled. Such an image serves as a literal expression of mechanized, meaningless death, for such a death resists transcendental and personal meaning. The apparent instant dematerialization of nearly an entire body violates one's innate image of the whole body, obliterates any conception of heroism, and haunts the mind long after its perception.

The terrible balance of *All Quiet's* one action sequence between attack and counterattack reflects the historical failure of World War I military strategy to anticipate or break the 360-mile-long snake of trenches that for four years lay across Europe. By denying Kat, Paul, and their fellows a clearly arranged and individualized position through the confusion of battle, Milestone dramatically challenges Hollywood's traditional reliance on evolving action and strategic agency in the war romance.

The different presentations of the zeppelin sequence and the *All Quiet* infantry battle, one staged strategically and one nonstrategically, offer enough contrast to justify the distinction between war romance and realist war film. However, the elements these two scenes share serve to limit any pure categorization of either film as romantic or realist, strategic or nonstrategic, myth-maker or demythicizer. Indeed, Milestone's attempt to delineate a simple relationship to war spectacle must be seen in light of the ongoing development of film sound in 1930 Hollywood. Robert Sklar raises a point against the typical belief that *All Quiet's* success was founded solely in its antispectacular realism:

At its most basic level, sound was noise, and noise itself could be a source of thrills. Hollywood did not tear down its boudoir sets overnight, but the possibilities of sound attracted filmmakers more and more to noisy settings. War was one, and Lewis Milestone's *All Quiet on the Western Front* became the big hit of 1930. Two world-war air spectacles—Howard Hughes's *Hell's Angels* and Howard Hawks's *The Dawn Patrol*—were also popular that year. (176)

This emphasis on sound is apparent in *All Quiet's* sound track, in particular the five-day bombing of the trenches and the infantry battle. The sound here is not only impressive (the density and distortion of the blasts), but also the sheer relentless repetition of blasts is remarkable. Also of note is the force of the sound of shelling to literally obliterate dialogue and other diegetic sound, a cinematic attempt to approximate the deafening potential of real shelling. In its sound, then, *All Quiet* is as spectacular as the air spectacles. This element provides support for the observation that it is impossible to film war without glorifying it through its inherent spectacles. If the air picture is disparaged for its emphasis on spectacle in general, and sonic spectacle in particular (recall that *Wings* was presented theatrically with a crude film sound system that triggered plane-like diving and roaring sounds from behind the screen, and that Hughes literally remade *Hell's Angels* in order to add the spectacle of sound to his film), then what critical stance is to be taken toward a lauded example of antispectacle such as *All Quiet*, which, to some degree, successfully exploited the rapidly developing sound technologies of its day?

Death in Spectacle and Antispectacle

Another forceful contrast is highlighted when the deaths of the central protagonists of *All Quiet* and *Hell's Angels* are analyzed side by side. Kat Katczinsky (played brilliantly by character actor Louis Wolheim) is a bullish, almost indestructible old veteran who shelters Paul and his young student volunteers as best he can. Near the end of the film, Kat is literally badgered and bombed to death by a single biplane during a sunny walk that reunites the old veteran with Paul, just back from leave. The greatest separation of the romantic and realist vision of World War I can be seen in comparing Kat's death in *All Quiet* and *Hell's Angels'* single image (twenty-five seconds) of trench warfare. *All Quiet* represses and distorts the air war just as certainly as *Hell's Angels* represses and distorts the ground war. Milestone and Hughes repress World War I content, and when they do briefly acknowledge the existence of the second arena of combat, the dialectic, they do so with extremely pointed staging and for narrative contrivance.

Kat's death scene begins with the veteran out searching for food (he might as well be berry picking). Paul sees his old friend and they meet and embrace. Low on the soundtrack is the drone of a single airplane. Milestone uses three cutaways of medium long shots to present a distant airplane. The shots are so distant that the plane and its flyer remain impersonal, almost gnat-like. The plane drops one bomb and wounds Kat. Paul hoists his large friend onto his back and begins carrying him to an aid station. While Paul consoles his friend, the plane drops another bomb, which kills Kat, although Paul fails to notice his friend's fatal injury and that the larger-than-life Kat has shielded his young friend from death—as he has so many times before. Remarque's novel stages Kat's death in much the same way, but without the single plane—indeed, it is apparently artillery shelling that kills Kat in the novel; however, just before Kat's death, Remarque includes this passage: "There are so many airmen here, and they are so sure of themselves that they give chase to single individuals, just as though they were hares. For every one German plane there come at least five English and American. For one hungry, wretched German soldier come five of the enemy, fresh and fit" (247). Milestone successfully turns the romantic flyer into a distant, mechanical weapon, chasing and destroying Kat, the most impressive embodiment of human survival and strength in the entire film. This is to pose the airplane as machine against man, where the air picture poses man embracing machine. Milestone has a biplane destroy not only Kat but the rebonding and comradeship of Kat and Paul. In this way, the last symbol of World War I romance becomes the murderer of *All Quiet's* only celebration: male (human) bonding in time of war.

Hughes's repression of trench warfare is even more extreme than *All Quiet's* denial of the air. It is only until the very last scene of the film, after Monty and Roy have given their lives in order to save hundreds of 7th Brigade infantrymen, that Hughes shows thirty seconds of ground combat. Only two shots are used, a costly long shot that involved 1,700 extras (Thomas 52), and a medium close-up of a British officer leading his men forward with, "Come on you 7th Brigade, we've got 'em now!" Following upon the previous scene where the stage Huns have carried out Roy's execution only to be immediately surprised by the 7th Brigade's surprise attack, *Hell's Angels'* final thirty-second intrusion of trench warfare is heavily tilted toward action and spectacle, and wrapped around the strategic agency of the film's central protagonists. From a four-year war composed primarily of stalemate and attrition, Hughes ends with the narrow moment when men go over the top and break the murderous balance of force, apparently because two airmen died gallantly.

Conclusion

In one instance World War I had taken its toll on a generation soon to be called lost, had left America fully engaged in postwar European problems, and introduced a self-absorbed public to the horrors of modern, global warfare. Thus, the development of pacifistic movements, nativism, the fight for the League of Nations, and the rise of realism and irony in America's postwar arts could provide *All Quiet* with a historical context that might sustain it. Simultaneously, *Angels* derived from another American historical context, one more fixed on dramatizing the present and imagining the future of aviation. After World War I, California was flooded with cheap, surplus military planes. With the equipment also came veterans and flyers—Laurence Stallings, Howard Hawks, William Wellman, John Monk Saunders, Ted Parsons, Dick Grace, and dozens of others—some who merely wanted to barnstorm or do Hollywood stunt flying, others, like Saunders who would make a career of scripting air pictures, or, like Wellman and Hawks, begin long careers that began by exploiting World War I experience.[4]

But it was probably Charles A. Lindbergh's instantly legendary flight from New York to Paris in May 1927 that helped further chart the romantic course of aviation in postwar America. New York citizens smothered Lindbergh in far more ticker tape than fell on the Armistice parade (Tindall 1,038), suggesting the force of aviation romance over Great War solemnity in postwar America. Producers of *Wings*, released just after Lindbergh's flight, wasted no time in slapping an opening title

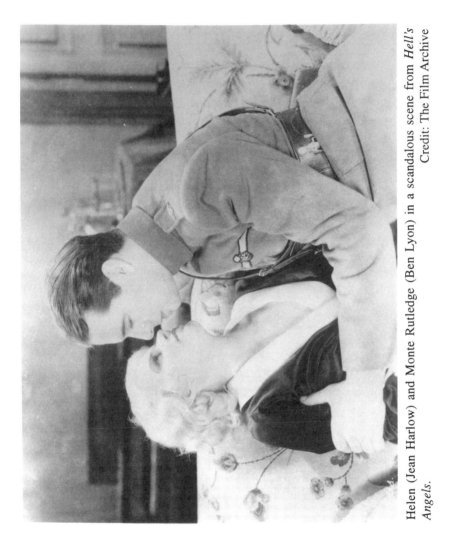

Helen (Jean Harlow) and Monte Rutledge (Ben Lyon) in a scandalous scene from *Hell's Angels.* Credit: The Film Archive

on their film, dedicating the work to Lindbergh and "those young warriors of the sky," and making the explicit connection across time and death between the still flying Lindbergh and the "young warriors" of World War I combat aviation, "whose wings are forever folded." Thus, it was not only the psychological dialectic of romance and realism that made possible the double vision of *Angels* and *All Quiet*, but also a double vision in postwar America, one that remembered World War I as a horror strong enough to "end all wars," the other selectively remembering those symbolic spoils that might usefully romanticize a present and a future that would certainly be more global, technologically dependent, and dangerous than the past.

Notes

1. Osborne's discussion of *All Quiet* is in marked contrast to his celebration of *Wings'* spectacle. *All Quiet* is a "savage antiwar film . . . grim and morbid . . . filled with scenes of machine-gun deaths, amputations, corpses, trench rats, starvation while fighting and other horrors of war" (23). The dialectic of realism and romance is solidly maintained: "Battle films have always rated well at the box office. It fascinates filmmakers and the public. *All Quiet* is a rare specimen: during its 140 minutes, there is not a single glorification of combat, no dashing charges, no thrill of victory, no heroics. Just the message: war is grim for those who have to fight it" (23).

2. Dominick Pisano expands his argument about the glorification of air warfare—and the vision of *The Dawn Patrol*—in chapter 4 of this book.

3. Both before and long after *Angels*, Hollywood filmmakers would utilize the zeppelin as spectacle, as a symbol of German militarism and technological superiority, and as a target of American anti-Nazi anger. In *The Rocketeer* (1991), which includes Howard Hughes as the designer of the film's rocket pack, Bill Campbell plays an All-American boy flyer who deflates the Nazi wonder weapon after dispatching villains in and atop the zeppelin. Steven Spielberg uses a passenger-service zeppelin in *Indiana Jones and the Last Crusade* primarily for spectacle and 1940s German ambiance. Indiana and his father are trying to sneak out of Germany by way of airship. When an SS officer comes aboard just before takeoff, searching for the Joneses, Indy "borrows" a steward's uniform and literally punches an SS officer out the window of the zeppelin, onto baggage below—Jones's quip to the startled passengers: "No ticket!" After a son-to-father chat aboard the zeppelin in flight, Indy notices the dirigible turning back toward Germany, their cover blown. Indy and his father run through the catwalks of the zeppelin and climb aboard a suspended biplane, only to fall into a duel with three single-wing Fokkers.

Right after *Hell's Angels* Hughes had planned to film something titled "Zeppelin L-27." According to Tony Thomas's *Howard Hughes in Hollywood*: "The zeppelin sequences continued to bring praise, and the doings of airships were in the news, especially the Atlantic crossings of the *Graf Zeppelin*. But getting a workable script and a reasonable budget together caused Hughes to abandon the idea" (76). Hughes shared his infatuation with the zeppelin with millions of Americans.

The U.S. Postal Service issued Graf Zeppelin stamps in 1930 (*Hell's Angels'* release date) both for mailing aboard the zeppelin and in 1933 to commemorate the zeppelin's arrival at the World's Fair in Chicago. Hughes's obstinate support and development of his own fixed-wing, but dirigible-sized Spruce Goose during World War II, in spite of many more practical and immediately useful military aviation advances, has almost always been interpreted as a symbol of an eccentric, Quixotic streak. Viewed in terms of Hughes's love affair with the zeppelin (and his insistence on having a massive German Gotha bomber in *Hell's Angels*), the Spruce Goose (conceived as a massive transport ship) might be seen as Hughes's American, home-grown substitute for the zeppelin. Impractical for day-to-day military and commercial aviation, these massive airships and gigantic biplanes were literally and symbolically larger than life and, thus, perfect icons where style mattered more than substance.

4. This impossible confusion of the realist and romantic modalities resonates with the stories of World War I airmen who, after the war, flew some of their most dangerous missions in improbable air pictures. Some, like Ormer Locklear, found death on the floor of the Los Angeles Basin while attempting to capture realistic footage of aerial combat. Howard Hughes himself nearly died on the set of *Hell's Angels* when he attempted a dangerous climbing turn in a Thomas Morse Scout. With the cameras rolling, Hughes took the plane up and quickly crashed. Apocrypha have it that Hughes was pulled from the wreckage unflustered, with stunt flyer Frank Clarke taking the punch line, "For a minute I thought we'd lost our meal ticket" (Thomas 41). Undercutting this bit of romance with the real story are biographers Barlett and Steele, "Hughes was pulled unconscious from the crumpled plane, one cheekbone crushed. He spent days in hospitals and underwent facial surgery. But his face, at least according to Noah Dietrich, was never the same" (63). One point that might be taken from this historical curiosity is that during peacetime, in a Hollywood world of model zeppelins and tinted flames, one of America's richest men nearly died trying to capture an illusion.

Works Cited

Rev. of *All Quiet on the Western Front*. *Variety* 7 May 1930.

Barlett, Donald L., and James B. Steele. *Empire: The Life, Legend, and Madness of Howard Hughes*. New York: Norton, 1979.

Botting, Douglas. *The Giant Airships*. Alexandria: Time-Life, 1981.

Frye, Northrop. *Anatomy of Criticism*. Princeton: Princeton UP, 1957.

Fussell, Paul. *The Great War in Modern Memory*. New York: Oxford UP, 1975.

Rev. of *Hell's Angels*. *Variety* 4 June 1930.

Keats, John. *Howard Hughes*. New York: Random House, 1972.

Leed, Eric J. *No Man's Land: Combat and Identity in World War I*. New York: Cambridge UP, 1979.

Morrow, John Howard. *The Great War in the Air: Military Aviation from 1909 to 1921*. Washington, D.C.: Smithsonian Institution, 1993.

Mosse, George L. *Fallen Soldiers: Reshaping the Memory of the World Wars*. New York: Oxford UP, 1991.

Osborne, Robert A. *Academy Awards Illustrated: a Complete History of Hollywood's Academy Awards in Words and Pictures*. La Habra, Calif.: ESE, 1975.

Pendo, Stephen. *Aviation in the Cinema*. Metuchen: Scarecrow, 1985.

Pisano, Dominick. *Legend, Memory, and the Great War in the Air*. Washington, D.C.: U of Washington P, 1992.

Remarque, Erich Maria. *All Quiet on the Western Front*. Trans. A. W. Wheen. Boston: Little, Brown, 1987

Robbins, Keith. *The First World War*. New York: Oxford UP, 1993.

Sklar, Robert. *Movie-Made America: A Cultural History of American Movies*. New York: Vintage, 1975.

Solomon, Stanley J. *Beyond Formula: American Film Genres*. New York: Harcourt, 1976.

Thomas, Tony. *Howard Hughes in Hollywood*. Secaucus: Citadel, 1985.

Tindall, George Brown. *America: A Narrative History*. Vol 2. New York: Norton, 1984.

6

The Fighting 69th:
An Ambiguous Portrait
of Isolationism/Interventionism

Daniel J. Leab

How does a President of the United States persuade his country to work actively—even at risk of war—against the leadership and policies of another land? President Franklin D. Roosevelt faced that problem in September 1939 when Germany invaded Poland. The American President, although seriously concerned about Japanese aggression in the Far East, looked on Führer Adolf Hitler and his Nazi followers as "gangsters who . . . would have to be restrained" (Burns, *Lion* 355). FDR felt that morality, as well as the best interests of the United States, demanded that it take a nonbelligerent stand against Germany and in support of Britain and France—the western democracies who went to war in support of Poland. But the President faced strong, determined opposition from isolationist forces. The backlash during the 1930s against American involvement in World War I had revived a long-standing isolationist tradition.

The Roots and Impact of Isolation

A significant part of the country's population wanted to avoid any activity—official or otherwise—that would obligate the United States internationally to fight against Hitler or any other international aggressor. Isolationism's roots ran very deep. All through the nineteenth century and the first decades of the twentieth, students learned that George Washington in his September 1796 Farewell Address had warned against "entangling alliances." Washington, in what was, in effect, a partisan political effort, had not used those exact words. He had urged the U.S. "to steer clear of permanent alliances" and to avoid "excessive partiality for one foreign nation," but he had pragmatically accepted the need for "temporary alliances for extraordinary engagements" (Commager I: 174). As diplomatic historian Robert Ferrell points out, even though nowhere in his address did Washington use the phrase "entangling alliances," this absence was "overlooked by political leaders and publicists who sought to show for their own purposes" that Washington was an isolationist and that the United States should heed his advice (Ferrell 84).

A striking exception to this tradition was the fervor marking U.S. involvement in World War I, participation that had to overcome very strong public feelings that the United States should follow its customary policies. Indeed, Woodrow Wilson had won reelection as President in 1916 with a campaign that boasted, "He Kept Us Out of the War" (which had begun in 1914). But in April 1917, only weeks after again taking the oath of office—for reasons about which historians still debate—Wilson obtained a Congressional declaration of war against Germany. In order to mobilize a divided United States, the Wilson administration undertook a massive propaganda campaign. Using what has been described as "every known channel of communication" (Mock and Larson 5), the government sold American participation as "a war to end war, a war to make the world safe for democracy, a people's war" (Blum 125).

Disillusionment set in rapidly after hostilities ceased in November 1918. The reasons for this disillusionment in the United States were many. Russia's newly established revolutionary government published transcripts of secret imperialistic agreements among America's associates belying claims of single-minded democratic opposition to German tyranny; the peace conference held in France at Versailles led to a treaty far removed from Wilson's idealistic war aims. Later, the U.S. Senate, bitterly divided about those treaty clauses committing the country to membership in an international organization dedicated to implementing many of these aims, failed to ratify the Versailles pact. (The United States signed a separate peace with Germany in 1921.) "Altruism," to use one historian's words, had "collapsed . . . the nation reverted to its normal isolationist behavior" (Osgood 112).

The United States did not remove itself entirely from the international scene. It remained very active economically, pursuing what economist Herbert Feis has described as "the diplomacy of the dollar" (qtd. in Degler 442). That diplomacy, however, continued to avoid commitment; U.S. policy thus isolated the country from the rest of the world. In 1933 President Roosevelt's message to the London Economic Conference, which had been convened to deal with the economic disarray caused by the Depression, disrupted it: he rejected the "old fetishes of so-called international bankers" and declared that "the sound internal system of a nation is a greater factor in its well-being." Isolationism was the order of the day even for such an internationally minded President (qtd. in Beard 133).

That concept was reinforced during the early 1930s by a flood of histories, journals, memoirs, and novels stressing the horror and futility of World War I as well as the putative nefarious reasons for U.S. involvement. A spate of publications (often with lurid titles—*Merchants of Death, Iron, Blood, & Profits*, "Arms and Men") charged that U.S. entry into World War I stemmed from a conspiracy between munitions makers who indiscriminately sold arms to both sides and bankers concerned lest Britain and France prove unable to repay the loans made for purchase of these arms. The United States, it seemed, had not entered World War I in defense of its rights as a neutral against Germany or for idealistic reasons; rather, a naive America "had been gulled into sacrifice of youth and treasure" (Filler 88).

The capstone for this conspirational view was put into place in 1934-35 as a result of hearings held by a special U.S. Senate committee. Chaired by the tenacious and energetic Gerald P. Nye (R-ND) and consisting mostly of Senators opposed to any U.S. international entanglements, this committee aroused public opinion. Realities of the war were forgotten in a crusade against past/future intervention. A satiric manifestation of the sentiment aroused by the Nye Committee was "the munitions-maker's night time prayer":

> Now I lay me down to snore
> I hope tomorrow there'll be war—
> Before another day shall pass
> I hope we sell some mustard gas.
> Bless the Germans, bless the Japs
> Bless the Ruskies, too, perhaps—
> Bless the French! Let their suspicions
> Show the need for more munitions!
> Now I lay me down to snooze
> Let the morrow bring bad news.

A more serious result was the enactment by Congress of legislation designed to "take the profits out of war." Roosevelt agreed with the isolationists and their supporters that America needed a "fixed policy" that would "embargo arms and loans to warring countries while at the same time protecting the U.S. from the baleful pressure of self-seeking economic groups" (Roosevelt qtd. in Parish 445). The legislation passed between 1934 and 1937 was designed to do just that: these laws, as a contemporary analysis averred, would "prevent the U.S. from being drawn into the next war" (Shepardson 258). The 1934 Johnson Act barred future loans to countries defaulting on their World War I debts to the United States. The Neutrality Acts passed between 1935 and 1937 prohibited shipment of arms or munitions to belligerents as well as forbidding them loans or credit.

In October 1937 Roosevelt—concerned about the economic and political threats that he believed faced the United States from an aggressive Germany, a militaristic Japan, and a truculent Italy—challenged the isolationist mood. He called attention to "a reign of terror and international lawlessness" which threatened "the very foundations of civilization" (*FDR Speaks*, Side 4, Band 2). FDR, without giving specifics, suggested quarantining "law-breaking nations . . . in order to protect the health of the community." The "Quarantine Speech" was a trial balloon that failed. The isolationists mauled the President, who was accused of warmongering and threatened with impeachment. Suddenly deserted by much of the Democratic Party, Roosevelt backtracked and disavowed the implications of his pronouncement. Later he confided to a friend: "[I]t's terrible to look over your shoulder when you're trying to lead—and find no one there" (Burns, *Crossroads* 157).

FDR thereafter, having decided "candor was . . . too risky" (Divine 29), publicly catered to the national mood. But, behind the scenes, he worked to move the country away from isolationism. Occasionally his intrigues showed. In January 1939 an experimental Army Air Corps bomber crashed in Los Angeles; among the injured was a French citizen who turned out to belong to a French mission purchasing American war planes. This business arrangement had been initiated by FDR without consulting Congress. It was perfectly legal, but it aroused the ire of isolationists.

World War II's outbreak nine months later did not shake their resolve or FDR's. He understood the nation's hostility to Germany and Hitler: public opinion polls in September 1939 showed only 2 percent of those queried favored "a Nazi triumph"; 82 percent considered Germany "responsible for causing the war; and 84 percent wanted "Britain and France to win." But an even greater percentage of Americans wanted "to keep clear" of what initially was "the last European war" (Lukacs 95). Overwhelmingly, those polled expressed "a stubborn, unyielding, unspectacular desire . . . to remain out of the war" (Lavine and Wechsler 42-43). Even Anglophilic Harvard wanted no part of any foreign conflict: the *Crimson* editorialized "we are determined to have peace at any price"; the student editors declared that "we intend to resist to the utmost any suggestions that American intervention is necessary to 'save civilization' or . . . 'democracy and freedom'" (Bethell 34). FDR publicly played to these attitudes. Notwithstanding his determined opposition to Germany and his continued behind-the-scenes activity, he found it expedient to declare on a broadcast at the war's outbreak that "I hate war." And he stated that the United States would "keep out and that every effort . . . will be directed to that end." But FDR, unlike Wilson on the outbreak of World War I, did not ask Americans to be "neutral in thought as well as in deed" (Williams II: 29). Said Roosevelt: "[E]ven a neutral cannot be asked to close his mind or . . . his conscience" (*FDR Speaks*, Side 5, Band 3).

Roosevelt's pleas for peace had absolutely no impact on the belligerents. The German blitzkrieg crushed organized Polish resistance in five weeks. Poland was partitioned between Germany and the Soviet Union. Britain and France limited their activity against the Germans on the ground to ineffectual sorties. The war dissolved rapidly into what was dubbed a "sitzkrieg." This "phony war"—to use a popular term of the day—did not end until April 1940, when the Germans began their assault on Western Europe. The only active hostilities on the continent during the winter of 1939-40 resulted from the Soviet Union's attack on Finland in December. To most Americans the war was, as one historian points out, "a distant conflict, one that might even dissipate for lack of action" (Herzstein 131).

It is important to note that there is much debate, even among Roosevelt's most zealous partisans, about just exactly what course the President planned at this time. As FDR scholar Warren Kimball argues, FDR in pursuit of these aims "by his own admission . . . was disingenuous, deceptive and devious. . . . Roosevelt reacted, shifted, rethought, and recalculated" (Kimball 8). Publicly, FDR assumed what a biographer calls "the role of honest broker" who attempted to achieve a negotiated settlement (Maney 116). Privately, the pro-Allied President determined to do what he could to aid Britain and France. A first step was to amend the neutrality legislation. Congress agreed to a "cash and carry" amendment which meant, as elder statesman Bernard Baruch put it, "cash on the barrel head and come and get it" (Schulzinger 1994). FDR, rather disingenuously, suggested that such a provision would help to keep the United States out of the war (no loans or necessity to fight for neutral rights as during World War I) but, of course, given the British Navy's control of the surface sea lanes and its extensive merchant marine, "cash and carry" clearly was a boon to the democratic Allies.

World War I and the Movies

FDR's appeals to public opinion carried the day but it was a hard fight. The public opinion that Roosevelt courted had been shaped by many forces—not least the movies. The number of moviegoers fluctuated substantially during the decade but always represented a significant percentage of the population. In 1939 a substantial percentage of the U.S. population of 130,000,000 went to the movies more than once a week. One estimate has it that as many as 85,000,000 people were weekly moviegoers. You could not escape the movies, for as one critic then pointed out, given the almost 17,000 movie theaters in more than 9,000 U.S. cities and towns, "it is difficult to get out of range of a movie . . . anywhere in the country" (Thorp 17).

The movies during the 1930s that dealt with World War I were, in historian Thomas Doherty's words, "elegiac in tone, pacifist in purpose, and cynical in perspective (91-92). Before 1934, when the industry's self-censorship dramatically tightened, the films dealing with the war were generally more outspoken. Typical were films such as *All Quiet on the Western Front* (Universal's 1930 adaptation of Erich Maria Remarque's pacifist novel); *A Farewell to Arms* (Paramount's 1932 version of Ernest Hemingway's tale of love and disillusionment), and *Broken Lullaby* (a sadly neglected 1932 Paramount antiwar film). These films were powerful statements against war. After 1934, as a recent study asserts, "introspective anti-war films were discouraged" (Black 130). But films dealing with aspects of World War I continued to be made. Admittedly more subdued, they still attacked the war and its impact. Even when World War I is touched on only tangentially, the treatment is critical: in *Alexander's Ragtime Band*, a 1938 Twentieth Century-Fox musical cavalcade built around Irving Berlin tunes, the leading lady in commenting on a character's war service record declares: "Oh, what a waste."

During the 1930s Warner Bros. became known for its productions of "socially conscious" films—what one industry historian describes as "movies with a genuine interest in the realities of life" (Finler 232). This interest would lead the Warner brothers, upset by Germany's anti-Semitic policies, to produce *Confessions of a Nazi Spy*. Released in spring 1939, *Confessions* was the first overtly anti-Nazi film made by a major American studio. Because of significant problems with the industry's self-censorship body and because of poor box-office returns, neither Warners nor any other major studio undertook similar productions for nearly a year.

Hard on World War II's outbreak, the industry self-censorship body urged the studios, in keeping with Roosevelt's neutrality policies, to avoid "hate" pictures. Will Hays, head of the industry's chief trade organization and a spokesman for Hollywood, declared that "today with European nations once more at each other's throats . . . no propaganda on the screen should be the contributing cause . . . of sending the youth of America to war" (qtd. in Colgan 513-14). In part, the industry's desire to retain access to European markets was behind this plea. It was months before a change came. According to Colgan, "as far as can be . . . ascertained, the relaxation of the policy seems to have occurred in January 1940" when various studios put forth anti-Nazi scripts for clearance (520). Hollywood, however, produced few such films until the victorious Germans in mid-1940 began to shut American films out of continental Europe.

Occasionally, political comment would seep through, and in the most unusual places. Warners' *Roaring Twenties* (the studio's 1939 Armistice Day attraction) was a big-budget, Runyonesque tale, a romanticized view of the life of Larry Fay, who "had been mixed up in rackets involving taxicabs, milk, booze and nightclubs" (Walker 245-46). It took 11 screenwriters to turn this concept into a slick film that was both a critical and a commercial success. In the opening sequence, a montage worked backward in time from 1939 to World War I. Ten percent of the completed film's 106 minutes dealt with World War I and its aftermath. These sequences, in keeping with 1930s attitudes, emphasized the cruelty and futility of the war, the greed of profiteers, the falseness of government propaganda, and the post-war indifference to veterans. Many contemporary reviewers dwelt on the veteran theme; Otis Ferguson declared that they "had saved the world but it's somebody else's oyster" (Wilson 278). A decade later the film was shown in the USSR with the title *The Fate of a Soldier in America*.

Less than nineteen months later, Warner Bros. released *Sergeant York*, a stirring flag-waver about a much acclaimed World War I American hero. Filmed during the first months of 1941, the film moved away from the traditional pacifist view of World War I: "preparedness" is endorsed; U.S. participation in World War I becomes a metaphor for current events as an initially reluctant and pacifist York serves his country in France. He accepted the country's call-to-arms, and was held up as an example to those conscripted by the nation's first peacetime draft, established in 1940.

Much of the stir the film caused resulted from its marketing, which was much more interventionist than the film. A typical press release referred to "World War II's menacing threat to American democracy" (Colgan 635). The studio issued statements over York's name asserting that "in the last war we won a lease on liberty . . . now after 23 years . . . Hitler tells us that lease is expiring" (Lee 635). An outraged Senator Nye, who had been called "Neville" by York, articulated the isolationist response when he angrily characterized *Sergeant York* as "a picture . . . rousing the American people . . . to be killed on a real battlefield" (Nye 721).

The Fighting 69th

Much more ambiguous in its response to World War I than films such as either *The Roaring Twenties* or *Sergeant York* was *The Fighting 69th* (1940). A transitional film, it could—and has been—read in a variety of ways. It has been judged as supporting isolationism and as propagating interventionism, as a depiction of the horrors of war, and as an argument for unthinking patriotism. The mixed response to *The Fighting 69th,* then and now, once again underscores a contention made over and over again, that "people of varying backgrounds find mixed messages in films, sometimes even reading them in ways contrary to the filmmakers' clear intentions" (Koppes and Black 12).

Certainly the response to the film at the time of its release reflects the dramatic changes which took place domestically and overseas in the months after its genesis. It was conceived in the heyday of isolationism during the spring and summer of 1939. The film was in production during the German conquest of Poland and premiered in January 1940 at the height of the "phony war." *The Fighting 69th* refers to a New York regiment that was part of the American Expeditionary Force (AEF) and suffered high casualties (one-third of its 3,500 men were killed in action). Designated the 165th Infantry well before the war, it had been organized in 1861 as the 69th New York and during the Civil War had earned the sobriquet "the Fighting Irish." Despite the renumbering, it was usually referred to as "the old 69th": the regiment's historian, poet Joyce Kilmer (killed in battle, 1918), averred that "only on paper was the name 165th in use" (Duffy 336). The regiment was federalized after U.S. entry into World War I, becoming along with other militia units part of "the Rainbow Division"—a composite of such units banded together to demonstrate the country's united commitment. The regiment had remained predominately Irish Catholic and was proud of that Celtic heritage. The unit's history also enthused that "we had three or four score Jews . . . but there was a Coen, a Leavy, and a Jacobs who were Irish" (Duffy 379).

Among the officers was the famous "Wild Bill" Donovan, subsequently a politically well-connected lawyer and intimate of President Roosevelt. (He served FDR during World War II as creator and director of the Office of Strategic Services.) One of the AEF's most decorated soldiers, he led one of the regiment's three battalions in combat. Another officer was Father Francis P. Duffy, a parish priest who later was dubbed a "hero chaplain" ("Comment" 122). As the regiment's spiritual counselor, he chose to go to the front with his flock. The film handled Kilmer, Donovan, and other real personages with care and respect. It dealt gingerly with Father Duffy, played by Pat O'Brien at his most "irreverently pious and patriotic" (Keyser 174).

Warners strove for authenticity, using four technical advisers—by one count "more than had ever been used in its productions to that date" (Karpf 177). *The Fighting 69th* showed the regiment in training at Long Island's Camp Mills, recreated in what has been described as "epic proportions" (Nash 843). The film demonstrated, perhaps too didacticly, the difficulty of creating a cohesive fighting force from disparate militia units. Once at the front lines, fluid cinematography, an army of extras, first-rate direction, and not inconsiderable expenditures resulted in a panoramic presentation of the terrors of trench warfare. Yet, for all of its use of real characters, *The Fighting 69th* centers on a fictional character, Private Jerry Plunkett (played by James Cagney).

Private Jerry Plunkett

The film follows Plunkett from his arrival for training as a raw recruit at Camp Mills until his death on the front lines. Plunkett initially is presented as a cocky, wise-cracking, street-smart, young tough from Brooklyn. He is a loner who resists training, does not understand the need for teamwork, and lacks respect for the illustrious history of the 69th. His main nemesis is "Big Mike" Wynn (played by Alan Hale), the sergeant in charge of Plunkett's platoon.

When Plunkett first encounters Father Duffy, he takes him for just another soldier. Subsequently a brawl breaks out between the men of the 69th and the soldiers of the 4th Alabama, who have come to Camp Mills to be integrated into the Rainbow Division. When Father Duffy helps to break up the brawl, Plunkett learns that his newfound friend is a priest and regimental chaplain. An uneasy relationship develops as Father Duffy tries to bind Plunkett to the Fighting 69th.

In the aftermath of the brawl Donovan addresses the men about the need for unity. In a speech that would be echoed in subsequent war movies, he stresses their need to work together: the outfits had been on opposite sides during the Civil War but, declares Donovan, "Now you're in a common cause. . . . We're all one nation now, a team." It is also during the scenes set at Camp Mills that Donovan, in effect harking back to an older view of the war, explains to Father Duffy that "war is a brutal business." The officer knows that he will be sending men to their deaths for uncertain reasons. And as the Camp Mills sequence ends and the troops march off for transport to France, Father Duffy offers a prayer.

Once in France, Plunkett, like the rest of the men, is anxious to "get a crack at the Heinies." In the trenches he does not have much chance. One night, angry at a German sniper who has creased his helmet, Plunkett (against orders) sends up a flare to get a view of the enemy. The Germans, fearing that the flare presages an attack, unleash a massive

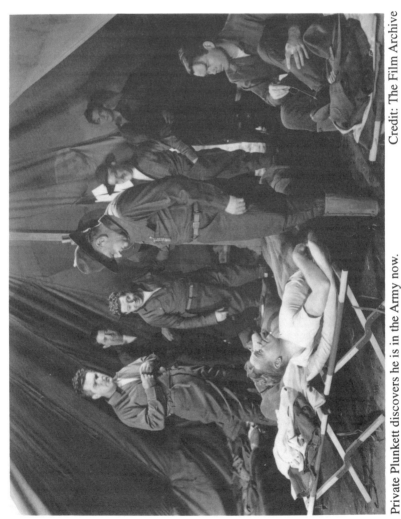

Private Plunkett discovers he is in the Army now.

Credit: The Film Archive

barrage that inflicts severe casualties. Plunkett panics and flees. Duffy quiets Plunkett and bravely is lowered into one of the collapsed bunkers to offer the trapped men the last sacraments.

Plunkett's unreliability alienates him from his comrades. Donovan wants to transfer Plunkett, but Duffy convinces the officer to give "the regiment" one more chance to "make a man" of the soldier. Back again in the trenches, Plunkett in conversation with Father Duffy explains his fear of death from an unseen enemy: "I've never been afraid of anything in my life before but this stuff, seeing what a bursting shell can do to human flesh and blood." He was being driven crazy, Plunkett told the priest. "Volunteered" by Donovan for a combat patrol, Plunkett runs when he sees the enemy, yells out when others on the patrol try to stop him, and—having given away its position—is responsible for the deaths of various members of the 69th, including Wynn's younger brother.

Court martialed, Plunkett—despite Father Duffy's efforts—is sentenced to be shot and is held in a storeroom adjacent to a makeshift hospital. A last-minute plea by Father Duffy to Donovan for a reprieve is rejected. The 69th moves up to the front. In a throwback to earlier views of the war, one officer describes the projected offensive as "mass suicide," to which Donovan replies, "Ours is not to reason why, ours is to do and die."

Father Duffy offers Plunkett spiritual help but refuses to help him escape. Shells hit the hospital area. The wounded soldiers begin to panic. Plunkett sees Father Duffy move among the wounded, calming them, and leading a group recitation of the Lord's Prayer. A few minutes earlier he had rejected Father Duffy's plea to join the 69th at the front, planning somehow to work his way back to Brooklyn. Now Plunkett nods knowingly to Father Duffy and dashes off to the front lines where the 69th is bogged down, suffering extensive casualties; even Donovan is wounded.

Plunkett arrives at the front, quickly grasps the need to blow a hole in the barbed wire and to neutralize the machine-guns pinning down the 69th. With the aid of wounded "Big Mike" Wynn, the "coward" uses a mortar to blast a path for his unit. They overrun the German position in a scene that previews the Hollywood heroics of World War II. Plunkett is then mortally wounded when he jumps on a grenade to save the sergeant's life. Father Duffy administers last rites to the coward-turned-hero; Plunkett apologizes to the sergeant for the death of his younger brother and tells the priest he's no longer afraid. Donovan looks down on the dying soldier and says, "And I thought this man was a coward." The last words Plunkett hears are the sergeant's response: "Coward, sir. From now on every time I hear the name Plunkett, I'll stand to attention and salute."

The film ends with a victory parade in New York City (including some of the same newsreel footage used in *The Roaring Twenties*), a tribute to Father Duffy, and a moving prayer by O'Brien as the priest asks us not to forget those who died. However one views the last reel of the film—and there are various, conflicting interpretations—it is clear that Plunkett has been regenerated by Father Duffy's homilies. Or to put it another way, the Cagney-O'Brien relationship found in many Warner Bros. films of the 1930s "simply moved . . . to the Western front" (Isenberg 185).

Behind the Scenes: Concept and Production

Initially the film was to concentrate on Father Duffy. On March 10, 1939, Bryan Foy—then head of the studio's "B" unit—wrote Jack Warner that "there is a picture in the life of Father Duffy," requested Pat O'Brien for the role, and suggested the title "The Fighting 69th" (Behmler 102). A month later Foy, realizing his "B" unit had no chance of utilizing a star like O'Brien or of getting a budget to make a large-scale war movie, wrote Warner that "you should turn this over to one of your 'A' producers because the story would make a great big picture" (April 10, 1939, Warner Bros. Archive). Twentieth Century-Fox executives certainly thought so, bought the rights to Duffy's life story, and announced *The Life of Father Duffy* (subsequently retitled *Father Duffy of the Fighting 69th*). An annoyed Warner wrote Fox production head Darryl Zanuck that "ten weeks or so before you made any announcement of your story, we already had announced ours. . . . I am sure you haven't any moral right to go ahead and make your picture" (Behmler 103). In any event, Warners got the edge by signing on as a technical adviser Captain John Prout. According to *The New York Times* he had "resigned from the 69th right after the war to fight in the Irish rebellion against the Black and Tans" and now had "obtained releases" for the studio "from all of the important officers in the regiment giving Warners . . . exclusive use of their names" (September 24, 1939).

The Fighting 69th had a fairly uncomplicated production history. The movie is the product of three screenwriters: Norman Reilly Raine, a contract writer who had worked on such other major Warner films as the very successful 1938 Technicolor spectacle *Adventures of Robin Hood;* Fred Niblo, Jr., a "B" picture specialist since 1931 whose recent Warners credits included the 1939 dull-witted comedy *Cowboy Quarterback;* and Dean Franklin, whose only other Warner screen credit, a 1939 Ronald Reagan programmer called *Code of the Secret Service,* was so bad that the studio "distributed the film in small towns where it had no chance to be reviewed" (Edwards 185).

Raine completed a first treatment ("Father Duffy and the Fighting 69th") at the end of July 1939, when cuts in Federal relief expenditures presaged greater spending on defense. Work on various drafts was undertaken by Franklin and Niblo during August. When World War II began in September, *The New York Times* reported that given the industry's skeptical attitude toward war films as well as FDR's request for Americans to be neutral in "deed" if not in "thought" it was "doubtful . . . *The Fighting 69th* will be made" (September 10, 1939). However, the project moved forward. Filming began soon after the Germans and Russians divided Poland, although the final script was not completed until the beginning of October 1939—just about the end of fighting there.

The film developed the Plunkett character at the expense of Father Duffy. This shift in focus may have resulted from the casting of Cagney as Plunkett, but it may well have been caused by concerns expressed by some Catholic clergy who had seen the script and felt that the depiction of the regimental chaplin was, in the words of a Legion of Decency official, "merely another cinematic attempt to beat more loudly the war drums" (Warner Bros. Archive, Father John McCafferty to Monsignor McIntyre, August 21, 1939). The film was completed during the "phony war." The studio had no problems with the industry's self-censorship body: the Production Code Administration readily granted its seal of approval notwithstanding its avowed determination to keep "America's screens neutral."

The final shooting script contained dialogue echoing traditional isolationist views of the 1930s: soldiers' comments about "the stench of dead bodies," the "everyday horror" of war, and "useless slaughter," as well as a Protestant chaplain declaring sadly to Duffy that "with all that's going on in the world—one half of it at the others throat—I wonder if Christianity hasn't failed" (*The Fighting 69th*, treatment by Niblo and Franklin, no date, 143, 24, 158, October 20, 1939, script insert Warner Bros. Archive). The writers put in scenes such as the one in which Donovan and Duffy mock the press for having made heroes of them. Yet none of this material made its way onto the screen. It either was not filmed or was deleted from the release print. But some very strange antiwar comments were added during the last days of shooting, such as Donovan's outburst to Duffy about orders to attack "regardless of the fact that it'll cost up probably 60 percent casualties." And enough antiwar sentiment remains to cast doubt on more recent judgments that the film's main purpose was "to stoke up the fires of war," that it fostered "an attitude of preparedness for war," that it "refought the war . . . on a more optimistic basis to detach it from its former downbeat tradition." Such comments attempt to reinterpret the past with the benefit of hindsight (Perlmutter 22; Sklar, *City Boys* 99; Basinger 96).

At the time, many indeed felt that *The Fighting 69th* took a strong stand against war. A Production Code administration reviewer described the film as a "Preachment against war—and a plea for peace. Shows death, destruction, and futility of war" (Motion Picture Code Administration Files). American film critics east and west judged it "a fine . . . document to promote peace," "an exhibit against war," "not . . . glorifying war" ("Critics Quotes"). Within parameters of what the Production Code and more official censorship boards then could allow, the film had enough graphic scenes that one reviewer declared that *The Fighting 69th* depicted war "at its most horrific . . . filth, squalor, and suffering" (Warner Bros. Archive). The preview trailer played up the combat scenes and the Cagney-O'Brien relationship, but the studio in its publicity also emphasized antiwar aspects. The press book quoted a "former head of the American Legion to the effect that *The Fighting 69th* was a preachment against war and the needless sacrifice of youth" (Warner Bros. Archive). Jack Warner—admittedly with his usual exaggeration—declared, "I believe it carries the strongest plea to keep America out of war that has been shown to our people" (Colgan 485).

It seems to me that *The Fighting 69th* is not only a transitional film but also in many ways an ideologically ambiguous one. The studio's confused search for an ending is an indication of that ambiguity. One of the later scripts had as the film's last line: "Who said we didn't fight for democracy?" Indeed the film ends with a montage of soldiers marching (characters we know have died and also those who survived), superimposed on the statue erected to Father Duffy in New York's Times Square with O'Brien's voiceover in character saying to rousing music:

O heavenly father hear I beseech you the prayer of this, America's lost generation. They loved life, too, O Lord. It was as sweet for them as to the living of today. They accepted privation, wounds, and death that an ideal might live. Don't let it be forgotten, Father, amid turmoil and angry passions when all worthwhile things seem swept away. Let the tired eyes of a troubled world rise up and see the shining citadel of which these giving lives formed the imperishable stones—America, a citadel of peace; peace forevermore. This I beg of you, through Christ, Our Lord. Amen.

Subsequently that plea could be seen as a pitch for "preparedness," but O'Brien's words seem consonant with the industry's neutral stance in the months after the invasion of Poland and before England stood alone.

Father Duffy brings forgiveness to the trenches.   Credit: The Film Archive

In a way the studio—like the industry generally—attempted to have it "both ways." However the film may be viewed in retrospect, at the time of its production and distribution both isolationists and interventionists could find something to support their side in *The Fighting 69th*.

Moreover, war meant that traditional foreign markets so important to Hollywood's economic well-being, might close down. Warner Brothers, like the other studios, therefore reacted cautiously on war's outbreak. Warners implemented various economies: Bryan Foy's "B" unit, for example, was furloughed for nearly two months. It may well be that the brothers Warner took more of an interest in domestic and international politics than did their peers, but the brothers remained "first and foremost businessmen" (Vaughn 43). Thus, despite the brothers' visceral, outspoken anti-Nazism, this film was neither explicitly nor implicitly anti-German. Nothing allegorical could be read into the few shots of German troops in the film; they are depicted simply as opponents to overcome; the enemy is not demonized. Indeed, there is little in *The Fighting 69th* to characterize them in any way.

This film was conceived, produced, and distributed in a period neatly described as "the last time" Americans believed in seriousness that "we could remain aloof from the problems of the world" (Ketchum viii). For many, as for Anne Morrow Lindbergh, "an established world was cracking, a long period of peace was coming to an end, and a dream of civilized order and unity was dying" (3). *The Fighting 69th* and other films like it at the time are marked by such attitudes. As a result there is in the film a conflict between what the French critic Jean Loup Bourget has dubbed the "movie's pretext—the script, the source and its text—all the evidence on the screen and the soundtrack" (192), a tension between the explicit statement and the implied argument. That dichotomy reflects the divisions that would disturb the United States in 1940 and 1941, until Pearl Harbor ended "the great debates . . . over America's international political and economic roles" (Liggio and Myles xi).

Obviously, the studio's management had major input. And one aspect of *The Fighting 69th* convincingly demonstrates this principle. There is no ambiguity about its treatment of Jews, a directness which I believe can be traced directly to Harry Warner's legitimate concerns about Nazi Germany. A few years earlier the studio had taken a very different tack in a film that dealt with anti-Semitism. In 1937 Warner Bros. had produced *The Life of Emile Zola,* centered on that French author's fight at the turn of the century against the railroading of Captain Alfred Dreyfus to the Devil's Island penal colony by anti-Semitic elements of the French army. The Dreyfus Case was a *cause celebre* and the Captain's Jewishness was well-known—yet barely mentioned in the film.

In *The Fighting 69th* there are many ambiguities but none about the Jews. The actor Sammy Cohen—physically a stereotypical Jew but one without any pronounced accent—plays Michael Murphy (actually "Moskowitz"), who adopted an Irish name so that he could join the 69th. He is a good man in the fisticuffs with the 4th Alabama, and obviously one of the boys. He converses disdainfully in Yiddish about "Big Mike" Wynn with Plunkett (no stretch for the authentic-sounding Cagney, who grew up in New York City and had spoken Yiddish in other films such as a 1932 Warners feature, *Taxi*). Murphy-Moskowitz is mortally wounded in combat and the ecumenical Father Duffy comforts him with a Jewish prayer as he dies. Given the almost total absence of Jewish characters from American films at this time, the role of Murphy-Moskowitz deserves recognition.

The Fighting 69th was a well-crafted product of the studio system. Its two lead stars played roles familiar to their fans. We can judge the film from various perspectives over a half-century later, for we have the benefit of a paper trail, oral histories, memoirs, and monographs on the studio, its products, and its talent. But in 1940 *The Fighting 69th*, however we may view it today, represented what Harrison's Reports, a respected and influential trade journal, called "Virile Melodrama" (13 January 1940: 6).

A movie like *The Fighting 69th* helps to make more comprehensive men and events about which there was both great national concern and serious agreement. An industry, such as the movies, tied to markets abroad (often the margin of a film's profit) and worried about censorship at home, well understood what has been called "the dangers of cinematic advocacy" (Neary 102). Filmmakers, even advocates such as the brothers Warner, adopted a policy of "watchful waiting." Under the spur of world events FDR felt compelled to act clandestinely to advance the policy he deemed best for America. Public attitudes changed, as gauged by various polls, in the months before Pearl Harbor because of German victories and Japanese mercantile policies. Yet it took considerable time for the movie industry to do more than follow in the wake of the national mood.

World War I ultimately would prove a perfect vehicle for those who wished to make movies commenting on current events, as *Sergeant York* would prove. But at the time of the making of *The Fighting 69th,* American public opinion was too ambivalent for even the outspoken brothers Warner. The film was part of the transition from isolationism to intervention; it was neither fish nor fowl. It seems to me, therefore, perfectly reasonable in the context of 1940 to sum up *The Fighting 69th* as "equal parts of blather, battle, and blarney" (Niderost 47), each of which had an ambiguous tinge.

Works Cited

"Arms and Men." *Fortune* Mar. 1934: 50-53.

Basinger, Jeanine. *The World War II Combat Film.* New York, Columbia UP, 1986.

Beard, Charles A. *American Foreign Policy in the Making, 1932-1940.* New Haven, Yale UP, 1946.

Behmler, Rudy, ed. *Inside Warner Brothers, 1935-1951.* New York: Viking, 1985.

Bethell, John T. "Harvard and the Arts of War." *Harvard Magazine* Sept./Oct. 1995: 32-48.

Black, Gregory D. *Hollywood Censored: Morality Codes, Catholics, and the Movies.* New York: Cambridge UP, 1994.

Blum, John Morton. *Woodrow Wilson and the Politics of Morality.* Boston: Little, Brown, 1956.

Bourget, Jean Loup. "Social Implications in the Hollywood Genre." *Journal of Modern Literature* April 1973: 16.

Burns, James MacGregor. *The Crossroads of Freedom.* New York: Vintage, 1989.

——. *The Lion and the Fox.* New York: Harcourt, 1956.

Colgan, Christine Ann. "Warner Brothers Crusade Against the Third Reich: A Study of Anti-Nazi Activism and Film Production, 1930-1941." Diss. University of Southern California, 1985.

Commager, Henry Steele, ed. *Documents in American History.* 9th ed. 2 vols. Englewood Cliffs: Prentice-Hall, 1973.

"Comment." *America* 15 May 1937: 122.

"Critics' Quotes." *Motion Picture Daily* 1 Feb. 1940: 3.

Dallek, Robert. *Franklin D. Roosevelt and American Foreign Policy, 1932-1945.* New York: Oxford UP, 1979.

Degler, Carl. *Out of Our Past: The Forces That Shaped Modern America.* New York: Harper, 1970.

Divine, Robert A. *Roosevelt and World War II.* Baltimore: Johns Hopkins UP, 1969.

Doherty, Thomas. *Projections of War: Hollywood, American Culture and World War II.* New York: Columbia UP, 1988.

Duffy, Francis P. *Father Duffy's Story.* New York: Doran, 1919.

Edwards, Anne. *Early Reagan.* New York: Morrow, 1987.

Engelbracht, Helmut C., and Frank C. Haulghen. *Merchants of Death: A Study of the International Armaments Industry.* New York: Dodd, 1934.

FDR Speaks. Edited and annotated by Henry Steele Commager. Washington Records, 1340 Connecticut Ave., Washington, DC, 1960.

Ferrell, Robert. *American Diplomacy: A History.* New York: Norton, 1975.

Fighting 69th. Harrison's Reports 13 Jan. 1940: 6.

Filler, Louis. *Vanguards and Followers: Youth in the American Tradition.* 1978. New Brunswick: Transaction, 1995.

Finler, Joel. *The Hollywood Story.* New York: Crown, 1988.

Herzstein, Robert E. *Henry Luce: A Political Portrait of the Man Who Created "The American Century."* New York: Scribner, 1995.

Isenberg, Michael T. *War on Films: The American Cinema and World War I, 1914-41.* Rutherford: Fairleigh Dickinson UP, 1981.

Karpf, Stephen L. *The Gangster Film, 1930-1940.* New York: Arno, 1973.

Ketchum, Richard. *The Borrowed Years, 1938-1941.* New York: Random House, 1989.

Keyser, Les, and Barbara Keyser. *Hollywood and the Catholic Church.* Chicago: Loyola UP, 1984.

Kimball, Warren. *The Juggler: Franklin Roosevelt as Wartime Statesman.* Princeton: Princeton UP, 1991.

Koppes, Clayton R., and Gregory D. Black. *Hollywood Goes to War: How Politics, Profits, and Propaganda Shaped World War II Movies.* New York: Free, 1987.

Lavine, Harold, and James Wechsler. *War Propaganda and the United States.* New Haven: Yale UP, 1940.

Lee, David. *Sergeant York.* Lexington: UP of Kentucky, 1985.

Liggio, Leonard, and James J. Martin, eds. *Watershed of Empire: Essays on New Deal Foreign Policy.* Colorado Springs: Myles, 1986.

Lindbergh, Anne Morrow. *The Wave of the Future.* New York: Harcourt, 1949.

Lukacs, John. *The Last European War.* Garden City: Anchor/Doubleday, 1976.

Maney, Patrick J. *The Roosevelt Presence: A Biography of Franklin Delano Roosevelt.* New York: Twayne, 1992.

Mock, James R., and Cedric Larson. *Words That Won the War: The Story on the Committee on Public Information, 1917-1919.* Princeton: Princeton UP, 1939.

Motion Picture Code Administration Files, Herrick Library, Academy of Motion Picture Arts & Sciences. Beverly Hills, CA.

Nash, J. Robert et al., eds. *The Motion Picture Guide.* Chicago: Cinebooks, 1986.

Neary, John James, III. "The Reality of Dreams." Diss. University of Maryland, 1961.

Niderost, Eric. "Hollywood Goes to War." *World War II* Mar. 1994: 721-23.

Nye, Gerald. "War Propaganda." *Vital Speeches* 15 Sept. 1941: 721-23.

Osgood, Robert Endicott. *Ideals and Self-Interest in American Foreign Relations.* Chicago: U of Chicago P, 1953.

Parish, Michael E. *Anxious Decades: America in Prosperity and Depression, 1929-1941.* New York: Norton, 1992.

Parrish, Thomas. *Roosevelt and Marshall: Partners and War—The Personal Story*. New York: Morrow, 1989.

Perlmutter, Tom. *War Movies*. London: Castle, 1974.

Schulzinger, Robert D. *American Diplomacy in the 20th Century*. 3rd ed. New York: Oxford UP, 1994.

Seldes, George. *Iron, Blood, and Profits. An Exposure of the World-Wide Munitions Racket*. New York: Harper, 1934.

Shephardson, Whitney, H., in collaboration with William O. Scroggs. *The United States in World Affairs in 1934-1935*. New York: Harper, 1935.

Sklar, Robert. *The City Boys*. Princeton: Princeton UP, 1993.

——. *Movie-Made America: How the Movies Changed American Life*. Rev. ed. New York: Random House, 1995.

Thorp, Margaret Farrand. *America at the Movies*. New Haven: Yale UP, 1939.

Vaughn, Stephan. *Ronald Reagan in Hollywood: Movies and Politics*. New York: Cambridge UP, 1994.

Walker, Stanley. *The Night Club Era*. New York: Stokes, 1938.

Warner Brothers Archives, University of Southern California, Los Angeles, CA. *The Fighting 69th*.

Williams, William A., ed. *The Shaping of American Diplomacy: Readings and Documents in American Foreign Relations*. 2 vols. Chicago: Rand McNally, 1970.

Wilson, Robert, ed. *The Film Criticism of Otis Ferguson*. Philadelphia: Temple UP, 1971.

7

"The Devil's Tool":
Alvin York and *Sergeant York*

Michael Birdwell

Known as the greatest American hero of World War I, Alvin C. York avoided profiting from his war record before 1939.[1] Although he was wooed at the war's end by Hollywood, Broadway, and various advertisers, York turned his back on quick and certain fortune in 1919, opting to go home to Pall Mall, Tennessee, to resume private life. Largely unknown to most Americans today is the fact that York returned to America with a single vision. He wanted to provide a practical educational opportunity for the mountain children of Tennessee. Painfully aware of his limitations, York dedicated the remainder of his life to education. Today York Agricultural and Industrial Institute, north of Jamestown, Tennessee, stands as a monument to his embattled dream. Therefore, when York finally agreed to allow a movie to be made about him, he insisted that the film emphasize his work since the war and not dwell on his fame as a war hero.

The nature of the country changed over the course of York's struggle to improve education. His campaign began during the flush time of the 1920s and he fought valiantly to keep the school open as funds dried up during the Depression. By the mid-1930s the clouds of war again loomed on the horizon and York, like most Americans, renewed his vow of pacifism. The specter of war reminded the public of the disappointments associated with World War I. With the world once again apparently on the verge of war, the official stance of the United States government proved reminiscent of York's initial attitude toward the World War I. America in 1939—and York in 1917—both had to be convinced that war was not only justifiable but sometimes necessary.

At the same time, the threat of war had rekindled the interest of some filmmakers, most notably Jesse L. Lasky, into reviving the story of York's exploits. Lasky, having witnessed the famous New York reception for the hero from his eighth-floor office in May of 1919, felt destined to tell York's story. While several studios found interest in the

121

saga in 1919, only Lasky of Famous Players-Paramount (later associated with Twentieth Century-Fox, and finally Warner Bros.) persistently pursued him (Lasky and Weldon 252-53). When York relented, he announced that the film would "be a true picture of my life . . . my contributions since the war. It won't be a war picture. I don't like war pictures" ("Sergeant York Surrenders"). He later declared: "Actually it's going to be more a story of our people up there in the mountains than it is of me. It's going to show how education has been taken into the mountains and how we're training our young people now to be good citizens. My part in the war should be presented only as an incident in my life" (Lee, "Appalachia on Film" 211-12). Despite York's ambitions, the film definitely *was* a war picture. The original screenplay presented the war as an epiphany that forced York to recognize his own lack of education but fulfilled his wish to improve himself and his homeland. Unfortunately, that film has never yet been made. The motion picture that arrived in theaters in July of 1941 not only signaled a profound change in York's pacifism but sounded a clarion call for American entry in World War II.

The York Story and Jesse Lasky

Ironically, Alvin C. York had applied for conscientious objector status in 1917, but the Fentress County Draft Board denied his request because it refused to recognize the Church of Christ in Christian Union as a legitimate Christian sect.[2] He fought reluctantly in the Great War and, once it ended, often spoke publicly against war. The laconic hero even conducted impromptu prayer meetings on his troopship, the *U.S.S. Ohioan*, as it returned home (York Papers, hereafter YP). His heartfelt belief that war represented moral evil never wavered before his association with Jesse Lasky and Warner Bros.

In 1916, Jesse Lasky and his partner, Adolph Zukor, created Paramount, one of the first studios in Hollywood. He served as its chief creative producer until 1931, when the Great Depression caused a massive overhaul of the studio. Not only was Lasky dismissed, but he lost his home and entire personal fortune (Lasky 73-78).[3] From 1931 to 1938 he bounced from studio to studio and even dabbled, unsuccessfully, in radio. He needed a hit movie to revitalize his career because Hollywood, noted for its short memory, deemed a person only as good as his last picture. So, "I began hunting for a story or theme important enough to serve for my second 'comeback' in the picture business" (Lasky and Weldon 253). An RKO executive rekindled his interest in Sergeant York, and Lasky turned once again to the possibility of a "biopic" based on the mountain hero.

The film community in 1939, perhaps more than any other segment of American society, anticipated the evil Adolf Hitler represented. Anti-Nazi European and Jewish artists, musicians, writers, and intellectuals fled to the United States, and by 1939 the list of prominent European expatriates included playwright Bertolt Brecht; intellectuals Theodor Adorno, Hannah Arendt, Herbert Marcuse, Max Horkheimer; novelists Heinrich Mann, Thomas Mann, Lion Feuchtwanger, Salka Viertel, Erich Maria Remarque; actors Peter Lorre, Marlene Dietrich, Luise Rainer, Albert Basserman; directors Fritz Lang, Billy Wilder, William Dieterle; composers Max Steiner, Erich Korngold, and many more. Some members of the film community favored American involvement abroad, while at the same time they were painfully aware that they could not outwardly advocate U.S. intervention (Cook 17-18, 30-32, 113-17; Colgan 29-198). Warner Bros. was the first studio to discontinue its business with the Third Reich. Harry Warner had wanted to curtail operations in 1933, but owing to contractual obligations had to wait until 1934 ("WB First U.S. Co. to Bow Out of Germany").[4] Ironically, Paramount, MGM, and Twentieth Century-Fox continued to distribute films in Nazi Germany and its territories until 1940.

As the world's political climate deteriorated, York's saga appealed to Lasky even more, and between October of 1939 and March of 1940 he plotted a storyline. It was no mere coincidence that Lasky pitched the idea to Warner Bros. Their reputation as anti-Nazi producers set them apart from the rest of Hollywood. Harry Warner encouraged employees to join the controversial Anti-Nazi League, and to brush up on their shooting skills at the studio's rifle range. He raised funds for British relief, purchased two Spitfires for the RAF, provided ambulances for the Red Cross, cared for British orphans, and more. They made the country's first antifascist films and were the first to mention Hitler and the Nazis by name (Birdwell 63-69).

For Lasky, York's heroism had a special resonance in the current troubled times. Part of the appeal was that York typified the nineteenth-century American hero. His exploit in the Argonne seemed larger than life, and he was often compared to Daniel Boone, Davy Crockett and Abraham Lincoln. Literally born in a log cabin and raised in the Tennessee backwoods, he lived a quasi-frontier existence that bore no resemblence to New York, Chicago, or Los Angeles, and York seemed to come from another time. As late as 1917 he hunted squirrel, racoon, quail, wild boar, and deer with a muzzleloader. York's life captured the American imagination not because of who he was but what he represented: a humble, self-reliant, God-fearing, peaceful man, who had fought his country's enemy only after great deliberation. His personal struggle in World War I found new urgency in an America at odds over Nazi aggression, for York personified isolationist-Christian-America wrestling with its conscience.

Just as Lasky's career was at a low point in 1939, so was York's. A big-hearted but inept businessman, York consistently gave away money to friends or strangers and rarely demanded repayment. Unfortunately, he lost control of his labor of love—York Agricultural and Industrial Institute—in 1933 due to chronic fiscal and political problems. In the late 1930s he tried, unsuccessfully, to establish a fundamentalist Bible school. The failure to get the new school going further demoralized him (YP).

Lasky made four trips to Tennessee, including sojourns to York's home in Pall Mall, between the summer of 1939 and the spring of 1940. He interviewed York's friends and family (*Sergeant York* File, hereafter *SY*).[5] Perhaps the most important person he met was Guy Williams, who, raised next door to the sergeant, knew York better than anyone. Williams told Lasky that York's religious denomination condemned movies as a sin, and until that problem could be resolved, it would be impossible to shoot a film. For obvious reasons, he warned the producer that once the Sergeant signed the contract, Lasky should mete out money to York on a piecemeal basis (Guy Williams interview; *SY*).[6]

In early February 1940, Lasky, confident that York would endorse a movie based on his life, leaked the story to nationally syndicated gossip columnist Louella Parsons. Anticipating the film's casting, she decided that Spencer Tracy should play the famed hero. She later changed her mind, suggesting that feisty James Cagney would make a more convincing mountaineer. Other columnists believed that Henry Fonda or Raymond Massey were perfect for the part, while York's personal choice of Gary Cooper was purposely kept from the press (*SY*).

Lasky softened the old warrior, though their negotiations proved intense. York had to be convinced that movies were not sinful in and of themselves as his church had declared. He wanted assurance that "the devil's tool would be used to do good works" (Guy Williams interview). Another equally serious and related problem concerned the fact that York contemplated a business partnership with Jews. Tennessee's Upper Cumberland had been practically devoid of Jews throughout its history. Due to his insular upbringing, York had been taught that Jews were untrustworthy, scheming pariahs, vile "Christ killers" (Guy Williams interview, Glass 63-76). Once God's chosen people, they had willfully rejected His promises; therefore Jews were beyond hope of salvation.[7]

While more traveled and enlightened than his neighbors, York still harbored suspicion of people from outside his immediate community.

Lasky faced a doubly daunting task: he had to win the confidence of the locals, proving he was not a threat to them or their way of life; and he had to convince York that association with Jews would not damn his soul to hell for eternity. The affable, diligent, and tenacious Lasky eventually accomplished both. If York's anti-Semitism initially created a barrier to the filming, Lasky clearly convinced him that Jews were not unregenerate, that they were worthy of his association, and that the film should be made. Lasky continued interviewing York's friends but found many of them frustrating because of their taciturn behavior:

We did manage to supplement our stock of York lore before returning to the Coast, but most of our inquiries about the sergeant's childhood among his backwoods neighbors elicited nothing more helpful than "Alvin, he's a good boy," or "Alvin, he'd never harm nobody." (Lasky and Weldon 258)

On March 24, 1940, York, though still skeptical, signed a contract with Lasky in the governor's office in Nashville.

Lasky agreed to pay York $50,000, in measured installments, as well as two percent of the box office gross, something practically unheard of during Hollywood's studio era. York's agreement, while a relief, created a series of complications. The first concerned his desire that Gary Cooper portray him. Although Cooper's contract belonged to Samuel Goldwyn, Lasky did not see that as an insurmountable problem since he was married to Lasky's sister, Blanche. Second, York had demanded that the actress cast to play Gracie could not drink, smoke, or swear—a hard thing to find at any time in Hollywood. Third, York had wanted editorial control over the screenplay. If the final product demeaned, insulted, or antagonized him, York could withdraw his support (*SY* and *YP*). Amazingly, Lasky agreed but explained that, for the sake of dramatization, some events had to be embellished and others omitted. He initially promised York that the film would not glorify his war years: "I wish to emphasize that this is in no sense a war picture . . . it is a story Americans need to be told today . . . [it] will be a document for fundamental Americanism" (Lee, "Appalachia on Film" 211). Lasky then presented York with a personal check for $25,000 as a token of good faith.

Why York demanded Gary Cooper is shrouded in a mystery of conflicting stories. Some argue that Lasky had planted the seed; both Hal Wallis and Jack Warner assumed credit; still others say that Cooper was the only movie star York knew by name. Cooper, though he would later win an academy award for his portrayal, looked and acted nothing like the Sergeant. York weighed over 300 pounds when he signed the contract; Cooper weighed 185. They were roughly the same height, but York had bright red hair and always wore a moustache. Cooper's hair was dark brown and he went clean shaven. Cooper was rather taciturn, while York "could talk the ears off a field of corn" (Guy Williams interview). In spite of their obvious differences, Cooper has come to embody for subsequent generations of Americans, the essence of their perceptions of Sergeant York.

From Story to Screenplay

Certain of the picture's success, Lasky began the task of bringing the story to the screen. On April 21, 1940, joined by writers Harry Chandlee, Julien Josephson and Abem Finkel, they cultivated friendships with locals by providing them odd jobs while gathering information to write the screenplay. Albert Ganier, a Nashville ornithologist and amateur photographer, shot still photographs of the Pall Mall area for set and costume crews to create the Wolf River Valley on a Burbank soundstage. Stenographer Agnes Seely transcribed the interviews. A skeleton film crew arrived in Pall Mall in October of 1940, and shot backgrounds and footage of locals going about their daily tasks to help the actors reproduce the mountaineers' mannerisms. Meanwhile, back at the studio, future *Dirty Harry* director Don Siegel scoured stock footage for pertinent images and pieced together the movie's montage sequences (*SY*). By that time Lasky had clearly won the Sergeant's trust; York loaned him the love letters he penned to Gracie while abroad, along with his treasured war diary. The numerous interviews, letters, photographs, and Congressional Medal of Honor affidavits became the key ingredients in writing the screenplay and lent genuine authenticity to the script (*SY*; YP; Wallis and Higham 68).[8] Chandlee and Josephson completed a twenty-nine-page rough treatment and submitted it to Lasky on May 8, 1940. It described the general storyline, and more importantly, drew attention to details that required fictionalization or alteration. On July 7, Chandlee and Abem Finkel submitted a revised final treatment titled *The Amazing Story of Sergeant York,* which York approved (*SY, YP*).

One change that the Sergeant willingly endorsed was the introduction of the fictional character, "Pusher," who represented his foil. A stereotypical Brooklyn subway worker, Pusher provided a reference point for urban viewers. He also depicted a nonexistent relationship between York and his former army buddies. Letters that the studio received, as well as location manager Bill Guthrie's experiences with the survivors, produced a very different drama than the one Pusher and York lived out on the screen, for York's pacifism and religious beliefs had alienated him from many of the men in his battalion. His best friend in G Company, Murray Savage, died in the October 8, 1918, melee. Being chosen as the lone hero of the battle only exacerbated the situation, and even though York always willingly gave full credit to his comrades, the army singled him out after George Patullo leaked his version of the story to the press.

While Lasky agreed to stick to the facts of York's life, events soon unfolded that made the promise impossible to keep, and over the course of the next year the emphasis of the movie, as well as York's attitude toward events in Europe, changed significantly. Because the film featured characterizations of people still living, obtaining their written consent was essential. Guthrie sought out family, friends, celebrities, and—most importantly—York's fellow survivors from G Company of the 82nd Division of the American Expeditionary Force. Secretary of State Cordell Hull, General John J. Pershing, Major George Edward Buxton, and men of rank willingly obliged, but others proved uncooperative.

Asbury Williams, York's father-in-law, refused to sign a release, even though York's friend and pastor, Rosier Pile (who condemned movies as a sin) willingly obliged. Pile, parroting Guy Williams, declaimed that the film's purpose was good, and the Devil's instrument could be used to do God's bidding. No amount of coaxing or coercion could budge York's recalcitrant father-in-law; as a result, the writers were forced to depict Gracie living in the home of her uncle, Elijah ("Lige") Williams. Other friends and family were reluctant to sign as well, among them York's own siblings. Although he was one of eleven children, only his brother George and sister Lucy were portrayed in the film, leading the audience to believe that York came from a small family (*SY* and YP).

Reasons for refusal varied. It appears that Asbury Williams never approved of York before or after the war, and abhorred York's marriage to his daughter. Aware of the antipathy between them, the first script made that conflict the centerpiece of the story. Lasky said that "in talking to Miss Gracie, who was sixteen when she married York, we discovered that his courtship had stirred up a feud between the two families. Her folks hadn't approved of her keeping company with a hell raiser" (Lasky and Weldon 258). Unconvinced of the sincerity of York's religious conversion, Williams felt that York did it only to be near his daughter.[9] So, the central plot motivation had to be changed at the outset which forced York to compromise once again.[10]

A touchier problem arose when Guthrie attempted to get permission from the survivors of Company G.[11] As early as 1928, when *Liberty* magazine serialized York's war diary, Corporal William Cutting (whose real name was Otis B. Merrithew; hereafter Merrithew) conducted a personal campaign to discredit York. Merrithew maintained that it was he, not "Corporal York," who captured the 132 Germans. Wounded during the famous engagement, Merrithew lay in a first-aid station as York marched the prisoners into U.S. Headquarters. Feeling robbed of proper credit, he wanted to set the record straight, for he believed that each of the seven survivors deserved recognition for their heroism. (Due to his unflagging efforts, he and Sergeant Bernard Early were belatedly awarded the Distinguished Service Cross in 1927.) As news of the Warner Bros. plan to make a movie based on York's life became public, Merrithew bombarded the studio with letters. A notarized "official version" of his own statement came to the attention of Roy Obringer, head of the studio's legal department. Unaware of the ongoing campaign against York, however, Guthrie continued his quest to find G Company survivors (*SY*).

First located was Percy Beardsley, who refused to sign until Guthrie agreed to pay him $20. This proved a costly mistake, for as Guthrie slowly found them, he discovered none willing to sign a release without compensation—$20 here, $50 there—all of which got back to Merrithew. When Guthrie found the brooding corporal, Merrithew demanded $250, which the location manager grudgingly paid. Promptly contacting his former comrades, Merrithew told them how much money he received and added that they had been cheated once again by "Corporal" York. Joining forces, the seven survivors petitioned Warner Bros. to stop production immediately and threatened a lawsuit (*SY*).

Later, as filming neared completion, Merrithew wrote Guthrie on March 11, 1941: "[The seven survivors] never remember signing affidavits for York. *All* of them in recent correspondence are willing to testify that they thought they were signing a 'supply slip' for some article of clothing that was issued to them" (*SY*). Threatening Guthrie with an incriminating recording of a conversation that had occurred on October 16, 1940, he wrote:

Why doesn't York come out with the true story and give the boys the right recognition that is due them? There is one point in particular that I wish to impress; if the picture shows the German major handing over his pistol to anybody but me as a sign of surrender, Warner Brother's will have a court case on their hands. In handing me that pistol the Major knew that *I* was in command and *not* York. (*SY*, his emphasis)

Casting and Shooting the Film

In spite of these recriminations the troubles with the survivors appeared minor compared to the byzantine contractual machinations transacted between Harry Warner and Samuel Goldwyn.[12] York wanted

Gary Cooper confers with the real Alvin York.

Credit: Birdwell Collection

Gary Cooper to portray him; what that meant was Cooper or no film—
period. Negotiations went slowly, however, and Lasky was forced to
confront the possibility that another actor might have to be substituted.
Lasky and producer Hal Wallis believed that if Cooper could not be
signed, they might be able to persuade York to endorse another actor.
Jack Warner told Lasky that he was "crazy to think that Goldwyn would
ever come through for the studio, and to find another actor" (Lasky and
Weldon 258). Facing the grim possibility that Cooper might be unattain-
able, on November 15, 1940, they shot a screen test with another actor—
Ronald Reagan (*SY*).

While Warner and Goldwyn parried, Lasky turned to the task of
casting other roles. Always enthusiastic when an idea hit him, Lasky
asked Obringer what he thought of Jane Russell playing Miss Gracie.
Obringer replied on January 3, 1941: "I agree with you that Jane Russell's very attractive but I hardly think she's the type for 'Sergeant York.'
She doesn't look much like the simple backwoods country girl to me"
(*SY*). Undaunted, Lasky examined the screen tests of four actresses who
fulfilled York's conditions: Helen Wood, Suzanne Carnahan, Linda
Hayes, and Joan Leslie. He settled on Leslie and broke the news to her
on her sixteenth birthday (*SY* and YP).

Meanwhile, Lasky's ex-brother-in-law kept stalling and further
frustrated the studio by constantly changing the date and conditions of
Cooper's availability. Finally on August 16, 1940, in a fit of pique Harry
Warner fired off a missive to Goldwyn's liaison, Reeves Espy, demanding that the matter be resolved by one o'clock the following Monday, "or
forget the entire transaction" (*SY*). The letter not only reflected the exasperation of the studio but also indicated the way Harry Warner conducted business. "You and Mr. Goldwyn know me," he wrote, "and that
when I say 1:00 Monday I don't mean 2:00. It will all be history as far as
we are concerned and I wouldn't take Cooper after that for nothing,
because with me a deal is a deal" (*SY*). Goldwyn relented and a contract
was hammered out on March 19, 1941, which satisfied both parties.[13]

Independent director Howard Hawks, drawing an $85,000 salary,
began work on *Sergeant York* on December 16, 1940, but filming did not
get underway until January. Like Lasky, York, and Harry Warner, Hawks
was accustomed to having things his own way. A perfectionist who considered himself something of a writer, Hawks regarded a script as an outline, not a finished product. He criticized the initial York script as a weak
story cobbled together by hacks. Since Asbury Williams' refusal to sign
a release undercut the central conflict of the original script and a new
plot device was needed, York's war experience seemed the obvious thing
to focus upon. Chandlee and Finkel, however, wanted to stay as true to

the original script as possible because York had approved it, and they resisted the director's desire to intensify the war sequences. Nevertheless, Hawks brought John Huston and his friend Howard Koch on board for the rewrites that Chandlee and Finkel refused to do (*SY*). Chandlee and Finkel were not totally opposed to focusing on the war story, and wanted the audience to recognize parallels between the current war and World War I. They feared Hawks, Huston, and Koch would blow the war story out of proportion, resulting in the loss of the PCA's seal of approval. Koch, whose screenplay for the Errol Flynn swashbuckler *The Sea Hawk* (1939) preached preparedness against a totalitarian threat, openly favored intervention. *Sergeant York* (1941)—and later, *Casablanca* (1942)—told similar stories of conversion and commitment. Both Alvin York and Rick Blaine would have to be convinced that war was necessary, and would reluctantly agree to do battle. The script changes introduced by Koch and Huston defined the interventionist theme of the movie delivered to theaters in 1941.

York's religious faith had to be handled carefully, and all agreed that it was central to the story. The first script placed more emphasis upon York's days as a hell-raiser and his education at state-line border bars called blind-tigers. Everett Delk, York's best friend, was killed in a shootout at a blind-tiger in 1914. Because York maintained that Delk's death had profoundly affected him, Chandlee and Josephson detailed the incident in the script but added a curious twist. At York's behest, they transformed Everett Delk into a fictional nemesis named "Zeke." After imbibing too much white lightning, York kills Zeke in a drunken brawl. The change served two purposes: it increased dramatic tension leading to York's religious conversion, and it fulfilled York's desire not to have the Delk family relive the pain of Everett's death.

York made the mistake of telling the screenwriters that his conversion "was like being struck by lightning" (YP). The first three scripts remained faithful to the conversion experience by having him repent after Zeke's death; however, that was not how it eventually played on the screen. In the movie, Gary Cooper was literally struck by lighting. The bolt sent him and his mule crashing to the ground, twisting the barrel of his muzzleloader, driving home the message, "Thou shalt not kill." York hated the sequence, saying it trivialized his conversion; the Production Code Administration disliked it as well. After reviewing the footage, Joseph Breen sent Hal Wallis a terse memo demanding the sequence be reshot because Americans would not stand for mules dying on screen. (In its final version the mule came miraculously back to life.)

York's religion posed other problems. Once he decided to go to war, "he believed that he had received a Divine communication approving his going and assuring him that he would not be killed" (*SY*). Though press releases informed the public that profits from the picture were earmarked for the creation of a Bible school, the religious issue would not abate because York constantly invoked God's name and assured everyone that the movie would be a testament to Christian values. Chandlee and Josephson informed Lasky that "if York's real religious attitude is included in the picture, there is great danger of his appearing to be merely a religious fanatic and thus lose heavily in audience understanding and sympathy" (*SY*). The screenwriters' problem was how to make York's spirituality convincing without offending audiences. They opted for a balance between godliness and patriotism as a screen image of true Americanism (*SY*).

Chandlee made two other major alterations in the script. He invented the scene on the rifle range where York proved his prowess as a marksman and concocted the scene where Major Buxton presented York with an American history textbook. Although "[t]his scene never happened in real life," it tempered the perceptions of York as a religious zealot (*SY*). In reality it took months of coaxing by Buxton and Captain Danforth to convince York to serve in a combat unit, but this sequence worked beautifully because it cut to what many considered the symbolic essence of America—the myth of its unique history as the new Eden in a fallen world.

That sequence drove home the notion that there were differences between just and unjust wars, and that York understood the distinction. Buxton asked York specific questions to determine his sincerity while using his own biblical knowledge to persuade York to examine the scriptures in a figurative rather than a literal way. York's first response was, "The book is agin' killin' . . . an' I'm a figgerin' killin' other folks ain't no part o' what He was intendin' fer us to be a doin' here" (*SY*). Like a pair of boxers sizing each other up, Buxton and York swapped scriptures that advocated either aggression or peace. After gaining York's confidence, Buxton clinched the sequence by discussing the uniqueness of America and York's own hero, Daniel Boone, while holding the Bible in one hand and an American history text in the other. York, surprised to know that anyone outside of the Valley of the Three Forks knew anything about Daniel Boone, marveled at the history book. Buxton said:

It's the story of a whole people's struggle for freedom—from the very beginning until now—for we are still struggling . . . You're a religious man, York. You want to worship God in your own way, plow your fields as you see fit, to raise your own family according to your own lights. Such things are part of our heritage as Americans, *but the cost of that heritage is high. Sometimes it takes all we've got to preserve it—even our lives* [emphasis added]. (Chandlee, Finkel, Huston, and Koch, *Sergeant York*, Revised Final Draft 109-10)

The point about military service was further driven home in the next sequence where York, home on furlough, struggled to reconcile God and country. The famous conversion sequence depicted York sitting atop the bluffs overlooking the Wolf River valley musing over the Bible and the history text while voice-overs supplied by Pile and Buxton plead with him saying, "for God" and "for country." The dilemma is solved when York stumbles upon the passage "Render unto Caesar that which is Caesar's and render unto God that which is God's." In its final version, this scene would become a powerful piece of propaganda.

As tensions mounted around the set, the original writers accused Hawks, Cooper, and the script doctors of unauthorized rewrites. The movie was supposed to be a picture of York as he saw himself, not some farce or superman story. Since any aspect of the film that did not meet with York's approval could mean financial disaster for Lasky and Warner Bros., the fact that York had a degree of veto power sometimes put him at odds with those whose primary objective was to produce a money-making feature. Hawks's tendency to tamper with the script forced Lasky and the original writers to dole the shooting script out in sections in order to reduce his embellishing the story line.

Finkel feared that York and his fellow Tennesseans would be outraged by the final product. Wild improvisations on the battlefield and disregard for the original intentions of the project sent him into a frenzy. In an agitated memo to Hal Wallis dated January 9, 1941, Finkel made his consternation known. He had developed a genuine affection for the rough-hewn people of the Wolf River Valley. Since he recognized their simple dignity, he was concerned about the violence they might carry out if their reputations were impugned. About the potentially offensive treatment of Tennessee he wrote:

The mass audience knows the mountaineer as an unwashed, unkempt yokel whom it finds amusing . . . we thought that in order to create understanding, and therefore sympathy for York it would be best to depict him and his fellow mountaineers as simple human beings with as much common sense as most people . . . To portray these people as a bunch of oafish clods for the sake of background color or for laughs would certainly antagonize York . . . to him the story of his life is no laughing matter. It took him twenty-five years to make up his mind to let someone put it in a picture. (*SY:* "The Sad Story of Sgt. York" 1)

He elaborated on an issue even closer to York's heart, the manner in which Huston and Koch had characterized Gracie:

York still refers to his wife as "Miss Gracie" . . . . Their romance was simple and idyllic. . . . The slightest hint that Gracie gave him the "come on" and vamped him into kissing her, even if it were not the tallest kind of corn, York would reach for his rifle gun and come a "'shootin'." You must remember that York knocked off 25 German machine gunners and he wasn't even sore at them. Can you imagine if he really got mad. ("The Sad Story of Sgt. York" 1)

What concerned him most was the real threat of arousing the litigious survivors from G Company. By that time many people at the studio were aware of their attitude and Finkel saw disaster written all over the movie if Hawks, Huston, and Koch continued to improvise. Feeling slighted both by history and the studio, the seven survivors were united in their disdain for the project. Finkel continued:

it is not only York that must be considered. . . . You must remember that most of the officers and men involved in York's exploit are still alive. Bill Guthrie can tell you how jealously they guard their contribution to York's exploit . . . they will all yell bloody murder if they are not given their due. ("The Sad Story of Sgt. York" 1-2)

Movie Synopsis

The film opens with Pastor Pile (Walter Brennan) conducting a prayer meeting while a drunken Alvin York (Gary Cooper) shoots his initials in a tree outside the church. Pile tries to console York's long-suffering mother (Margaret Wycherly) who comments on the precision of her tipsy son's shooting skills. The first third of the film examines York's life as a barely literate good-for-nothing hell-raiser. In the interim he falls in love with Gracie Williams (Joan Leslie) and competes with his nemesis Zeke (Clem Bevans) for her hand and is foiled in the attempt to buy a piece of property. Angered, he crosses the state line to Kentucky where he drinks and brawls; as he returns in the rain, he is hit by a bolt of lightning that bends the muzzle of his rifle. Taking this experience as a sign, he goes immediately to the Wolf River church.

The second third of the movie examines a reformed York, who quits drinking and carousing and finds steady employment. Now a pacifist, York recieves his draft notice and applies for conscientious objector status. His request is denied and York reports to Camp Gordon, Georgia, for basic training. Tested by his comrades who believe him to be a coward, York's prowess on the rifle range brings him to the attention of his company commander, Major Buxton (Stanley Ridges). Buxton interviews York to assess the sincerity of his pacifism, and tries to persuade York that it is sometimes necessary to fight. York struggles with his conscience during a brief furlough at home and finally decides that America needs his efforts on the battlefield.

The last third of the film examines York's famous exploit in the Argonne and his elevation to a national symbol. The battlefield sequences stand in stark relief to the Tennessee scenes, and the last third of the film moves at a faster and more intense pace. Upon York's return to America, he is bombarded with offers to capitalize on his fame, but he chooses to return home to his sweetheart, Gracie Williams.

Sergeant York and Interventionism

As world affairs changed during the course of the filming, York—through his close contact with Jesse Lasky and Harry Warner—began to pay more attention to the international scene. Warner and Lasky convinced York that Hitler represented not only a military threat to the world but was evil incarnate; no one, neither Christian nor Jew, was safe from the barbarity of Nazi Germany (YP, Dinnerstein 113). Subsequent changes made in the script which placed greater emphasis on York's war experiences were made with his approval. As a result Lasky could write general sales manager Gradwell Sears: "We in the studio sense a great picture in *Sergeant York*, especially in view of present world conditions, and in our treatment of the story we are taking advantage of world events and are making it timely and patriotic to a degree" (*SY*). Earlier Chandlee and Josephson wrote that "We all realize that this should not be a war picture in the usual sense of the word" (*SY*). That same memo clearly indicated the studio's intention of playing up the war angle in light of the current political situation in Europe, for by that date the American people recognized York as an interventionist. Casting off his pacifist cloak, he spoke out for increased defense spending, a beefed-up air force, military training in the CCC, and American support of Britain. York's conversion to belligerency was reflected in the script (*SY* and YP).

Other developments during the filming pushed York toward intervention. On September 16, 1940, President Roosevelt signed a provision calling for the creation of a peacetime draft. General George C. Marshall testified before Congress that the times were such that America needed to be on guard; because the United States had been unprepared for the last war, many lives were needlessly lost. York wholeheartedly agreed with the general. To the chagrin of local political leaders in Fentress County, Governor Prentice Cooper approved York's endorsement by naming him chief executive of the Fentress County Draft Board (YP).

The film premiered successfully in New York on July 2, 1941, at Broadway's Astor Theater. Bill Rice and Charles Einfeld of the Warner Bros. publicity department orchestrated an elaborate opening, including a VFW parade down Fifth Avenue to the theater, while York and Lasky made their triumphal entry in a convertible limousine. Among those in attendance were Wendell Willkie, General John J. Pershing, Tennessee Governor Prentice Cooper, New York Mayor Fiorello LaGuardia, Gary Cooper, and Joan Leslie. Walter Winchell lavished praise on the picture, and Norman Vincent Peale wrote Jack Warner telling him that not only was *Sergeant York* the most important film of the year, but that Warner Bros. may have just saved the country (*SY*). *Newsweek* praised the picture:

In such times and in less capable hands . . . [York's story] might have been a jingoistic cross between *Billy the Kid* and *The Fighting 69th*. Instead it is an engrossing and humorous record of the American way of life in a backwoods community, as well as a timely drama of the inner struggle of a deeply religious man who weighs his horror of killing against what he feels is the greater necessity to stop all killing. ("Sergeant York" 61-62)

York and Lasky spent the next several weeks on the road promoting the film. They held a special screening for President Roosevelt, invited members of the government, and the military. FDR noted that the film arrived at a propitious time but flippantly remarked that he did not approve of so much killing in the film ("Sergt. York Visits with the President"). Lasky sent the Warners telegrams describing the Washington premier: "We came. They saw. We conquered" (*SY*). By July 17, Einfeld was convinced that the movie was "potentially the most important picture ever made in our industry" (*SY*).

The outraged seven survivors disagreed, however, and placed a notice in the July 14, 1941, edition of the Boston *Globe*, a portion of which follows:

I wish to inform you that none of the survivors are in agreement with Warner Brothers or with Sergeant York's version of what really happened "over there" . . . we never recall signing any affidavit . . . that would be against our grain as we always had figured Sergeant York out to be "yellow" and not a conscientious objector. (*SY*)

The irate survivors went on to say that if they signed anything "we probably thought it was a supply slip for underwear or something" (*SY*). Merrithew stated that the movie might be a hit in the South but it "wouldn't wash" in the Northeast where he, Beardsley, Early, and Wills lived (*SY*).

Their protest proved negligible, for the film continued to draw crowds, turned a steady profit, and was popular even in New England.

At least one critic agreed with the seven survivors. Otis Ferguson panned the picture in *The New Republic*. The film was too long, too preachy, and too militant for his taste. He disliked York's conversion "from hoodlumism to shouting hallelujah," finding the religious aspects of the film uncomfortable; more significantly, he wholeheartedly disapproved of York's conversion to militancy. The film was "nothing but a memorial screed" (404-05).

Newly politicized, York became more outspoken in his attitudes toward the war raging in Europe. Convinced by Harry Warner that the United States could not sit idly by while Europe fell beneath the heel of the Axis powers, York grew more bellicose. Speaking on the *Hello America* radio program in 1941, he told his listeners that he finally consented to a movie based on his life because he felt that Warner Bros. and Jesse Lasky were the best qualified to do so. He demonstrated his considerable change of heart when he recalled the Jews, Italians, Slovaks, Swedes, Poles, and Portuguese who made up his unit in World War I and said, "The Old World backgrounds were forgotten . . . we were all Americans united in a common cause." He remembered that, though they worshipped differently, they were united by a common faith—a faith in "American principles." Now Great Britain alone fought to defend the concepts of freedom and democracy as Hitler spread totalitarianism across Europe; therefore, Americans owed a debt to England and should be ready to help. "Yes, we hear it said that our boys won't go to war no more. Don't fool yourself." As he summed up his speech calling for vigilance, he quoted his new friend Harry Warner, saying, "Friends let us all fall in line for the defense of our country and do all we can to help put out all 'isms' but Americanism." (All quotations from "Sgt. York's Speech 'Veterans of Foreign Wars' *Hello America* Program," 1941.)

Conclusion

Sergeant York proved to be the most important film produced by Warner Bros. to focus on the intervention debate. The film accurately captured the atmosphere of the country as it pondered its responsibilities to a world at war. It dramatically presented York's transformations from backwoods-hellion to pacifist-Christian to Christian-soldier who fought for the Christian ideal of peace (Combs and Combs 42). *Sergeant York* stood at the forefront of a group of films in the summer of 1941 that heightened awareness of the world political situation, marking a new phase in the struggle over preparedness (Steele 81). (The list includes such films as *Martial Storm, Fire Over England, Dispatch from Reuters,* and *Foreign Correspondent.*) In a variety of ways, these films asked Americans to appreciate cultural threads binding England and America. Like Harry Warner, they begged American audiences to assume responsibility for their actions and not to remain aloof. *Sergeant York* appealed to Americans because the story of his life restated a common belief that all Americans are potential heroes because of the strength of their religious and political heritage.

It was York's second conversion, the conversion to interventionism that Americans needed in 1940-1941. The movie allowed American audiences to abhor violence and uphold Christian values at the same time—while still reveling in the vicarious thrill of battlefield action. Audiences could claim pacifism and isolationism, while coming to the realization that some conflicts did require American intervention.

Through his association with Hollywood, Alvin C. York had undergone a profound change of heart. His politics had turned from pacifistic isolationism to advocacy of armed intervention. His association with Hollywood executives had brought about his increasing admiration and respect for the Jews across the globe; his gradual awakening to the evil of the European war was a reflection of the growing change in America toward intervention. In the end, York's choice would be vindicated, and *Sergeant York* became one of the most important calls for arms in World War II.

Notes

1. On October 8, 1918, Corporal Alvin Cullum York and sixteen other men under the command of Sergeant Bernard Early were dispatched to capture the Decauville railroad near Chatel-Chehery in the Meuse-Argonne. After a brief firefight (nine Americans died in the melee) the confused Germans surrendered to what they believed to be a superior force. In all, 132 Germans were captured by the seven survivors led by Corporal York. The army singled out York as the greatest American hero of World War I and presented him with the Congressional Medal of Honor, but overlooked the other seven. See Patullo, "The Second Elder Gives Battle," and Lee, *Sergeant York: An American Hero.*

2. Guy Williams once described the Church of Christ in Christian Union in the following way: "Take the Church of Christ and the Nazarene and put them both together and then take out all the fun that either one allows—that's the Church of Christ in Christian Union."

3. When Paramount fired Lasky, Harry Warner bought Lasky's home and loaned him $250,000. Lasky had introduced Warner to his nephew, one of the studio's most successful directors, and Harry Warner's son-in-law, Mervyn LeRoy.

4. Jack Warner declared that the studio severed ties with Germany due to the death of an employee: Joe Kauffman, a Warner newsreel cameraman, was beaten to death by Brown Shirts at the 1936 Berlin Olympics. This story simply is not true. No employee named Joe Kauffman worked for Warner Bros.; the studio had no newsreel division; and, most important, Harry Warner demanded that their business in Germany come to an end on July 15, 1934—two years before the death of the fictional employee and the Olympics. See Colgan 8-9, 40-41.

5. Discrepancies abound between versions of the movie's creation and the archival records. Autobiographies of Jesse Lasky, Jack Warner, Hal Wallis, and Howard Koch prove problematical as well and should be read with some skepticism. Koch remembered writing *Sergeant York* in 1943—after he had written *Casablanca*—which would have been impossible.

6. Though York's church deplored movies, and York said he did not like war pictures, he indicated some familiarity with such popular entertainments.

7. One cannot overstate the seriousness of this situation. In interviews, York's friends and relatives always refer to the fact that the Sergeant did business with "a bunch of Hollywood Jews." When the author first interviewed Guy Williams, he took a long pull on his cigar and said, "Jesse L. Lasky. He was a Jew, you know. Short too." Lasky, the first Jew many of these people had ever seen, made a deep and positive impression on York and his neighbors.

8. The finished sets consisted of a mountain peak on a carousel that could rotate 360 degrees, a 200-foot mountain spring, three stationary peaks, three forests, a farmyard, cabins, church, and general store. There were 123 sets in all, eight outdoor locations, and an 80-acre battlefield on the Calabassas ranch.

9. York said that church was the only place he could legitimately see Gracie. Unfortunately, his conversion put him in direct opposition with members of his own family. Raised as Methodists, they viewed York's conversion with disdain.

10. The central conflict ended up being York's feuding over Gracie's hand and his attempt to buy some bottomland to prove himself worthy. To folks in Fentress County this solution was ludicrous, since *all* the land in Pall Mall was bottomland.

11. The seven survivors of the victorious attack were Percy Beardsley, Corporal William Cutting, Sergeant Bernard Early, Harry Parsons, Joe Konotski, George Wills, Feodor Sok, Michael Saccina, and Mario Mussi.

12. Harry Warner earned the Sergeant's respect and friendship. Both were unabashedly religious. Both had grown up exceedingly poor, had quit drinking and smoking, recognized the value of an education, and were devoted family men. Harry Warner's patriotism and religious zeal impressed York and fostered empathy for the plight of the Jews as he became more aware of their oppression in Europe.

13. The agreement specified that Warners would lend Jack Carson, Donald Crisp, Lester Cole, and Bette Davis to Metro for one picture each, while they would receive Gary Cooper and his sidekick Walter Brennan for twelve weeks for $150,000 and $85,000 respectively. If the picture went over schedule, Warners agreed to pay an additional $12,500 per week for Cooper's services. Goldwyn demanded that Warners take Miriam Hopkins at a cost of $50,000 even though the studio had no project for her. The picture that Davis shot at Metro, *The Little Foxes,* earned her a Best Actress Oscar.

Works Cited

Birdwell, Michael E. "Celluloid Soldiers: Warner Bros., Alvin York and the Coming of World War II." Diss. U of Tennessee, 1996.

Colgan, Christine Ann. "Warner Brothers' Crusade Against the Third Reich: A Study of Anti-Nazi Activism and Film Production, 1933-1941." Diss. U of Southern California, 1985.

Combs, James E., and Sara T. Combs. *Film Propaganda and American Politics: An Analysis and Filmography.* New York: Garland, 1994.

Cook, Bruce. *Brecht in Exile.* New York: Holt, 1982.

Dinnerstein, Leonard. *Antisemitism in America.* New York: Oxford UP, 1994.

Ferguson, Otis. "In the Army, Aren't We All." *New Republic* 105 (29 Sept. 1941): 404.

Finkel, Aben. "The Sad Story of Sgt. York." Los Angeles: Warner Bros. Archives.

Glass, William R. "Fundamentalism's Prophetic Vision of the Jews: The 1930s." *Jewish Social Studies* 47.1 (1985): 63-76.

Koch, Howard. *As Time Goes By: Memoirs of a Writer.* New York: Harcourt, 1979.

Lasky, Jesse L., and Don Weldon. *I Blow My Horn.* Garden City, New York: Doubleday, 1957.

Lasky, Jesse L., Jr., *What Ever Happened to Hollywood?* New York: Funk, 1975.

Lee, David D. "Appalachia on Film: The Making of *Sergeant York*." *Southern Quarterly* 19.1-2, 3-4: 211-212.

——. *Sergeant York: An American Hero.* Lexington: UP of Kentucky, 1985.

Patullo, George. "The Second Elder Gives Battle." *Saturday Evening Post* 26 Apr. 1919: 3-4, 71-73.

Sergeant York File, Boxes A-51 and A-52. Los Angeles: Warner Bros. Archives.

"Sergeant York." *Newsweek* 14 July 1941: 61-62.

"Sergeant York Surrenders." *Time* 1 Apr. 1940: 70.

"Sergt. York Visits with the President." *New York Times* 31 July 1941: 13.

Steele, Raymond W. "The Great Debate: Roosevelt, the Media, and the Coming of the War, 1940-1941." *Journal of American History* 71.1 (1984): 69-92.

Wallis, Hal, and Charles Higham. *Starmaker: The Autobiography of Hal Wallis.* New York: Macmillan, 1980.

"WB First U.S. Co. to Bow Out of Germany." *Variety* 17 July 1934: 1.

Williams, Guy. Personal Interviews. Allardt, TN: 1988-1991.

York, Alvin C. York Papers. Pall Mall, TN.

8

Military Incompetence and the Cinema of the First World War:
Paths of Glory

Andrew Kelly

Few speak well of the generals in World War I: popularly seen as
spectators rather than fighters, well-fed and luxuriously housed, the generals demanded the impossible and seemed ready to accept massive
losses for minor gain. It is little wonder that such epithets as "blimps"
and "donkeys" have been leveled at them. In his classic study of the subject Norman Dixon states: "Only the most blinkered could deny that the
First World War exemplified every aspect of high-level military incompetence. For sheer lack of imaginative leadership, inept decisions, ignoring of military intelligence, underestimation of the enemy, delusional
optimism and monumental wastage of human resources it has surely
never had its equal" (80).

Dixon's comments could well serve as a summary of *Paths of Glory*
(1957), Stanley Kubrick's film about military incompetence and the brutality and slaughter it engenders. Much of the film attacks the oppor-
tunism and greed of the French High Command, though, by implication,
it is a condemnation of all military authority. It is also a comment on
class conflict as the basis of warfare. Ultimately, however, it is about
humanity, illustrating the capacity of some men, even after two years of
bitter conflict, to retain a belief in justice as well as a degree of empathy
with the enemy.

The Story

The film opens in 1916. Two years of trench warfare and the lives
of hundreds of thousands of men have resulted in stalemate on the Western Front. General Georges Broulard (Adolphe Menjou) visits the opu-
lent château headquarters of the ambitious General Paul Mireau (George
Macready) to bring orders to take the key strategic position of the "Ant
Hill" within forty-eight hours. A veiled offer of promotion persuades

143

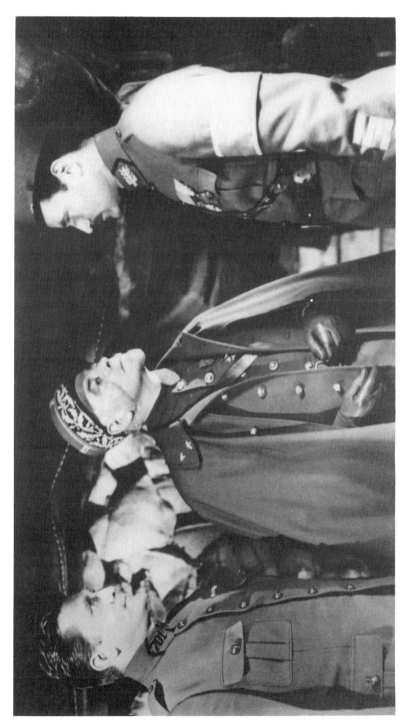

Attack the Ant Hill? Col. Dax, Gen. Mireau, and Maj. Saint-Auban discuss the futile mission.   Credit: The Film Archive

Mireau to force his already exhausted and devastated troops through another assault.

Mireau and his sycophantic adjutant, Major Saint-Auban (Richard Anderson), take the orders to Colonel Dax (Kirk Douglas), a battle-hardened commander respected by his men. Dax objects to the attack and agrees only on threat of being removed from command. That night a reconnaissance patrol consisting of Lieutenant Roget (Wayne Morris), Corporal Phillipe Paris (Ralph Meeker), and Private Lejeune (Ken Dibbs) go into no man's land. An unstable and fearful alcoholic, Roget sends Lejeune ahead but becomes jittery and throws a grenade. Corporal Paris, upon finding Lejeune's smouldering body, returns to the trench and accuses Roget of murder. Roget points out the impossibility of bringing such complaints against an officer—a status that seems to be above the law.

Next morning the attack begins despite unfavorable weather and the lack of sufficient artillery and reinforcements. Dax leads the assault but hundreds are killed and he returns to the corpse-strewn trench where the second wave remains, Roget amongst them. Watching from behind the lines, a disgusted Mireau—believing his troops are cowards—orders the artillery to fire on his own men; fortunately, the battery commander refuses to obey such an order.

After the failure, Mireau demands a court martial and insists that ten men from each company be executed for cowardice. He finally settles for three: Paris (picked by Roget to quiet him about the death of Lejeune), Private Pierre Arnaud (by lot), and Private Maurice Ferol (for being a social undesirable). Though Mireau protests, Dax is appointed defense counsel (in civilian life he is a prominent criminal lawyer). Despite previous citations—which Dax is prevented from introducing— and evidence of the men's brave action during the assault, they are found guilty. That night a priest (Emile Meyer) visits the men. A bitter Arnaud attacks him but Arnaud's skull is fractured when he is slammed against a wall by Corporal Paris.

Dax orders a reluctant Roget to take command of the firing squad. As Roget leaves, Rousseau (the battery commander) tells Dax of Mireau's order to fire on the trench. After obtaining further evidence, Dax visits Broulard at a ball at General Mireau's château. Broulard, shaken by Dax's revelations, orders him to leave. The execution takes place.

Broulard, Mireau, and Dax then meet over breakfast. Broulard reports the accusation, forcing an indignant Mireau to walk out. Broulard offers Dax Mireau's job—which he refuses vehemently. Dax returns to his room, but on the way hears cheering. Some of the men are in a tavern where they are entertained by an innocent and frightened German girl. At first they jeer but, as she sings, they begin to hum and cry. Dax, disgusted with the men's initial response, is heartened and allows them a few more minutes rest before returning to the front. He is unique in the chain of command in honoring the humanity of the ordinary soldiers under his command.

Stanley Kubrick and *Paths of Glory*

Alexander Walker has described *Paths of Glory* as Kubrick's graduation piece, a similar description given by Eisenstein to Milestone's *All Quiet on the Western Front* (Walker 82). Prior to *Paths of Glory,* Kubrick had made three features, two shorts, and had enjoyed a distinguished career as a photographer for *Look* magazine. He was still in his twenties. His first feature, *Fear and Desire* (1953), an antiwar film about four soldiers lost behind enemy lines, was an apprentice effort and has disappeared without a trace, no doubt encouraged by Kubrick who remembers it with embarrassment. His second film, *Killer's Kiss* (1955), a violent thriller about a boxer in love with the wife of a dance hall boss, received some critical acclaim. His third film, *The Killing* (1956), the story of a racetrack robbery brilliantly told from the viewpoints of the main characters, won widespread attention.

Among those impressed was Kirk Douglas who asked Kubrick if he had any other screenplays. Kubrick had written a script based on the novel *Paths of Glory* by Humphrey Cobb, which had made a great impact on him when he had read it at the age of fourteen. Douglas loved the script and helped raise the finance. Hitherto no studio had shown any interest, claiming that its lack of romance and Kubrick's plans to film in black and white made the project uncommercial. However, the participation of Douglas and his Bryna Production Company led a previously reluctant United Artists to post the budget of $900,000 of which Douglas received $350,000 (Walker 23).

The problem of the film's uncommercial nature was not lost on Kubrick who wanted the film to make money. Douglas said that after the film had been approved, Kubrick rewrote the script with Jim Thompson, the thriller writer (the two would share the final credit with Calder Willingham). The rewrite substituted a happy ending where the general arrives just in time to stop the execution and commutes the men's sentence to thirty days in jail. Douglas rejected this *deus ex machina* and demanded a return to the original, an action vindicated for him with the result being "a truly great film with a truly great theme: the insanity and brutality of war" (Douglas 282). It should be noted that Kubrick and Douglas had a stormy relationship on both *Paths of Glory* and

Spartacus. (In his autobiography Douglas describes the young director as a brilliant director but "a talented shit" [333].)

Humphrey Cobb and *Paths of Glory*

Humphrey Cobb was a veteran of the Great War. He had joined a Canadian regiment in 1916 and was both shot and gassed in combat. His novel was first published in 1935. It had received widespread prepublication interest and was an immediate bestseller despite some reviewers casting doubt on the veracity of the events portrayed. Cobb had anticipated such criticism and ensured that references to newspaper articles covering such trials for cowardice were included in the book (Cobb 265). However, having missed the classic pacifist phase in the early 1930s, *Paths of Glory* was quickly forgotten. The book impressed Hollywood sufficiently to hire Cobb as a screenwriter soon after publication, though little seems to have resulted. In a September 1940 *New York Times* interview he said that he had spent the last five years working for high rates of pay, or not working at all. He was also bitter about Hollywood politics, and was dismayed to discover that the various anti-Fascist groups he had supported were really Communist fronts (Van Gelder). He died in 1943.

It took 22 years for Cobb's novel to reach the screen. Bosley Crowther said it had "been a hot potato in Hollywood" since its original publication (Crowther, *New York Times*). The *New York Times* reported in late 1935 that Paramount had struggled for many months to make the picture, but feared offending the French government. The studio was also reluctant to make an avowedly antiwar film in a climate "seething with the spirit of aggressive nationalism," sensing that even if governments and censorship boards allowed exhibition, audiences would be hostile. A suggestion was made to situate the action in the Czar's army prior to the 1917 revolution. This compromise would have satisfied most objectors, including the Soviet government. Indeed, the *New York Times* felt the only opposition was likely to come from "such fugitive White Russians as still possess the price of a movie ticket." The idea was shelved (Sennwald).

Cobb's book influenced William Faulkner in his screenplay for *The Road to Glory* (and also his later allegorical novel, *A Fable*). A play written and produced by Sidney Howard did result, but its inability to translate battle scenes to the stage led to poor reviews and it closed after twenty-three performances on Broadway. One reviewer to buck the trend was Brooks Atkinson who predicted that someday "the screen will seize this ghastly tale and make a work of art from it" (qtd. in Alpert).

Novel into Film

Cobb's antimilitaristic novel is a realistic portrayal of war, sparing few of the gruesome details. It was, as Stephen Tabachnik recognized, written in cinematic terms (267-304). Indeed, parts of the screenplay were taken verbatim from Cobb's work. However, there are many differences between the book and the film. In general the novel allows greater character development and, unlike the film, reveals much more about the troops—their backgrounds and feelings. As is the case with most adaptations, a number of characters were either discarded or combined in the film. The crucial difference is the film's placement of Colonel Dax at center stage. In the book he occupies an important but not central role (he even appoints another captain—Etienne—to undertake the men's defense at the court martial). Kubrick added or amended a number of important scenes, particularly following the execution at the end of the novel. First, Dax appoints Roget as captain of the firing squad (in revenge for having picked Paris), thus making him indirectly responsible for his death. Second, Broulard turns on Mireau for his order to fire on his own trench and orders a court of inquiry with the implication that Mireau's career is ruined. (In the book, Dax states that he knew of the order, has been arguing the point with the general for some time, but is likely to get demoted for his trouble.) Third, there is the coda where the men go from the execution to the tavern—reestablishing the band of humanity with their enemy, with Dax, and with the audience.

The novel covers in considerable detail the choosing of the men for the court martial. One divisional commander—not wishing to sanction such an injustice—refuses to participate and disappears for the afternoon. Another chooses Ferol for being a social undesirable. The third is chosen by lot, though in a bizarre twist, it has to be redrawn as the first choice claims his number could be either 68 or 89.

Kubrick's additional scenes insure that the central theme of humanity emerges. Dax is seen as a man of honor and his men are shown to move from abuse and hatred for the enemy to empathy. Even General Broulard has the morality left to order an inquiry into the "friendly fire" incident. The book portrays a more bitter view. All characters are seen to be brutalized by the war: rather than being offered it, Mireau asks for promotion as his reward for attacking the Pimple (Cobb's name for the Ant Hill), Didier (Paris in the film) tries to shoot Roget while on patrol and, after returning, has breakfast before accusing him of Lejeune's murder. Nowhere is the cynicism more evident than in the order to attack the Pimple. This command is made on the basis of a communiqué already issued saying the target has been taken. Even Assolant (Mireau) resents this: "You are going to ask me to take with my bayonets what a

G. H. Q. ink-slinger has already inadvertently captured at the point of his pen!" (Cobb 21).

The Critics' Reaction

Paths of Glory opened in New York on Christmas Day 1957, having already had its world première in Munich on September 18. In general reviewers were impressed, praising its realism and the high standards achieved by the actors and production. Many were appalled with the story. *Variety* (November 20, 1957) described it as "a starkly realistic recital of French army politics." The *Film Daily* (November 19, 1957) said it was a "Relentlessly powerful drama. . . . Superbly conceived and executed."

In contrast to this praise were the fears of many reviewers that there were limited prospects for the film as it went against prevailing Hollywood trends in the 1950s. There was also some criticism that a film about the First World War was out of place in a nuclear age. *Time* (December 9, 1957) commented that "made 20 years ago, [the film] might have found a sympathetic audience in a passionately pacifist period, might even have been greeted as a minor masterpiece. Made today, it leaves the spectator often confused and numb, like a moving speech in a dead language."

Hollis Alpert recognized, but rejected, these problems. He found the film's message of universal relevance.

It is a wonder, in this time of unsettled conditions in the film industry, that *Paths of Glory* was made at all. It has none of the elements or gimmicks in it that are supposed to be box-office. It will not be shown on a large screen; it is in black and white; and its subject, an attack on the military command mentality, can hardly be expected to have vast popularity at this time. Its war, World War I, seems like primitive combat in these days of ICBMs with hydrogen warheads. But there is never anything untimely about an appeal to the human conscience, and this *Paths of Glory* makes. (31)

He predicted that the film would "take its place, in years to come, as one of the screen's most extraordinary achievements" (31).

Finally, *Paths of Glory* was released at a time when Europe was more divided than ever with the creation of new economic and military power blocs: the Warsaw Pact on the one side and NATO and the European Community on the other. With this background, and with many countries in Europe under virtual military occupation, it is little wonder that the film caused such controversy in many countries outside the United States.

Censorship and Protest

There were few problems with domestic censorship, although the Motion Picture Producers and Distributors Association (MPPDA) said that care had to be taken with the portrayal of the priest, suggested that some profanities were removed and insisted that the woman's blouse was not cut too low. But these changes did not prove enough to stop the film being banned in United States military bases at home and overseas.[1]

In Europe the film created a storm of protest, leading to censorship and bans in many cities and countries. It ran into immediate trouble in West Berlin when France threatened to withdraw from the July 1958 Berlin Film Festival were it not removed. It was eventually banned following the protests of General Gaze (who was able to invoke a clause in the four-power occupation treaty) and public disturbances by French soldiers in the British sector. The decision was condemned by German newspaper editors. The film's exhibition in Brussels was also stopped following demonstrations by French veterans, although it was reinstated after students from the Free University of Belgium protested against the ban. It may have been at this stage that discussions took place between the U.S. State Department and the French Foreign Ministry leading to the insertion of a foreword by the distributors, which stated: "This episode of the 1914-1918 war tells of the madness of certain men caught in its whirlwind. It constitutes an isolated case in total contrast with the historical gallantry of the vast majority of French soldiers, the champions of the ideal of liberty, which, since always, has been that of the French people." However, the film was again stopped in Brussels this time following student protests at French policy in Algeria.

There were also problems in Switzerland. The Ministry of the Interior banned the film as "subversive propaganda directed at France [and] highly offensive to that nation." There followed protests from the Swiss media, particularly when the government refused to screen the picture for journalists. It also ordered United Artists, under threat of confiscation, to export immediately all prints from the country. The film was not shown in Switzerland until the late 1970s.

Paths of Glory faced problems in Israel where the official film censorship board—invoking its policy of preventing exhibition of any film that ridiculed another government—placed a ban as it "disparaged the French Army" (*New York Times*, October 26, 1958.) Finally, the Australian, New Zealand, and British censors ordered cuts to the shot of Lejeune's smouldering body and extensive deletions to the execution scene.

The French Reaction

The greatest problems for the film, not surprisingly given its subject, were reserved for France.[2] The French government was reluctant to allow films highlighting embarrassing political and historical issues, particularly in the Fifth Republic under General De Gaulle. Jim Harris, Kubrick's co-producer, had been warned by the MPPDA in January 1957 of the likely objections of the French, though these had been dismissed as both Warner Bros. and MGM (potential production companies at that stage) were willing to take the risk. In addition, there was the possibility of a French partner in the venture.

The film—*Les Sentiers de la Gloire*—was regarded as undesirable by the government board of film censors. According to André Astoux, then director of the Centre National de la Cinematographie, "a discrete and effective act of dissuasion" prevented it from being released, though no total ban was ever announced. By 1972 the situation had improved. After the success of Kubrick's *A Clockwork Orange* a French arts society decided to ask for approval to show a subtitled version. However, United Artists, seemingly following Kubrick's advice, refused to produce the print. The film was finally released in 1975, according to *Box Office* (May 5, 1975), although *Variety* reported (July 19, 1978) that it was not seen in Paris for another three years. As in Brussels, the major problem for the film—in the early stages at least—seemed to be the war that the French were fighting in Algeria. It may also have been the case that it dredged up nightmares of the Dienbienphu failure in 1954 and the memories of the betrayal by Marshal Pétain in 1940 (both examples of High Command incompetence). Both Dienbienphu and Algeria had proved to be major crises for the French army and politicians. By 1957, Algeria was proving to be a particularly intractable problem: at one point over 500,000 troops were in the country, some of them conscripts. Like Vietnam (for the United States, later) there was criticism at home about the war. However, there was also discontent in the army leading to fears of a *coup d'état*. It is impossible now to think of these officers without comparing them with General Mireau: both seemed out of control, divorced from reality, and pursuing only one honour—the glory of France.

Paths of Glory and Antiwar Cinema

Whatever its aims and the interpretations placed upon it, *Paths of Glory* is undeniably a film which opposes war. It is important to state however, as Alexander Walker has said, that Kubrick cannot simply be classified as a pacifist (35). Kubrick himself, in a *Playboy* interview, said that he was unsure about the meaning of pacifism: on the one hand, he says, would it have been right to submit to Hitler to prevent the Second World War; conversely, "there have also been tragically senseless wars such as World War One" (Agel 350).

The opposition to war is evident right from the start. Although no comment is made on the origins and need for the war, the opening narration—spoken over views of the château and following the ironic use of the Marseillaise over the credits—points out that two years of conflict have resulted in the deaths of hundreds of thousands of men for very little gain. The film then examines three main areas: first, the ambition, incompetence, and brutality of the High Command; second, a realistic and horrific portrayal of war; and third, an argument on the class basis of conflict.

Dramatic contrasts are used to demarcate the characters of the High Command represented principally by General Mireau and General Broulard. The motivations, rationale, and actions of these two officers differ markedly with those of Colonel Dax who, though always a soldier and loyal to the system, is concerned about his men and accepts Mireau's order to attack only because he hopes to save lives by remaining in the chain of command.

General Mireau is the main character representing the High Command. In a superb performance, George Macready is duplicitous, utterly contemptible, self-aggrandizing with an almost psychopathic contempt for his troops. Early in the film he is sympathetic, concerned that with all that they have suffered hitherto, his men will be unable to take the Ant Hill. It does not take much for Broulard to change his mind and, even though there is no promise of artillery support and reinforcements, the mention of promotion to the Twelfth Corps and an extra star for his uniform, persuades him to attack. Mireau's tour of the trenches highlights how distant he is from the men and their reality of battle. Although he dislikes armchair officers it is clear that Mireau prefers to stay away from the front. He is more animated than the others when shells burst near the trenches. His "bonhomie" with the troops and the denial of the existence of shellshock show how far removed he has been from the suffering his troops experience daily.

Mireau's inability (or refusal) to identify the problems his soldiers will face is highlighted when he views the Ant Hill through binoculars. At this level it seems near and achievable, a view belied when Dax is in no man's land and sees the target as far away as ever. This failure of perception by the High Command is neatly summarized by Dax in the novel: "Rarely does a soldier see with naked eyes. He is nearly always looking through lenses, lenses which are made of the insignia of his rank" (Cobb 103). Alexander Walker also praises Kubrick's use of binoculars: "Each time it allows the military command to look on what are (or will be) the horrifying consequences of their orders without suffering the moral responsibility of physical involvement" (108). Despite his early concern, Mireau has a cavalier attitude to his men, willing to sacrifice whatever is necessary to take the objective. He tells Dax of the likely casualties—he expects 60 percent of the men to die. Dax is incredulous—over half his men will be killed—and although Mireau agrees it is a terrible price to pay, he must have the Ant Hill.

The change from Mireau's concern for the men to contempt is exacerbated when the attack begins to fail. The order to fire artillery on his own troops highlights his inability to understand the war he is fighting or to sympathize with the men under his control. The soldiers are now cowards. From this point Mireau hates the men who have cost him his promotion. He demands ten from each company—100 in all—to be tried for cowardice.

Dax protests and persuades Broulard to reduce the numbers—even offering himself as a sacrifice—and Mireau agrees to three men, one from each company in the first wave. Mireau now has someone to blame and sits smugly at the court martial. He only receives his comeuppance after the execution when Broulard confronts him with Dax's revelations.

The portrayal of General Broulard is also an attack on the High Command, though in different ways. It was an apt choice to cast Adolphe Menjou in the role: World War I veteran, debonair actor, enthusiast for right-wing causes (invaluable in his interpretation of the role according to Kubrick) (Walker 24). Broulard is shrewd, calculating, and well-versed in the realities of war. He gets all he needs from the attack and its aftermath, while avoiding any of the blame. By ordering the attack—which he later admits to Dax was probably impossible to implement—he deflects newspaper and political pressure at home. When it fails, he is able to place the blame firmly on the men—although he is not so strident in his criticism as Mireau. He is also careful to be absent from the court martial (anticipating the problems it could cause in the future) by telling his general it is best he handles it alone. Following Dax's revelations he realizes Mireau is a liability and ensures his dismissal—and probable suicide. He is unable to stop the executions, however, as that would be a sign of weakness. As indicated earlier, he even offers Dax Mireau's post which Dax rejects, to Broulard's surprise. Indeed, neither general can understand Dax's motives and sense of duty.

Broulard is also portrayed as having little sympathy for the men, although he recognizes, from the numbers of dead, that there must have been a considerable effort to take the Ant Hill. He sees great value in the executions in helping the troops morale *pour encourager les autres:* "these executions will be a perfect tonic for the entire Division," he says. "There are few things more fundamentally encouraging and stimulating than seeing someone else die."[3]

Colonel Dax is the only senior officer to emerge with any semblence of honor. In a marvellously underplayed performance (which, despite his own reservations, is one of the best in a distinguished career) (Walker 24), Kirk Douglas plays a man cynical of the High Command who dislikes false patriotism and respects—even loves—the foot soldiers of his regiment. At one point he quotes Samuel Johnson's comments to Mireau that "patriotism is the last refuge of the scoundrel" though the point is lost on the man.

Despite the praise lavished by reviewers, some commentators have criticized Dax's role. Robert Hughes claimed that "spectators leave the film with the impression that if only guys like Kirk Douglas could lead us, we could kill each other in good conscience" (8). Kubrick himself seemed to want a degree of ambiguity in the character. In a note for distributors regarding the synchronisation of the film in foreign language release he stated:

The voice should be cultured and educated but not to the point of being snobbish. However it should also be strong and manly. Be careful not to let . . . Dax ever wear his heart on his sleeve. Despite the conflict with his commanding officers he is always a soldier; *and never let him indulge in self-pity, or, for that matter, never let him break his heart* over the injustice being done to his men. His actions express his sympathy for his men fully enough. It would be disastrous to over-emphasize his indignation or his pity.[4]

Despite the differences in interpretation of Dax's role there is no doubt that he rediscovers his belief in humanity at the end. Up to then his faith had been totally shattered and, as he listens to the initial jeers of his men in the tavern, a look of utter disgust covers his face. But the disgust fades as the jeers lessen and the men hum, sing, and cry with the German girl. As the reviewer in the November 23, 1957, *Motion Picture Herald* said: "Threaded through . . . is the idealism of one man and the hope that it holds for mankind [is] epitomised by the final scene . . . in which Douglas, embittered and defeated, sees in a single flash the understanding compassion of man." Like Dick Williams, reviewer in the *Mirror-News*, we know that the "barbarities of war have not permanently captured men's souls" (December 21, 1957). That his tired men can appreciate the pathos and humanity of the singer is evidence that there is hope for humankind.

In contrast to the officers, and different from the novel, the ordinary soldiers are not portrayed in any detail, Kubrick preferring to use them as symbols of the common suffering of the eternal soldier in the war. This has led one commentator, Adrian Turner, to criticize the film in the *Guardian* as

a stacked deck of liberal idealism which is never convincing. . . . We know these hapless soldiers will be executed and we, like Kubrick, couldn't care less. They exist, not as characters, but as targets. Kubrick loves the generals who . . . have the best lines and give the best performances. Kubrick is enthralled by their control and their authority, for they demonstrate his themes of universal and inherited evil. (December 23, 1988)

This is a point also recognized in Dilys Powell's contemporary review. "The film invites compassion for the herd of soldiers, helpless, wavering between callousness and self-pitying sentimentality. But the invitation is made intellectually, from the outside. And except for a moment or two in the performance of Timothy Carey as a pathetic, bemused prisoner the characters are characters from a novel, not from life" (146).

The fate of the doomed men is of great interest; few viewers could fail to be moved by the miscarriage of justice and the execution. The rationale behind the order to attack, the assault, the court martial, and the actions of Mireau all highlight the brutality of military incompetence. This is confirmed with the execution. As if their suffering were not enough, the three men are brought to their deaths in front of the remains of the regiment, press, and invited dignitaries. Paris walks upright, resigned to his fate but able to avoid the blindfold so that he can condemn Roget and the bureaucracy; Ferol, distraught, is helped to his death by the priest; Arnaud—who earlier in the film said that he was more afraid of pain than of being killed—is carried, barely alive, on a stretcher; his cheeks are pinched so that he can at least be awake at his death. "The men died magnificently" Mireau tells Broulard over a sumptuous breakfast.

No other film about war has been able to convey in a single scene how needlessly men died to satisfy and hide the whims, ambitions, arrogance, and mistakes of the High Command. *The Hollywood Reporter* found it praiseworthy: "The final big scene is a long and grotesque one, horribly impressive, in which the glory that is France is summoned up to execute the three wretched individuals and thus redress French military honor" (November 18, 1957).

The reassertion of humanity is also present in the final scene with the men in the tavern. Up to this point in the film, the troops—battle weary and fatalistic—have made no comment on the trial and the execution, glad they were spared in the arbitrary nature of the decision-making. As they sit, a frightened German teenager is brought onto the stage—the first manifestation of the enemy yet seen—and her singing provides a cathartic release for their loss, fears, and memories of loved ones back home. Clearly moved, Hollis Alpert commented "we know that Colonel Dax and his soldiers have made their odyssey and arrived home safely" (32).

The antiwar nature of the film is also contained in the realistic portrayal of the horrors of war. Kubrick, an assiduous researcher and planner, was keen to attain verisimilitude in his picturing of the trenches and no man's land. Impossible to make in France, the picture was filmed in and around Munich, with the interiors at the Bavarian Geiselgasteig Studios and the court martial in Schleissheim Castle. For a battlefield, the filmmaker rented 5,000 square yards of land and there created credible trenches, barbed-wire defenses, and shell holes.

This re-creation of reality proved a great achievement; many reviewers praised the battle scenes for their resemblance to war newsreels and photographs. As the reconnaissance patrol sets out, it clambers over dead bodies, barbed wire, shell holes, mud and water; the battle scenes (with extras provided by the West German police force) are skillfully achieved and highlight the brutal noise, death, and suffering—what an enthusiastic recruit in the novel calls "The Orchestration of the Western Front"—of full-frontal assaults on heavily fortified enemies (Cobb 75). Winston Churchill, who knew more than most about the results of military incompetence, praised the film's authenticity.

There is a third element in the film. The stark contrast between the officers in the château and the men in the trenches epitomizes class struggle, and is resonant of von Clausewitz's dictum of war being the continuation of politics by other means—albeit in a more brutal fashion than the philosopher of war intended. The film is making a similar point to that of *La Grande Illusion* (1937), where the differences between people are not those of nation and language but of class. Mireau and Broulard represent the upper-class rulers, those in control, who are able to abuse those under them as mere pawns in their power games.

Dax's defense of the troops against this cynicism is characteristic and he is the only military man to straddle the officer/soldier divide. But it is clear which side he is on. Alexander Walker has also recognized the point of class struggle. The film, he writes:

takes its stand on human injustice. It shows one group of men being exploited by another group. It explores the social stratification of war. No man's land is

Despite reservations, Col. Dax prepares "to go over the top" with his troops.

Credit: The Film Archive

not really the great dividing barrier between the two sides . . . the "two sides" actually wear the same uniform, serve the same flag, and hold the same battle line, though in vastly differing degrees of comfort. The actual division, the deeper conflict, is that between the leaders and the led. It exists whether there is a war or not, but a war situation widens the division fatally. Only by implication is *Paths of Glory* a protest against war as such; it is much more pertinently an illustration of war as the continuation of class struggle. The paths of glory in the title are not the ones that lie across the battlefield; they are the avenues to self-advancement taken by the generals in command, with the utmost indifference to the fate of the men in the trenches. (84)

Kubrick's attack on military incompetence, the slaughter that results and the humanity that can remain, makes it one of the great antimilitarist statements. It came at an important time for public perceptions of conflict resolution. In the mid-1950s the world was torn apart in a Cold War that could have resulted in near total destruction. *Paths of Glory* said—at a time that needed prophets—that war was not a method for resolving disputes. Few films have matched its message and its power.

Notes

1. All information from the MPPDA is taken from research in the Margaret Herrick Library in the Academy of Motion Picture Arts and Sciences in Los Angeles.
2. Much of the information on the French release was provided by the Centre National de la Cinematographie.
3. All quotations from the film have been taken from the copy of the screenplay held in the New York State Archives, Albany.
4. An insert contained in the screenplay.

Works Cited

Burgess, J. "The 'Anti-militarism' of Stanley Kubrick." *Film Quarterly* 18.1 (1964).

Cobb, Humphrey. *Paths of Glory.* New York: Viking, 1935.

Crowther, Bosley. Rev. of *Paths of Glory. New York Times* 26 Dec. 1957.

Dixon, Norman F. *On the Psychology of Military Incompetence.* London: Futura, 1979.

Douglas, Kirk. *The Ragman's Son: An Autobiography.* New York: Simon and Schuster, 1988.

Hughes, Robert. "Murder: a 'big problem.'" *Film: Book 2. Films of Peace and War.* Ed. Robert Hughes. New York: Grove, 1961.

Powell, Dilys. *The Golden Screen: Fifty Years of Film.* London: Pavilion, 1989.

Sennwald, A. "The Paths of Glory." *New York Times* 27 Oct. 1935.

Van Gelder, R. "A Talk with the Author of Paths of Glory." *New York Times* 22 Sept. 1940.

Walker, Alexander. *Stanley Kubrick Directs.* London: Abacus, 1973.

9

Johnny Got His Gun:
Evolution of an Antiwar Statement

Martin F. Norden

With the 1939 publication of *Johnny Got His Gun*, a novel about a veteran whose face and limbs had been blown away by an artillery shell on the last day of World War I, Dalton Trumbo established himself as one of the preeminent antiwar voices of his generation. A Hollywood screenwriter since 1935, Trumbo began writing *Johnny* at a time when fascism was on the rise and war seemed imminent. Unlike many of his leftist peers, however, Trumbo wanted to avoid U.S. engagement in the escalating events overseas and developed the project as a plea for the country not to get involved. "If the book is any good at all it is good as an argument against war," he wrote his agent in February 1939, shortly after completing the manuscript, "and it will be utterly valueless if the country is either in war or in favor of war by the time it is published" (qtd. in Cook 130). Published eleven days after the signing of the Nazi-Soviet Non-Aggression Pact and a mere two after the outbreak of war in Europe, the stunning novel won an American Booksellers Award and left critics tripping over themselves with superlatives. In addition to going through seven printings that year, *Johnny* was serialized in *The Daily Worker* to much acclaim by the American left and led a kindred spirit named Arch Oboler to dramatize it as an hour-long NBC radio play in 1940 with the popular movie actor James Cagney in the lead role (Cook 300, MacDonald 57). Those who had been railing at the prospect of American intervention in the war on the other side of the Atlantic had found a new hero.

Encouraged by all the attention and aware that pacifistic themes had guided the greatest of the Great War movies—among them, *The Four Horsemen of the Apocalypse* (1921), *The Big Parade* (1925), *What Price Glory?* (1926), and *All Quiet on the Western Front* (1931)— Trumbo quite unsurprisingly began exploring the possibility of turning *Johnny Got His Gun* into a film. He would have no way of anticipating the lengthy and tortuous route that this dream would follow, however, or

161

the reaction it would receive; the movie did not appear until 1971 and left viewers extremely divided over its merits. This study provides a much-needed framework of understanding for Trumbo's complex novel and namesake film by tracing his experiences as they informed the content and structure of both works, his decades-long struggle to bring *Johnny* to the screen, and the highly mixed responses that resulted.

Early History and Influences

Born in Montrose, Colorado, in 1905 and brought up in the small city of Grand Junction about sixty miles away, James Dalton Trumbo was raised a Christian Scientist but doubtless saw his faith shaken after witnessing the return of home-town World War I veterans, many now with permanent disabilities. As a youth, Trumbo worked in a Grand Junction bookstore run by a young man who had been blinded in the war, and he later acknowledged that his daily encounters with this disabled vet were among the first influences on him for *Johnny Got His Gun* (Cook 37-38). His belief in the power of faith healing received a further jolt in 1925 when his father died of a blood disorder at age 51. "There was nothing we could do for him in any event," noted Trumbo, who then hinted at his shifting perspectives by adding: "This was a couple of years before the liver extract cure for pernicious anemia had become known" (qtd. in Cook 53).

Though a belief in "miracle cures" continued to find expression in many cultural products of the postwar period,[1] Trumbo like so many others no longer found it a viable strategy for coping with life's hardships. A major turning point in his development as a writer (to say nothing of his development as a human being) occurred years later when he learned about two WWI veterans who had suffered injuries so severe that they precluded any hope for recovery: a British major who had been so mutilated that the army reported him missing in action to his family, and a Canadian soldier left dismembered, blinded, deafened, and tubefed by the conflict. As Trumbo described the latter's story: "In the mid-thirties, the Prince of Wales visited a military hospital in Canada. At the end of a hallway, there was a door marked 'No Admittance.' 'What's in there?' he asked. 'We'd rather you not go in there,' they told him. But the Prince of Wales insisted, and when he came out of the room, he was weeping. 'The only way I could salute, the only way I could communicate with that man,' he said, 'was to kiss his cheek'" (qtd. in Flatley 11). The stories of these vets made such an impact on Trumbo that, even while working steadily as a Hollywood screenwriter, he began writing a novel that would reveal the absurdities and cruelties of war and would daringly be told from the perspective of such a veteran.

One of Trumbo's first tasks was to come up with a title, and he decided to let the spirit of the early war years be his guide. "God, but we were all crazy about the first World War," he said. "The enthusiasm . . . I remember young boys going to Canada to volunteer in the Canadian Air Force. They just couldn't wait for the United States to get into the war. Europe was mad with pleasure. The Germans were insane with joy; the French marched gaily off to slaughter. Dogfights in the air, the dropping of wreaths over the wounded" (qtd. in Flatley 11). In particular, Trumbo drew on George M. Cohan's immensely popular "Over There," a 1917 war tune that became a veritable rallying cry for countless Americans. ("Funny about them giving me a medal. All I wrote was a bugle call," Cohan contemplated in retrospect [qtd. in Morehouse 126].) Some of the song's lyrics are reproduced below:

> Johnnie, get your gun, get your gun, get your gun,
> Take it on the run, on the run, on the run;
> Hear them calling you and me,
> Every son of Liberty.
> Hurry right away, no delay, go today.
> Make your daddy glad
> To have had such a lad,
> Tell your sweetheart not to pine,
> To be proud her boy's in line.[2]

Cohan's lyrics contributed to the spirit of what might be called the "front end" of the war for America, a time when a sense of chivalry and noble duty clouded the horrors of a conflict that had been raging in Europe for almost three years. With Trumbo's selection of "Johnny Got His Gun" as his title, his interest in representing the "back end" of the war—the lingering, ignoble consequences that people created for themselves and others after "Johnnie" indeed got his gun—was clear. As his wife, Cleo Trumbo, noted, "In *Johnny Got His Gun* it was not his purpose to revel in pain. His purpose was to tell a story that might challenge the concept of the glories of war. The story said: *This happens*. The story said: *This happens because of us*" (ix-x).

With a title in hand and the stories of the two severely disabled vets as his point of departure, Trumbo threw himself into the project and began fleshing out the narrative details. Though not a veteran himself, he infused *Johnny Got His Gun* with numerous autobiographical and familial elements; not only did he endow his lead character, "Joe Bonham," with his paternal grandmother's maiden name,[3] but he also had the youth grow up in a Colorado town, attend Christian Science rallies, move to

Los Angeles with his family, see his father—a beekeeper and expert at raising crops in parched environments—die at age 51, and work in a bakery to help the family make ends meet. All these things had happened to Trumbo, who identified so much with his literary construction that as a part of the creative process he began to perceive the world from that character's perspective. "In 1938, almost immediately after Trumbo and I were married, he started writing *Johnny Got His Gun*," Cleo Trumbo remembered many years later. "I didn't know anything about writers. We had bought a small place up in the mountains. He worked all night. I watched flashes of Johnny appear at breakfast. I learned—if not about writers—about Trumbo. In order to write *Johnny*, he had to *become* Johnny" (ix).

An additional factor that helped shape the writing of *Johnny Got His Gun* was Trumbo's experience as a screenwriter. At the time he wrote most of the novel, he was living at his so-named "Lazy-T" ranch up in California's Ventura mountains some eighty miles outside of Los Angeles. Far from the bustle of Hollywood (indeed, he did not even have a telephone), Trumbo nevertheless drew heavily on the craft of Hollywood scriptwriting by bestowing a conspicuously cinematic quality on his novel; it relies strongly on such movie devices as voice-over narration, motivated flashbacks, and sound montages to propel it. Bernard F. Dick perhaps put it best by suggesting that in many ways *Johnny* is a disguised script:

Trumbo makes liberal use of flashbacks introduced by quick cuts or slow dissolves, and fragments the plot into discrete narrative units that are more like film sequences than chapters. In fact, he had to use flashbacks; when the main character is a double amputee [*sic*], fed intravenously, deaf and speechless with a gaping hole for a face, and confined to a hospital bed where he is an object alternately of pity and disgust, there is not the remotest possibility of a plot without them. (186)

Thus, the strategies that Trumbo learned as a screenwriter eventually coalesced with the stories of the two "basket cases," his early encounters with disabled veterans, and other elements of his life to form the narrative vehicle that became the book and, years later, the film.

A Dream Deferred

Trumbo entertained thoughts of developing *Johnny* into a movie after its publication but soon realized the timing was terrible; the Nazi invasion of Russia in June 1941 and the American entrance into the war later that year smashed any production hopes for the foreseeable future.

"After Pearl Harbor its subject matter seemed as inappropriate to the times as the shriek of bagpipes," he noted (*Johnny* n.p.).[4] Aware that the movie industry had adopted a pro-war stance in part to protect its profitable overseas markets, he sensed correctly that no studio would touch such an impassioned antiwar plea as *Johnny*. Leftists were now lining up with others against fascist aggression, and Trumbo proved no exception; a number of the screenplays he turned out during those years fervently supported the war effort. An example was his script for *Thirty Seconds Over Tokyo* (1944), an MGM flagwaver about the famous air raid masterminded by Lt. Col. James H. Doolittle in which sixteen American B-25s bombed Tokyo and other cities, inflicting minimal damage on their targets but creating untold morale boosting value and affecting Japanese defensive strategy. Though *Thirty Seconds* dealt extensively with issues of wartime disablement—its heroic lead character, Ted Lawson (Van Johnson), loses a leg as a result of a crash landing after the raid—its tone differed significantly from that of *Johnny Got His Gun*; none of the novel's disillusionment, sense of absurdity, and generally bitter quality had found its way into the script.[5]

In 1946, after the war was over and his novel went through another printing, the time seemed right for *Johnny* to be made into a film and Trumbo pursued the possibility in earnest. His dream was shelved once again, however; this time, the delay resulted from the House Committee on Un-American Activities hearings dedicated to ferreting out "subversives" in the movie industry in 1947 and the blacklisting era that ensued. Trumbo was a member of the Communist Party at the time of the hearings (he had joined in 1943 and would remain a member until 1948) and resolutely refused to cooperate with the Congressional committee. "I have never been able to convince myself that I can retain any dignity as a man, as an American, if I yield to the committee's demand for compulsory revelation," he argued (*Additional* 502). Trumbo became the most famous member of the Hollywood Ten, the unfriendliest of the so-termed "unfriendly witnesses" who appeared before the committee and were jailed for their convictions.

After serving ten months in a federal penitentiary in Ashland, Kentucky, for contempt of Congress, Trumbo emerged to find that no studio would hire him. Forced to go underground, he continued to write screenplays but under assumed names and received only a fraction of his preblacklist salary; his per-script fee, once among the highest in Hollywood at $75,000, tumbled to as low as $3,000.

Though Trumbo was unable to use his own name on his scripts from 1947 to 1960, his antiwar novel seemed more timely than ever during and after the new war in Korea. Indeed, the Liberty Book Club published a new edition in 1952 and seven years later, after the country had had a chance to gain some chronological distance on the Korean War, the publishing concern of Lyle Stuart brought out yet another edition that featured a new introduction by Trumbo and went through nine printings.

The blacklist was broken in 1960 with Trumbo playing no small part; he had humiliated the Academy of Motion Picture Arts and Sciences in 1957 by winning an Oscar for *The Brave One* under the pseudonym "Robert Rich," and in 1960 not only did Otto Preminger openly hire him as principal screenwriter for the movie adaptation of Leon Uris's *Exodus*, but he also worked with Kirk Douglas and Stanley Kubrick on the big-budgeted historical epic *Spartacus*. Within several years, Trumbo was back on top of his profession and again commanded high screenwriting fees for such films as *Lonely Are the Brave* (1962), *The Sandpiper* (1965), and *Hawaii* (1966). As *New York Times* reporter Peter Bart noted in 1966, Trumbo's "last four scripts alone reportedly yielded over $1 million. He is in constant demand" (13).

Though Trumbo obviously welcomed the opportunity to return to the screenwriting field under his own name, he never felt quite at ease with his rather odd dual status: a refugee from the far left who profited handsomely from a medium known for its mainstream values. "I still think of myself as a radical," he noted in 1966. "But I suppose if I were really as radical as I think I am, I would sell this house, live on $10,000 a year and donate the rest of my salary to protest movements" (qtd. in Bart 13). Some of his Hollywood peers were critical of what they perceived was the writer's complacency. "Trumbo used to be full of fight," said a fellow writer. "Maybe he's become too rich and slick" (qtd. in Bart 13). Unbeknownst to them, however, Trumbo had quietly revived the idea of turning *Johnny Got His Gun* into a movie. While living in self-imposed exile in Mexico during the blacklisting era, he had encountered a like-minded leftist in the personage of Luis Buñuel, the famous Spanish surrealist then in the midst of his "Mexican period." Buñuel, who claimed that Trumbo's novel "struck me like a bolt of lightning" (193), was the author's choice to direct the movie and in 1964 the two of them worked together on a script. As Buñuel remembered it:

In the early 1960s, I was supposed to make this movie; the producer Gustavo Alatriste was ready to put up the money, and Trumbo, then one of the most famous scriptwriters in Hollywood, worked with me on the screenplay (I talked and he took notes). Even though he incorporated only a few of my ideas, he insisted that both our names appear in the credits. For a variety of reasons, however, the project was shelved. (193)

What followed after the funding fell through was a long line of rejections; no less than seventeen Hollywood companies turned it down as "too depressing," in Trumbo's words. "I'd be happy to think they rejected it because of my political past, but I fear otherwise," he said (qtd. in "Trumbo's" 20). The movie finally got off the ground in 1970 after a longtime friend of former blacklistees, the aptly named Simon Lazarus, brought the project back from the dead by raising $750,000 for the film's production. To keep costs down, Trumbo decided to direct it himself; at age 65, he had become in his words "the oldest new director in Hollywood" (qtd. in Mount 21). He pursued other cost-cutting measures: all of the performers felt so strongly about the film that they agreed to defer their salaries until after the film's release (indeed, Donald Sutherland, who had recently starred in the antiwar megahit *M*A*S*H*, worked for nothing at all), and in a virtually unprecedented action the unionized crew members deferred their overtime pay as well. "I think that's the first time in the history of American cinema that's ever happened," the director said with some astonishment (qtd. in "Trumbo's" 20). Trimming expenses even further, Trumbo turned *Johnny* into something of a family affair; his son Christopher served as an associate producer, daughter Melissa shot photographs for the movie, wife Cleo developed the prints, and Trumbo, who wrote and directed the film, also played the bit role of a medical director who happily notes the speed by which wounded veterans can be returned to the front. With the guidance of producer Bruce Campbell, who also happened to be Trumbo's son-in-law, and a distribution deal with Cinemation Industries, *Johnny Got His Gun* began playing in movie theaters the following year.

In some ways, the timing of the movie's release was auspicious. Though Trumbo claimed that he wanted *Johnny* to receive no advance publicity—he said he wanted the film to "make it on its merits or not at all" (qtd. in Mount 23)—by accident or design he had become a lightning rod for news-media attention the previous year. *Esquire* not only published "The Happy Jack Fish Hatchery Papers," an exchange of humorously pointed letters between Trumbo and Steve Allen, but also "Diary of a Dead Bavarian," a lengthy piece by a disgruntled *Johnny* extra named Jerry Zinnamon. More conspicuously, an anthology of Trumbo's correspondence from 1942 to 1962 titled *Additional Dialogue* had just been published to much acclaim, and his suggestion that there were "only victims" during the blacklisting era, given in a speech after he received the Writers' Guild annual Laurel Award, generated considerable controversy.[6]

Perhaps more significant than these developments in 1970 was the publication of yet another edition of *Johnny Got His Gun*. Bantam had republished the book in 1967 to little attention, but when it brought out a new edition three years later, featuring an introductory addendum by Trumbo that specifically invoked the Vietnam War, the novel served once again as a galvanizing force for the American left.[7] "Numbers have dehumanized us," he wrote in his addendum. "Over breakfast coffee we read of 40,000 American dead in Vietnam. Instead of vomiting, we reach for the toast" (*Johnny* n.p.).[8] With all the attention Trumbo had called to himself that year, to say nothing of the moral imperative created by the film's Vietnam context, the stage was set for his directorial debut.

Not Just Your Average Joe

The focus of the film is of course Joe Bonham (played by Timothy Bottoms), who before the movie begins has been hit by an artillery shell on the last day of World War I. The early passages are distinguished by cinematographer Jules Brenner's gritty black-and-white imagery as doctors, photographed from a very low angle suggesting the disabled veteran's point of view, examine Joe and declare him a "completely decerebrated" individual who cannot "experience pain, pleasure, memory, dreams, or thoughts of any kind." Completely obscured to the audience by bedclothes draped over him, Joe is far from a vegetable, however; he provides frequent voice-over narration that informs the audience—but not the other characters—of his thoughts and feelings. ("Where am I? It's dark in here," he says in voice-over, soon after a doctor has proclaimed him as "unthinking as the dead.")

Joe learns with mounting horror that the injury has left him legless, armless, and faceless, his abilities to see, hear, smell, and speak destroyed. Frequently under the spell of sedative drugs, he fends off the waves of revulsion that ensue by retreating into memories and fantasies—the first and only time he made love to his girlfriend Kareen (Kathy Fields), his final meeting with his dying father (Jason Robards), and many more—which Trumbo had Brenner shoot in color to contrast with the monochrome horror of Joe's present circumstances. Trumbo often enhanced the surrealistic qualities of these sequences by showing Joe as he appeared before the accident but having him talk about subjects that happened after it. After a heavily sedated Joe imagines that a rat is crawling on him, for example, a fantasy sequence shows him attired in battle fatigues and discussing his rodent dream with Jesus Christ (Donald Sutherland) while the latter, dressed in carpenter's garb, prepares grave markers in the shape of crosses.

Following a series of such "conversations" with his dream and fantasy figures, Joe discovers a way to communicate with his medical attendants; he taps out S.O.S. messages in Morse code with his head on his pillow. The doctors regard his movements as simple muscle spasms, but a sympathetic nurse (Diane Varsi, identified in the credits simply as "Fourth Nurse") finally understands and shares her knowledge with the doctors. Joe communicates through his head-tapping that he wants the army to put him on display in carnivals to show everyone the terrible cost of war, a request the army of course denies. Following that, Joe pleads to be killed and, to his chagrin, that request is denied as well.

Trumbo's use of religion and Christ imagery in particular adds considerable resonance to the film. As played by Donald Sutherland, Jesus Christ is a hippie-like cynic who, in a reflection of Trumbo's shift away from Christian Science, is unable to help Joe in any way. When the young soldier refers to himself as "a piece of meat that keeps on living" during the rat-discussion scene noted above, Christ responds by saying, "Since your real life is a greater nightmare than your dreams, it would be cruel to pretend that anyone could help you. What you need is a miracle." None comes, however, and Joe instead becomes something of a Christ figure himself.

The film underscores this idea at several points. When Joe as a boy asks his father how he would feel if he (Joe) ever went off to war, the elder Bonham invokes one of the Bible's most famous passages, John 3:16, by intoning that, "for democracy, any man would give his only begotten son," for instance, while his mother declares him a "perfect reflection of God's reality"—a comment that takes on new meanings aplenty in the context of Joe's current state. The film clearly suggests that Joe has been sacrificed on behalf of his society, but unfortunately he is unable to redeem it. Interestingly, the movie does not borrow from the novel's powerful concluding screed that reads in part: "He had a vision of himself as a new kind of Christ as a man who carries within himself all the seeds of a new order of things. He was the new messiah of the battlefields saying to people as I am so shall you be" (240). Trumbo opted instead for a low-key approach; the camera simply and slowly backs away from Joe, his face and body obscured by a mask and bed-sheets, while his words "S.O.S., help me" repeat and then fade out on the soundtrack. With no hope for either a didactic role or a quick death, Joe ultimately becomes a stark reminder of his society's inability to comprehend what he represents and learn from him. A doctor's line uttered early in the film—"There is no justification for his continued existence, unless we learn from him how to help others"—thus takes on a exceptionally bitter quality: the physicians who insist on keeping Joe alive ironically fail to see how this horribly mutilated man could "help others" beyond the level of furthering medical knowledge. The audiences watching his film, Trumbo no doubt hoped, would not be nearly as foolish.

Aftermath

Johnny achieved phenomenal success at several early film festivals. At Cannes in May 1971, it won the International Critics Prize, the Special Jury Prize, and World Council of Churches Protestant Prize, with Trumbo, the film itself, and Luis Buñuel (who made a special appearance at Cannes on behalf of Trumbo and *Johnny*) each receiving a lengthy standing ovation. The following month, the film won the Atlanta International Film Festival's top award, the Golden Phoenix, as well as the Golden Dove for best film dealing with pacifist issues ("Trumbo's" 20, Kay 11). A favorable review by *Variety*'s "Mosk" at Cannes (17) set what Trumbo hoped would be the tone for the critical reactions to follow.

Heady with these early successes, Trumbo soon began developing follow-up projects. By July of that year, he and Campbell were already talking about their next film, a tale of a young midwesterner who searches for his identity during a momentous trip to New York City (Weiler 13), and by early August Trumbo announced plans for a trilogy of which *Johnny* was the initial installment. *Johnny*, he said, "could be subtitled 'On the Pleasures of War.' The next picture, which is called *Morning Glory*, is on the pleasures of being black in America. The third, which is extensively outlined, is called *Post Meridian* and is on the pleasures of being poor" (qtd. in Cooper 72).

Trumbo never made any of these films, however, for then the bottom to *Johnny* fell out. Though the movie continued to garner favorable comments (positive reviews appeared in such publications as the *New York Post, Rolling Stone, New York Daily News,* and *Newsday*), they were soon overshadowed by vitriolic condemnations. "On any terms that I might recognize and possibly credit, *Johnny Got His Gun* is a stultifyingly bad movie," wrote the *New York Times'* Roger Greenspun, who went on to suggest that Diane Varsi as the sympathetic nurse may have given "one of the worst performances in the history of movies" (25). *Commonweal*'s Colin Westerbeck called the film "an anthology of all the fallacies to which anti-war films are subject. . . . It's too bad that watching the film doesn't allow us to share any of the satisfaction [Trumbo] must have taken in making it" (62). Writing in *Saturday Review*, Hollis Alpert dismissed *Johnny* as "far less a profound sermon on the obscenities of war than a bathetic study of a man's ultimate loneliness" and concluded by opining that "as film art it is simply bad" (48).[9] The negative word quickly spread, and Trumbo soon found himself losing thousands of dollars of his own money on the film. *Johnny Got His Gun* was "his undoing," wrote Ring Lardner, Jr., a longtime friend of Trumbo and fellow Hollywood Ten blacklistee. "It was a downright failure at the box office. His investment of time and capital in it, added to the costs of the cancer and heart disease which killed him in 1976, brought him at the end to where he had so often lived, the brink of insolvency" (5).

Several projects associated with *Johnny* did little to improve the latter's image. In late 1971, several months after the film's debut, Jane Fonda and Donald Sutherland staged "Fuck the Army" (which also went by the laundered title, "Free the Army"), an antiwar revue that they produced near military bases in Hawaii, Okinawa, the Philippines, and Japan. They recorded their program of sketches and songs in a 1972 documentary film simply titled *F.T.A.*, one part of which featured Sutherland somberly reading the concluding passage from Trumbo's novel. In addition, an intrepid soul named Bradley Rand Smith adapted *Johnny* into a one-person play and staged it in New York in 1982 with Elinor Renfield as director and Jeff Daniels as star. In 1989, the rock group Metallica created the singularly titled "One," a music video with an antiwar theme that drew on *Johnny* for about half of its visuals. These spinoffs were hardly memorable, however; *F.T.A.* was rarely screened and is today something of a relic from the period, while the theatrical incarnation of *Johnny* disappeared quickly after mostly negative reviews. "Mr. Smith has not come up with an adequate stage equivalent of Bonham's interior monologue," wrote Mel Gussow in the *New York Times*. "As a work of theater, *Johnny Got His Gun* does not amply engage our emotions" (16). The music video "One," which achieved a ranking of 77 in MTV's top 100 video countdown of 1989, generated little enthusiasm even among the musicians who appeared in it. "When people first saw it, they were scratching their heads, going, 'Well, this is their video,'" said Kirk Hammett, a Metallica guitarist. "Obviously it's a very different video and it sticks out like a sore thumb, but, uh, y'know, I'm . . . I'm happy with it" (qtd. in MTV).

Critical reaction to the film itself seemed only to worsen with age. Richard Corliss published an anti-auteur, pro-screenwriter book called *Talking Pictures* in 1974, but far from offering a defense of the longtime screenwriter he proceeded to rake both Trumbo and the film over the coals (254-62). When *Johnny* finally had its network television debut in 1983 on PBS, *TV Guide*'s resident film critic, Judith Crist, flagged audiences off of it. "The intentions of the film and the intensity of its message are praiseworthy," she wrote, "but for this viewer it is so cloddish and naive in its execution, so simplistic and self-consciously righteous that it vitiates its virtues" (5). In his encyclopedic overview of 1970s cinema written from a mid-1980s point of view, Marc Sigoloff echoed the perceptions of many by calling it "a pretentious anti-war drama" laden with dreams and fantasies that "appear to be poor imitations of Fellini," and concluding that "Trumbo may have been a good writer, but the same cannot be said for his abilities as a director" (155).

Conclusion

From a perspective decades after the film's original release, it is clear that time has not been kind to *Johnny*. Several moments ring false, such as an early scene in which the father of Joe's girlfriend urges the young man to make love to her, while others are simply slipshod. Jules Brenner's cinematography during the opening and closing scenes is undeniably haunting, but the rest of his work, mainly representing Joe's dreams and nightmares, is at times shockingly amateurish. (Lighting instruments mounted on ceilings are plainly visible for long stretches of time in several scenes, for example.) In addition, the film features a terrible sound mix in which the dialogue, recorded after the film had been shot, was synchronized to the imagery with minimal ambient sound, resulting in an effect similar to that created by poorly dubbed foreign-language movies.

I would argue that the initially strong response to *Johnny* was intimately connected to the film's historical context. *Johnny* appeared during the latter stages of U.S. involvement in the Vietnam War, and a number of people were so eager to embrace this antiwar film by a famous longtime social activist that they tuned out its deficiencies. They were simply stunned by the film's intensity and uncompromising position, qualities that were hardly accidental. As Trumbo himself noted, "The intellectual attack on war has been going on for a couple of thousand years and has failed. I decided one should try an emotional attack, and that is what I attempted to do" (qtd. in Cooper 72).

It is worth noting that *Johnny* was among a number of Hollywood films appearing during the late 1960s and early 1970s that were not explicitly about the Vietnam War but nevertheless offered veiled commentary on it. As Linda Dittmar and Gene Michaud noted, "Policymakers' determination to escalate the fighting allowed for only covert, highly mediated, and murky expressions of concern" (2) and those expressions included such films as *Little Big Man, Soldier Blue, Catch-22,* and *M*A*S*H*, all of which appeared in 1970, and of course *Johnny Got His Gun. Johnny* was one of the last films in this short-lived tradition, however, and it is likely that, after the initial hoopla surrounding the film had died down, other audiences found little patience with a film that covered what was by then highly familiar territory and that offered its arguments in sledgehammer fashion. During the beginning stages of *Johnny's* American release, *Newsweek's* Arthur Cooper illustrated the film's difference from some of the other antiwar movies of the period by noting that *"Catch-22* and *M*A*S*H* deftly scored their points with satire and black humor. They evoked uneasy laughter at the grisly horror of war they portray. *Johnny Got His Gun* hits squarely in the guts with the impact of a recoiling howitzer" (70). According to Bernard F. Dick, this same distinction led to the film's disastrous box office: "Trumbo thought the film would be equally timely [as his novel had been in 1939], since the Vietnam protests were at their height, and the flower children were finding the road to peace tough going. He may not have realized that the flower children wanted the message leavened with satire and dark humor, and they already had it—in *M*A*S*H*" (218).

If viewers then and after found it easy to reject *Johnny Got His Gun* for its heavy-handedness and occasional crudeness of construction, few would deny the passions and rightness of purpose that motivated it. Though unquestionably a marred film, *Johnny Got His Gun*—like the book that inspired it—was and is a powerful and timeless reminder of the horrific effects of war.

Notes

The author presented a slightly different version of this essay at the 1995 University Film and Video Association conference in Keene, NH. He would like to thank Gary Burns of Northern Illinois University and Maurice Rapf of Dartmouth College for their help.

1. Norden, *Cinema* (57-68, 72-74) discusses movies within this trend.

2. Cohan in turn may have borrowed from Robert Burns's poem, "Hoch Time in the Auld Town," which contains the following lines: "Lives of great men all remind us/Rose is red and violet's blue; /Johnny's got his gun behind us/'cause the lamb loved Mary too."

3. Trumbo also used "Bonham" for a check-clearing account during the blacklisting years.

4. This quotation appears in Trumbo's unpaginated introduction, included in all editions of *Johnny* since 1959.

5. For further discussion of *Thirty Seconds Over Tokyo* as it relates to issues of physical disability, see Norden, "Resexualization."

6. The Laurel Award speech is reprinted in *Additional* (569-70). Fellow blacklistee Maurice Rapf wrote of Trumbo's contentious "only victims" remark: "I think it has merit, but, along with his wife, Cleo, I disagree with it and have said so on many occasions. Maybe there were few heroes, but there were plenty

of villains and, even if we feel compelled to resume relations with any of them, as I have, there is no reason to forget" (letter to the author).

7. In his 1989 film *Born on the Fourth of July*, Oliver Stone suggested a sense of *Johnny*'s importance to the nascent anti-Vietnam War movement in a "tip of the hat" gesture to Trumbo. During the scene in which a doctor tells Ron Kovic (Tom Cruise) he will never walk again, Stone's camera glides past Kovic to reveal a copy of *Johnny Got His Gun* on a tray near the veteran's bed.

8. The unpaginated "Addendum 1970" follows the introduction.

9. A compendium of additional reviews may be found in *Filmfacts*, 14.22 (1971): 582-85.

Works Cited

Alpert, Hollis. "Poor Johnny." Rev. of *Johnny Got His Gun. Saturday Review* 28 Aug. 1971: 38.

Bart, Peter. "The Highly Unlikely Dalton Trumbo." *New York Times* 11 Dec. 1966: B 13.

Buñuel, Luis. *My Last Sigh*. Trans. Abigail Israel. New York: Knopf, 1983.

Cook, Bruce. *Dalton Trumbo*. New York: Scribner, 1977.

Cooper, Arthur. "The Spoils of War." *Newsweek* 9 Aug. 1971: 70, 72.

Corliss, Richard. *Talking Pictures: Screenwriters in the American Cinema*. Woodstock: Overlook, 1974.

Crist, Judith. "This Week's Movies." Rev. of *Johnny Got His Gun. TV Guide* 25 June 1983: A 5.

Dick, Bernard F. *Radical Innocence: A Critical Study of the Hollywood Ten*. Lexington: UP of Kentucky, 1989.

Dittmar, Linda, and Gene Michaud. "America's Vietnam War Films: Marching Toward Denial." *From Hanoi to Hollywood: The Vietnam War in American Film*. Ed. Linda Dittmar and Gene Michaud. New Brunswick: Rutgers UP, 1990. 1-15.

Flatley, Guy. "Thirty Years Later, Johnny Gets His Gun Again." *New York Times* 28 June 1970: B 11, 27.

Greenspun, Roger. Rev. of *Johnny Got His Gun. New York Times* 5 Aug. 1971: 25.

Gussow, Mel. "Theater: World War I, 'Johnny Got His Gun.'" Rev. of *Johnny Got His Gun. New York Times* 11 Aug. 1982: C 16.

"The Happy Jack Fish Hatchery Papers." *Esquire* Jan. 1970: 73-77, 166, 168, 170-72, 174.

Kay, Terry. "Trumbo's Film Wins Top Prize." *Atlanta Journal and Constitution* 27 June 1971: B 11.

Lardner, Ring, Jr. "Will 'Johnny' Finally Have His Day?" *New York Times* 8 Aug. 1982: B 4-5.

MacDonald, J. Fred. *Don't Touch That Dial!: Radio Programming in American Life, 1920-1960*. Chicago: Nelson-Hall, 1979.

Morehouse, Ward. *George M. Cohan: Prince of the American Theater*. Philadelphia: Lippincott, 1943.

"Mosk." Rev. of *Johnny Got His Gun*. *Variety* 19 May 1971: 17.

Mount, Douglas N. "Authors & Editors." *Publishers' Weekly* 5 Oct. 1970: 21-23.

MTV Top 100 Music Video Countdown, 1989.

Norden, Martin F. *The Cinema of Isolation: A History of Physical Disability in the Movies*. New Brunswick: Rutgers UP, 1994.

——. "Resexualization of the Disabled War Hero in *Thirty Seconds Over Tokyo*." *Journal of Popular Film & Television* 23.2 (1995): 50-55.

Rapf, Maurice. Letter to the author. 26 Nov. 1995.

Sigoloff, Marc. *The Films of the Seventies: A Filmography of American, British and Canadian Films 1970-1979*. Jefferson: McFarland, 1984.

Trumbo, Cleo. Foreword. *The Night of the Aurochs*. By Dalton Trumbo. New York: Viking, 1979.

Trumbo, Dalton. *Additional Dialogue: Letters of Dalton Trumbo, 1942-1962*. Ed. Helen Manfull. New York: Evans, 1970.

——. *Johnny Got His Gun*. 1939. New York: Bantam Windstone, 1982.

"Trumbo's 'Johnny Got His Gun' Is Screened at Cannes Festival." *New York Times* 15 May 1971: 20.

Weiler, A. H. "Dalton's 'Darling Girl.'" *New York Times* 11 July 1971: B 13.

Westerbeck, Colin L. Rev. of *Johnny Got His Gun*. *Commonweal* 15 Oct. 1971: 62.

Zinnamon, Jerry. "Diary of a Dead Bavarian." *Esquire* Dec. 1970: 68, 70, 72, 74, 76, 78.

10

Parallels or Continuities
in *Goodbye Billy* and *The Frozen War*

Peter C. Rollins

I am saying that there seems to be one dominating form of modern
understanding: that it is essentially ironic; that it originates largely in
the application of mind and memory to the events of the Great War.
—Paul Fussell, *The Great War and Modern Memory*

World War I and Vietnam:
Beguiling Parallels or Telluric Continuities?

The most important contribution of Paul Fussell's *The Great War
and Modern Memory* (1975) was to identify World War I as a continuing
presence in contemporary consciousness. By examining both the *belles
lettres* and popular literature produced by the war—serious poetry and
prose by Siegfried Sassoon, Edmund Blunden, and Robert Graves, as
well as popular poems, wartime rumors, and trench folklore—Fussell
unearthed fundamental notions that originated in the Great War and continue in our time—what I call telluric continuities. Some of these ideas
include our loss of innocent faith in establishment culture and politics;
our sense that we are victims of history rather than its heroic shapers;
our perception that machines and technology do not guarantee progress
for the whole of humanity; our frustration that language has been disjoined from truth; and, finally, our reluctant acknowledgement that war
is the quintessential expression of twentieth-century civic culture.

Certainly Fussell is correct in arguing that the differences between
the work of an early war poet such as Rupert Brooke (d. 1915) and a surviving postwar poet such as Siegfried Sassoon (d. 1967) register a loss
of innocence as do the endless ruminations since World War I about "the
future of tragedy."[1] Complaints about the disjuncture of language from
thought and from reality were epitomized for the 1920s by Ogden and
Richards in *The Meaning of Meaning*.[2] Three generations of readers and
two generations of moviegoers know Ernest Hemingway's protagonist in

177

A Farewell to Arms (1926), Lieutenant Frederic Henry, learned that "abstract words such as glory, honor, courage or hallow were obscene" while retreating from Caporetto in 1917.[3] Any number of historians would endorse Fussell's conclusion that the Victorian faith in Progress was nullified when the First Battle of the Somme (June-November, 1916) resulted in 1,265,000 casualties.[4] Yet readers of *The Great War and Modern Memory* often miss Fussell's fundamental point: the mental shelling from Flanders Fields to the Italian Alps was not restricted to the immediate postwar era, wounding the spiritual life of a single lost generation. The battlefield traumas—and resulting modes of thought—still affect us.

Even casual digging for similarities between World War I and Vietnam unearths matching shell fragments. The loss of innocence by American boys in Vietnam is the central theme for most of the novels, personal narratives, and films from the war.[5] From the perspective of popular culture, the loss of innocence was driven home by a hit song, "19"—the title refers to the average age of the combat soldier in Vietnam. The perversity of language was a constant issue in the 1960s. Cynicism about official pronouncements was revealed in flipflop expressions such as "the Saigon Follies" (used sarcastically to describe daily press briefings in Saigon); "hearts and minds" (used by President Johnson in a serious way, but in 1974 reinterpreted by filmmaker Peter Davis to mean America's insensitivity to Vietnamese culture); "free fire zone" (used by the Army to describe an area clear of civilians, but perversely transformed by antiwar activists to [falsely] describe how American troops shot anybody anywhere). Nearly 40 percent of Noam Chomsky's *American Power and The New Mandarins* (1969) is devoted to debunking the language of social scientists who thrived on war-related projects—further evidence to support Fussell's concerns about the duplicities of language in our time. Junior officer Philip Caputo, in *A Rumor of War* (1977), repeatedly cites Wilfred Owen and Siegfried Sassoon in comradely homage to the Great War's trench poets. In Vietnam, devotees of President Kennedy's "New Frontier" found themselves bogged down in a noxious quagmire, sinking deep into what Pete Seeger satirized in song as "The Great Muddy." With all of these thematic parallels between World War I and Vietnam, how could Cadre Films conduct their historical reconnaissance without wandering along some well-trodden paths? In Fussell's own language, the cinematic exploration of World War I brought the makers of *Goodbye Billy: America Goes to War, 1917-18* (1971) and *The Frozen War: America Intervenes in Russia, 1918-20* (1973) into contact with at least five major themes of "our own buried lives" (335).[6] What they explored were more than beguiling parallels

lels with their own times, the 1960s; they dramatized themes with telluric continuities reaching back to the Battle of the Somme in 1916.

Goodbye Billy: America Goes to War, 1917-18

Goodbye Billy's title gives some idea of the duality of this historical compilation film's approach. The second half of the title refers to the way in which the film focuses on the moods of the American nation as it evolved through three discernible emotional stages during the Great War. In the opening ten minutes, *Goodbye Billy* evokes the innocent spirit of American enthusiasm as the country prepares to fight another "splendid little war." During the second third of the film, the experience becomes more complex: aural and visual elements are juxtaposed to reflect the confusion Americans felt once they confronted the realities of war. The final segment of *Goodbye Billy* further exploits the tool of cinematic irony to conjure up the post-war *angst* of a lost generation.[7]

To convey these three phases of the national mood, Cadre Films avoids using a didactic narrative and instead creates rapid juxtapositions of images and sounds, employing what Sergei Eisenstein called collision montage. Early in part one, sheep graze on the White House lawn; this shot from archival footage is followed by a shot of Woodrow Wilson looking out a window. Later, in part two of the film, the same shot of Wilson is juxtaposed with a shot of troops climbing out of trenches and trudging off into no man's land like "lambs to the slaughter." Halfway into part one, there is a particularly clever use of sight-sound irony. Charles W. Eliot, president emeritus of Harvard University, condemns German militarism aurally; the juxtaposed visuals contradict the statement by showing an American patriotic society (the Knights Templar) in elaborate military regalia as they parade along New York City's Central Park West. In the final segment of the film, the New York Philharmonic Orchestra plays Charles Ives's haunting "Unanswered Question" while two portions in the soundtrack vie for attention. In the aural foreground, a young voice reads from the last chapter of John Dos Passos's novel *1919*, a chapter entitled "The Body of an American." In the background is President Warren G. Harding speaking at the grave of the Unknown Soldier. The implication is that a generation gap has opened. Young people, divested of faith, must now make their way through a cynical, post-war world.

While the nation passes through moods of optimism, confusion, and despair, the representative soldier, Billy, has his own story. He has a caring mother, a proud father, and a fiancée who becomes increasingly anxious he will be gone "for a long, long time." At the opening of the war, Billy shares in the war fever, but the reality of battle alters his view.

While the protected civilians back home are still beating the drums of war with blind enthusiasm, he witnesses the horrendous impact of technology. Despite his efforts to maintain morale through horseplay and desperate, black humor, his spirits decline as the war "progresses"; finally, after he is slaughtered like an animal, he is brought back to become the nation's Unknown Soldier. While his family and fiancée mourn for Billy, politicians use him—even in death—as a symbol to justify their war. Like Billy Pilgrim of George Roy Hill's film, *Slaughterhouse Five* (1972), the protagonist of *Goodbye Billy* is the consummate victim of the war machine.[8]

The Frozen War: America Intervenes in Russia, 1918-20

As the last American combat troops were leaving the Republic of South Vietnam, Cadre Films came forward with a follow-up to *Goodbye Billy*. In 1918, an American Expeditionary Force (AEF) was ordered to land at Vladivostok, Russia. Concurrently, a second force was dispatched to the Russian city of Archangel, another major Russian port on the White Sea, some six thousand miles away from Vladivostok. Some said the ten thousand troops were there to protect American civilians and property; more zealous "frozen warriors" claimed the challenge to America posed by the Bolsheviks must be met early, lest the contagion spread. In the end, American presence in a foreign land fostered conditions which increased, rather than attenuated, human suffering.

Luckily, Cadre filmmakers found a veteran from the Expedition. With his wonderfully expressive voice, Lynn McQuiddy is a more effective historical witness than the implied hero of *Goodbye Billy*. The challenge for the new film became how to convey the shock for a young American entangled in such an imbroglio.

To convey this theme as a film experience, *The Frozen War* used anti-Bolshevik cartoons, newsreels of Attorney General A. Mitchell Palmer's famous "Red Scare" raids, and films of the Expeditionary Force from the Army Signal Corps collection at the U.S. Archives. By juxtaposing popular songs of the 1920s against Russian religious and concert music, the filmmakers evoked the clash between Western and Eastern cultures. But the real challenge of this picture involved using the archival footage to communicate the sense of alienation and repulsion of the protagonist, Lynn McQuiddy. Like Billy on the western front, McQuiddy is on the cutting edge of foreign policy where he can gauge the distance between official rhetoric and the painful consequences of misguided policy.

Themes Common to World War I and Vietnam
in *Goodbye Billy* and *The Frozen War*

Loss of innocent faith in establishment culture and politics.
Early in *The Great War and Modern Memory,* Paul Fussell describes the citizens of England during World War I as "those sweet, generous people who pressed forward and all but solicited their own destruction" (19). Fussell admires Philip Larkin's elegiac poem "MCMXIV," a work that concludes there never will be "such innocence again." This same "loss of innocence" theme pervades novels and films about Vietnam. Typically, the American GI leaves a placid, civilian environment to fight in a war that leaves him emotionally spent. Ron Kovic's *Born on the Fourth of July* (1976) is a representative text. The media shape young Kovic's attitudes toward war; after high school, the Marine Corps adds its corrupting influence. When the stress of combat further degrades his spirit, Kovic reaches a dead low: he kills a friend by accident and participates in the accidental shooting of Vietnamese children. His spinal wound comes as a blessing of sorts—through it, he learns to fight back against the official authorities. Caputo's *A Rumor of War* follows a similar spiritual devolution in its effort to exculpate a young lieutenant from the guilt of his war crimes. At the climax of *Vietnam-Perkasie,* another tale of disillusionment, W. D. Ehrhart participates in the battle for Hue with demented fury:

I fought back passionately, in blind rage and pain, without remorse, conscience or deliberation. I fought back . . . at the Pentagon Generals and the Congress of the United States, and the *New York Times;* at the draft-card burners, and the Daughters of the American Revolution . . . at the teachers who taught me that America always had God on our side and always wore white hats and always won; at the Memorial Day parades and the daily Pledge of Allegiance . . . at the movies of John Wayne and Audie Murphy, and the solemn statements of Dean Rusk and Robert MacNamara. (246-47)

From the opening scene of Oliver Stone's *Platoon* to the closing scene of Stanley Kubrick's *Full Metal Jacket,* the motif of corrupted innocence is shared by nearly all major books and films that deal with Vietnam.

In the first third of *Goodbye Billy*, the filmmakers use symbolism to establish America's naivete. U.S. Signal Corps footage of troops aboard ship is edited with a rousing pro-war ditty entitled "The Yanks Are At It Again." As the soundtrack tells of how "Kaiser Bill will surely get/His due before we're through," young soldiers aboard ship participate in a childish pillow fight. The event is clearly part of a "field day" exercise to keep the soldiers busy, but Cadre has transformed the images into a developed symbol for the lack of understanding on the part of the young Americans. In a montage described earlier, sheep—traditional symbols of Arcadian innocence—are shown on the White House lawn with footage taken by the Signal Corps to show that even the White House was conserving vital resources. When edited with a picture of Wilson looking out over them, the collision montage becomes more negative: America's soldiers are indeed mindless sheep being sent to the slaughter by a well-intentioned, but naively idealistic leader. These fascinating moments in *Goodbye Billy* resonate with meaning for both World War I and Vietnam.

In *The Frozen War*, McQuiddy admits he participated in the Vladivostok expedition with youthful enthusiasm. He speaks of being in "an adventurous mood." However, second thoughts quickly develop. McQuiddy discovers America's involvement in the Russian revolution is exacerbating the agony of a society that will inevitably go through many painful transformations. As an eyewitness, he is able to attest to the failure and irrelevance of the incursion. We may laugh with McQuiddy when he remembers the inadequacy of supplies or complains about not taking a proper shower for three months, but we are deeply moved as he amasses details about human suffering. His reports about disease, hunger, dislocation, and simple cruelty—intensified and amplified by archival footage—inculcate a profound loathing of the rhetoric used to justify U.S. intervention.

Woodrow Wilson, "the Peacemaker," may have sent us in to protect American property, but in the process of saving a few flivvers, thousands of Russian civilians died of disease or met more violent ends. The American ambassador to Moscow may intone that "we are not at war with the Bolsheviks," but McQuiddy has fought them and even taken some as prisoners. This might not be war on the ambassadorial level, but it is war enough for any participant with a life to lose. The word "innocence" in this context has a very negative connotation; it applies to the blundering efforts of a State Department whose misdirected policies will result in murder, rape, and starvation. Viewed from the Vietnam era, contemporary parallels must have been hard to avoid for Cadre in 1972; there certainly are reverberations for Bosnia in the 1990s.

We are the victims of history.

The Great War and Modern Memory focuses upon this theme as perhaps the most important factor in modern consciousness. Fussell argues the Western world moved from an heroic self-image to one involving what literary scholars call "dramatic irony." (In a situation characterized by dramatic irony, the protagonist is unaware of his fate while the audience is painfully aware of the incongruity between the individual's hopes and his certain defeat.) Such a world allows no heroes, only victims.[9]

Fussell compiles convincing evidence about how such a world view took shape during the slaughter. German troops did so "well" in their aggressive—but costly—assaults that their casualties quickly depleted the army of its finest junior officers and senior noncommissioned officers. Along the 400 miles of trenches on the western front, "the main business of the soldier was to exercise self-control while being shelled" (46). Through black humor, the troops tried to endure the war of attrition, but their sense of "bondage, frustration [and] absurdity" produced a new image of man in modern literature: "A standard character is the man whom things are done to. He is Prufrock, Jake Barnes, Charlie Chaplin" (313).

Fussell makes a great number of comparisons between the sensibility produced on the western front (1914-18) and the world of Yossarian (1943-45), protagonist of Joseph Heller's *Catch-22* (1961). It is a world in which nature and society seem bent on destroying an individual who is spiritually—and sometimes even physically—naked. Interestingly, *Catch-22* is referred to more frequently by Fussell than is the poetry of Rupert Brooke—a revealing imbalance. Fussell's point is that the connections go deeper than parallelism. In fact, even Yossarian's "primal scene" with the wounded gunner, Snowden, was culled from the writings of R. C. Sherriff retaining "all its Great War [dramatic] irony" (34). The primal scene "embodies the contemporary equivalent of the experience offered by the first day on the Somme, and, like that archetypal original, it can stand as a virtual allegory of political and social cognition in our own time" (35). This is not a matter of mere likeness; it is continuity. Finally, *Catch-22* is considered by many to be the quintessential Vietnam war novel—despite the fact that it was written four years before American troops landed in Southeast Asia and despite its World War II setting. Fussell's argument that the ironic vision stems from the Great War helps to explain the confusing discrepancies.[10]

Dramatic irony suffuses the last two-thirds of *Goodbye Billy*, frequently in the form of music hall patter. During the opening third, the humor is light and irreverent. Pat asks Mike about the "story about the wooden man who swallowed the whistle." Mike doesn't understand at first; Pat explains the result: "He wouldn't (wooden) whistle." In part two, the humor darkens. Pat has been hit. Mike tells us the "humorous" result: first, he "wooden whistle," and now "he can't stir!" Vietnam veterans will savor the special irony in an exchange about tours of duty: Pat asks Mike how long he will be fighting the war. Mike answers that he enlisted for seven years. Pat responds, "Aw gee, you're lucky. I'm for the duration." Men as inanimate objects and victims, men in uniform forever—these notions are part of the legacy of World War I and the subsequent regimentation of society.[11]

The futility of America's intervention is questioned many times during *The Frozen War*. The film makes much out of the postwar industrial boom stimulated by the automobile. In two or three places, Ford Motor Company footage and cartoons are edited to imply Americans see political problems as flat tires requiring patching. *The Frozen War* argues that nations are not so easily repaired and steered along the turnpike of history. When it comes to a Model T, we can "patch it up with anything, chewing gum or a ball of string and the little Ford will travel right along." Much to their chagrin, Americans should have learned after World War I that the world was not as susceptible to amateur tinkering.

The Frozen War concludes with a winter scene of Vladivostok harbor held in freeze frame. Large chunks of ice have halted boat traffic while fog drifts over the frigid waters. Through these images, the filmmakers attempt to relay a message about intervention. McQuiddy states with some exasperation, "I have had to wait for fifty years to tell this story. Anything that doesn't have a future to it . . . What the hell good is it?" Not only was the water at Vladivostok "frozen" in the sense of taking place in Eastern Siberia some hundred miles north of Korea; in addition, the policy of intervention was "frozen" in the sense of being inflexible to the complex realities of civil war.

Even the issue of the neglected Vietnam veteran is discernable in *The Frozen War*. One of the final shots looks down a railroad track at a minuscule figure. The music and his gait suggest a contemporary comic whose reputation grew in stature as film comedy evolved beyond slapstick. The link to Fussell's notion of victimization seems clear: this is a cinematic allusion to Charlie Chaplin. The men of the American Expeditionary Force were doing their job, but like "the little tramp," they were forgotten by the folks back home. (Consumer fixations of civilians are satirized in a song entitled "The Harem.") Like the Vietnam vets, the AEF troops have been left out in a "frozen war." The accumulating ice and snow symbolize the fruitlessness of the entire effort.

Machines and technology do not guarantee progress.
The introduction of technological innovations to the battlefield in World War I could hardly have been seen as "progress." The machine gun, the tank, poison gas, the airplane, barbed wire, and the submarine thrust mechanization into an horse-and-buggy context. With the intro-

duction of "indirect fire" techniques, artillery made great "advances" so that weapons could be hidden deep behind friendly lines; from these protected gun positions, they could lob shells upon the enemy. Using aiming stakes, maps, and forward observers connected to the batteries by radio or wire, shells weighing up to a ton could be dropped on targets as far away as fifty miles. (Germany's so-called Paris gun was mounted on railroad cars and lobbed shells into the French capital from a range of seventy-five miles.) This unequal clash between machines and flesh amplified existing questions about the benefits of industrialism. Observers began to speak of a "war of attrition" (Fussell 9); whatever their speculations, Fussell says the war became "a hideous embarrassment to the prevailing Meliorist myth which had dominated the public consciousness for a century. It reversed the Idea of Progress" (8).

In an effort to show progress in Vietnam, the government (and echoing them, the press) made much of "body counts." Without definite front lines to measure progress, this cruel offspring of attrition tactics seemed to help provide "light at the end of the tunnel." An HBO Special entitled *Dear America: Letters Home from Vietnam* (1988) introduces body counts as a motif to convey the sense of mounting human tragedy in Vietnam—as opposed to hailing progress through such figures. Vietnam veteran and Desert Storm commander General Norman Schwartzkopf carefully avoided the progress-through-numbers approach during the Gulf War despite continual requests by the press that he somehow quantify the American victory.

Fussell observes that World War I writers often develop dramatic contrasts between a pastoral prewar life style and the meatgrinding efficiency of the war machine; these same kinds of contrasts enhance the power of Vietnam films and books. Many reviewers were frustrated by the long homefront segment of *The Deer Hunter* where filmmaker Michael Cimino lavished detailed attention upon the intricate patterns of life and love among second-generation immigrant steel workers. What reviewers neglected to appreciate was that Cimino was imitating the rhetorical success of D. W. Griffith in his epic feature, *The Birth of a Nation* (1914). Both Griffith and Cimino understood that audiences could not properly respond to the disruption caused by war if they were not fully apprised of the harmonies of antebellum life. On the literary front, the very title of Ehrhart's *Vietnam-Perkasie* highlights the clash of the warfront/homefront values. The infamous Russian roulette scenes from *The Deer Hunter* have been interpreted in many ways, but one valid interpretation is that they are microcosms of victimization. Francis Ford Coppola's *Apocalypse Now* (1976) hypes more obvious symbols of American machines in the Vietnam garden. Helicopter assaults to the strains of Wagner's "Ride of the Valkyrie" suggest all kinds of ironies about technological "progress."

Goodbye Billy addresses the issue of technology. During the optimistic opening section of the film, Samuel Gompers, president of the American Federation of Labor, proclaims, "The final outcome will be determined in the factories, the mills, the shops, the mines, the farms." In other words, industrial and technological potency will prevail. During this preparedness speech, images of ships, tanks, and troops fill the screen. Musically, a somewhat sinister industrial leitmotiv is introduced, although, at this point, it appears to be assertive rather than threatening. Sections two and three define the limits of technology. Pictorially, the film shows a team of horses attempting to extricate an Army truck from a sodden field; reintroduction of the industrial leitmotiv over these pictures defines an America bogged down in its first "Big Muddy." At the close of part two, the industrial leitmotiv is again introduced over pictures of massive urban destruction, conveying the notion that potentially constructive industrial might can quickly be retooled for war.

In *The Frozen War,* footage of Americans awkwardly training for ski-borne operations in Russia is used to portray American interventionists as inept Keystone Cops. The clear message is that America cannot play the European game of power politics without suffering a number of diplomatic pratfalls. In a dejected moment, the narrator of *The Frozen War* describes our efforts as "burlesque antics in fantastic side shows."

Language has been disjoined from truth.

There were many recriminations after World War I, but certainly one of the major concerns of the 1920s was that propaganda misled decent people on both sides. Fussell speaks of a new distrust for language stemming from the "collision . . . between events and the public language used for a century to celebrate the idea of progress" (169). Early in *The Great War and Modern Memory,* he provides a list of terms that became "casualties of the war" (22). Prior to the trauma of 1916, soldiers did not enlist, they "joined the colors"; rather than dying, they "perished"; soldier's were "warriors"; and, rather than bleed, they lost "the red/Sweet wine of youth" (21-22). Post-war cynicism had not set in:

Indeed, the literary scene is hard to imagine. There was no *Waste Land*, with its rats' alleys, dull canals, and dead men who have lost their bones: it would take four years of trench warfare to bring these to consciousness. . . . There was no "Valley of Ashes" in *The Great Gatsby.* One read Hardy and Kipling and Conrad and frequented worlds of traditional moral action in traditional moral language. (23)

Postwar consciousness would focus on the need for a new language to describe a new world. As I. A. Richards and C. K. Ogden would explain in their *Meaning of Meaning* (1923), "Words were never a more common means than they are today of concealing ignorance and persuading even ourselves we possess opinions when we are merely vibrating with verbal reverberations" (262).

The Vietnam record shows concerns about the dangers of euphemism and doublespeak. On the positive side, servicemen devised an entire vocabulary of black humor to distance themselves from the deadly facts of life. The Pentagon in Washington, where plans and programs were concocted, was "Disneyland East." Saigon-based tacticians were called "chairborne commandoes" or "REMFs" (Rear Echelon, etc.). Up North, in the I Corps Area, the Demilitarized Zone (DMZ) became known to local infantryman as the "Dead Marine Zone." After My Lai, the inept Americal Division gained a reputation for being "the butcher brigade." (The Americal Division was quietly disbanded after the war.) Lonelier than astronauts in outer space, young Americans counted every day in the 365 days of their tour until they "derosed" (Date of Expected Return from OverSeas or DEROS) back to "the world" (home).

Noam Chomsky attempted to demystify pseudoscientific jargon in his critique of Pentagon-supported social scientists. According to the feisty MIT linguistics professor, much of the work by people like Samuel Huntington, Daniel Bell, and Ithiel Pool was not true social science. Thus Chomsky argued that so-called pacification was really a matter of starving uncooperative villagers and forcibly removing troublesome leaders (37). "Modernization" in this context meant tearing apart the fabric of a traditional society which had expressed no desire for change (57). "Nation building" meant imposing America's political institutions on others (59). Chomsky explained the purpose of such language was not to deal with human problems, but to legitimize the work of "experts" who could wield social science "as a new coercive ideology with a faintly scientific tone" (58). In the title sequence of his novel, Joseph Heller explored the gap between language and reality with devastating wit, capturing the notion of Everyman as a prisoner of language. Having succeeded in the West, Chomsky saw America's "liberal technocrats" attempting to impose their linguistic bureaucratese on the Third World.[12]

Like those who speculated about the deviousness of language in the 1920s, *Goodbye Billy* takes a harsh look at the gap between the rhetoric of propaganda and battlefront realities. Part two of the film culminates with a scene in which visuals and sound embellish this theme. As the orchestra plays "The Washington Post March" out of tune, we see visuals of a destroyed Zeppelin. Under the defining influence of music, the image becomes a developed symbol: the gas of propaganda has been released and the vaporousness of its promises revealed. A pan of a cemetery tallies the deaths caused by the manipulation of patriotic symbols, a tragic result further dramatized by solarized shots of afteraction rubble at Ypers (a Belgium transportation hub of some 20,000 citizens totally destroyed in late 1914). Although the war was sold as a crusade "to make the world safe for democracy," in the end, *Goodbye Billy* concludes that it was just another war smelling of "pukey dirt-stench." In its most powerful segment, the closing minutes of *Goodbye Billy* juxtaposes President Warren Harding's official dedication at the Tomb of the Unknown Soldier with the "real" version from John Dos Passos.[13]

McQuiddy constantly questions Washington-based policies in *The Frozen War*. In the opening montage, Ambassador Francis expresses his own exasperation: "Cable indicates State Department has heard that Soviet leaders acting under direction of German general staff. Regard suggestion of German control of Soviet government as absurd and impossible. If Washington credits this contention, why are we wasting time representing U.S. here in Moscow?" Shortly thereafter, the film shows American troops disembarking at Vladivostok, a screen action edited to coincide with President Wilson's saying that the "United States could not enter." In these opening minutes, we begin to sense that, just as Wilson falsely proclaimed he was "too proud to fight" prior to 1917, so with the Russian incursion, he will be dragged into some form of military involvement. (Viewers have noted parallels here to the 1965 Gulf of Tonkin incident and the escalation that followed.)

If Noam Chomsky had possessed a better grasp of American cultural history, he might have observed that his quarrel with social science and with the misuses of language had roots in the years immediately following World War I. Walter Lippmann's *Public Opinion* (1922) and George Creel's *How We Advertised America* (1920) share Chomsky's insights into the ways in which governments manipulate their citizens. The telluric continuities from Lippmann to Chomsky are implicit in an expression that came to symbolize our failed crusade in Vietnam, the famous statement "We had to destroy the village in order to save it." Probably invented by Associated Press correspondent Peter Arnett, the paradoxical explanation took hold and decades later is reiterated on TV talk shows as the quintessential soundbite for Vietnam. At first, the statement looks original in its mordancy, but the black humor involved clearly stems from the ironic mode which entered our culture after 1916. It is obvious that Australian Peter Arnett formulated the statement to reflect his repugnance at the nation-wide damage of the 1968 Tet offensive; yet, in shaping this cynical aphorism, could his "modern memory" have been reaching back to the military reversal suffered by Australian troops fifty-three years earlier at Gallipoli?

War is health for the twentieth-century state.
Fussell believes the current regimentation of society began with the World War I draft. He describes the Military Service Act in Britain as "an event which could be said to mark the beginning of the modern world" (11). Such a perception would make sense in the 1960s when the director of the Selective Service, General Louis Hershey, was threatening to draft anyone reported burning his draft card. In *Hair* (play 1968, film 1979), an innocent Oklahoman named Claude (John Savage of *The Deer Hunter*) dies in Vietnam not long after being drafted. Brutally torn from the "Age of Aquarius," he is the ultimate soldier/victim.

Goodbye Billy devotes a number of scenes to the draft. In part one of the film, the selection of names and the processing of recruits goes smoothly, but part two stresses the cruelty of chance and resentment against "the system." Samuel Gompers' comments on industrial might are visually supported by images of young men performing calisthenics. The implication is that youths are just more fuel for the War Machine. In *The Frozen War,* McQuiddy is cannon fodder but, fortunately for him and for us, he has survived to share his version of the fiasco with us.

Fussell believes militarism has dulled our moral sensibility. Citizens now passively accept repression needed to keep the war-machine operating: "[T]he war would literally never end and would become the permanent condition of mankind. The stalemate and attrition would go on indefinitely, becoming, like the telephone and the internal combustion engine, a part of accepted atmosphere of the modern experience" (71). In the Vietnam setting, the movie *M*A*S*H* (1970) (as well as the TV series to follow) screened a powerful metaphor of modern humanity caught in such a Catch-22. Indeed, the enduring appeal of the series can be accounted for by its success in shaping such a lively metaphor for our world. In *Going after Cacciato,* Tim O'Brien carried the Vietnam patrol metaphor all the way to the streets of Paris, thereby acknowledging the accuracy of Fussell's insight. While Oliver Stone's *Platoon* revealed a counterculture making headway (viz. Sergeant Elias and his squad), his *JFK* illuminated the deadly commercial imperative of a military-industrial complex.

Goodbye Billy contains a number of montage sequences that focus on advertising. Cigarette and automobile manufacturers—even the makers of Pepto Bismol—try to tap patriotic emotions. The film's message seems to be that war helps those who help themselves. In the most ironic commercial appeal, a newspaper ad pitches dynamite as "the builder of Civilization." Within the montage of *Goodbye Billy,* the slogan is a powerful exposé quotation. *The Frozen War* explores how exaggerated Red Scare propaganda short-circuits America's ability to understand the aspirations of revolutionary societies.

From Fussell's point of view, the result has been a general moral disenfranchisement: "Thus the drift of modern history domesticates the fantastic and normalizes the unspeakable . . . the catastrophe that begins it is the Great War" (74). The immediate occasion for this observation was a 1972 headline from the *New York Times* reading, "U.S. Aides in Vietnam See an Unending War." Fussell believes such reflections link Saigon to the Somme. These are not beguiling parallels or superficial similarities, but telluric continuities connecting the static defense at Khe Sanh to the trenches in Flanders' Fields. They explain how *Goodbye Billy* and *The Frozen War* explore both their ostensible subjects—World War I and America's thwarted attempts to bring a liberal consensus to Europe and Asia—and the concerns of America during the Vietnam era. Indeed, to explore these two films in the light of Fussell's categories may be the first step toward reinterpreting the last seventy-five years of our cultural life.

Notes

1. The loss of innocence, from the point of view of someone who lived through the period, is explored by Joseph Wood Krutch in *The Modern Temper: A Study and a Confession* (1929). Krutch observes that moderns can no longer see themselves in a tragic mode because "Tragedy arises when . . . a people fully aware of the calamities of life is nevertheless serenely confident of the greatness of man, whose mighty passions and supreme fortitude are revealed when one of these calamities overtakes him" (84). Faith in the greatness of man had been blown up on the Western Front. Fussell's ideas about the damage will be explored in this essay. In *The Modern Temper,* Krutch could only predict "progressive [spiritual] enfeeblement" (159).

2. I. A. Richards spent an entire career exploring the postwar problems of communication, with special interest in the function of artistic language in a scientific age. In a chapter entitled "Linguistic Abuse and Linguistic Reform," Max Black's *The Labyrinth of Language* (1968) gives a brief overview of some of the panaceas offered after World War I: the General Semantics Movement, the nostrums of Ogden and Richards, as well as other reforms/reformers of the period.

3. For Hemingway's views on language and style, especially in regard to his skepticism about Victorian ideals, see Harry Levin's article. In *A Farewell to Arms*, Frederic Henry discovers that life is really controlled by chaos, a force which he cannot even describe in English; he resorts instead to the Spanish word for nothingness, "Nada" (249, 327-28). He goes on in the famous quoted passage to observe, "I was always embarrassed by the words sacred, glorious, and sacrifice and the expression in vain . . . I had seen nothing sacred and the things that were glorious had no glory and the sacrifices were like the stockyards at Chicago if nothing was done with the meat except to bury it. There were many words that you could not stand to hear and finally only the names of places had dignity. Certain numbers were the same way and certain dates and these with the names of the places were all you could say and have them mean anything" (184-85).

4. S. L. A. Marshall's *World War I* describes the first battle of the Somme as "the most soulless battle in British annals. . . . It was a battle not so much of attrition as of mutual destruction" (180). Siegfried Sassoon observed the battle from a distance, finding it "a sunlit picture of Hell" (Marshall 196).

British losses for the entire campaign were 420,000. The French sector lost 195,000. In the meantime, the Germans lost some 650,000 soldiers, to include most of their best frontline leaders. Ironically, the Germans lost most of their troops during heroic—and "successful"—counterattacks. As a result, according to R. Ernest Dupuy, the German army "would never be the same again" (1053). Such experiences cut deep into the patina of Victorian optimism.

On August 21, 1916, a British documentary entitled *Battle of the Somme* opened at thirty-four London theaters. Public interest in the film was keen, perhaps because the authenticity of the production had been attested to by the king. In any case, Samuel Hynes believes that the widely seen film imparted a new image of war: "In this film, war is not a matter of voluntary acts, but of masses of men and materials, moving randomly through a dead, ruined world towards no identifiable objective; it is aimless violence and passive suffering, without either a beginning or an end—not a crusade, but a terrible destiny" (125). All of these details support Fussell's contention that the Battle of the Somme—as fact and as film—made an indelible impression on Western culture.

5. See my *American Quarterly* article for details about this motif in Vietnam books and films. At critical points in American cultural history, the notion has been celebrated and attacked—and, sometimes, such as in the 1840s and 1850s, both celebrated (Emerson) and attacked (Hawthorne). *The American Adam* by R. W. B. Lewis is a *locus classicus* for discussion of this offspring of American Romanticism. Looking at the 1960s in *Gates of Eden,* Morris Dickstein believes that by translating "the Edenic impulse . . . into political terms . . . [the youth movement stressed] man's right to happiness in the here-and-now" (viii-ix). Vietnam would become the nemesis for this revival of the Adamic spirit.

6. Prior to moving into description and detail of the two films, I wish to stress that I am *not* arguing that the filmmakers were shaped by 1960s issues to interpret the war as they did. I *do* wish to push Fussell's argument to its limits, asserting with him that the Great War shaped the structure of modern memory. The Cadre Filmmakers—and their contemporaries—interpreted *both* World War I *and* Vietnam the way they did because of the categories built into modern sensibility *by* World War I. This notion is a radical one with implications only partially explored by Fussell in *The Great War and Modern Memory.*

7. Scholars wishing assistance in dissecting this fine short film should consult the text by Harris J. Elder. It contains a detailed outline of the film and useful descriptive detail. In addition, Raack and Malloch made an extended radio documentary which was recorded on a two-sided long-playing record. *The Stars and Stripes and You* is sold with the complete lyrics and narration for the documentary, 80% of which were used in *Goodbye Billy.* In writing this paper, I was particularly aided by the record's printed transcript. (The record itself is a fascinating item and deserves its own critique.)

8. The film version of *Slaughterhouse Five* is an adaptation of Kurt Vonnegut's novel of the same title. Within the context of this discussion, it is important to note that the film leaves out the Vonnegut-as-historian character who constantly reflects on the story as it develops. This *persona* allowed the author to explore the actual processes of "modern memory." The five themes explored in this paper could be fruitfully applied to the novel and film versions of *Slaughterhouse Five,* perhaps revealing that Vonnegut is a victim of time-tripping, but not the futuristic type he celebrates in his novel. Actually, Billy's experience and the author's acts of memory are emotional regressions shaped by the legacy of the Great War.

9. The word "irony" is used many times in this article. Most historians probably consider irony to be identical with *sarcasm*—which is often the case. On the other hand, film scholars know that *film irony* or *cinematic irony* refers to situations in film in which the visual track and the sound track conflict with each other. Sergei Eisenstein was an early proponent of this device to disorient viewers and to make them think. (Both *Goodbye Billy* and *The Frozen War* frequently use this cinematic technique.)

Fussell and literary scholars explore other possibilities for the term "irony." When we use *rhetorical irony,* we mean the opposite of what we say. Fussell most often uses the word to mean *dramatic irony:* individuals may think that they are important and that the universe heeds their aspirations; unfortunately, World War I bombed that idea. In the new world of the lost generation, human beings are pathetic victims who are no longer in charge of their own destiny.

Again, *The Modern Temper* by J. W. Krutch is a *locus classicus* for this postwar confession of powerlessness.

10. Black humor pervades literature and entertainment during the 1960s from the Jewish-American commentary of Mort Sahl and Lenny Bruce to the literary perspectives of Philip Roth, Woody Allen, and, of course, Joseph Heller and Kurt Vonnegut. In his important study of the 1960s, Morris Dickstein comes to the conclusion that "[o]ne effect of Vietnam and Watergate was that the official organs of our society lost much of the respect and credence they had commanded. Even middle-Americans began to live with less of a mystified and paternalistic sense of Authority. The disillusionment, and ruthless skepticism— really spoiled idealism—of *Catch-22*, outlived the sixties to become a pervasive national mood" (118). It is Fussell's purpose in *The Great War and Modern Memory* to show that the roots of this skepticism go back farther in time.

11. As a volunteer in the Italian ambulance service, Ernest Hemingway— like the protagonist of *A Farewell to Arms*—was wounded by incoming fire. The trauma became a symbol to Hemingway of the wound borne by all postwar humanity and recurs as a motif in his short fictions and novels. Readers will recall that, in the words of *Goodbye Billy,* Jake Barnes of *The Sun Also Rises* (1924) suffers from "the worst wound of all." For more on the "symbolic wound" in Hemingway, see Hoffman's *The Twenties.*

12. During the 1960s, academics drew parallels between Chomsky's combined moral and philosophical critique with a very similar debate during World War I between Randolph Bourne and John Dewey. (Christopher Lasch has written an excellent description and analysis of the latter collision.) Dewey, as the leading spokesman for pragmatism, argued that his followers in the managerial class should support the war effort in order to reform American society from within. War powers in their hands could yield long-term improvements for the nation. Bourne, previously a disciple of Dewey, opposed his mentor on very pre-pragmatic moral grounds. In a manner anticipating Chomsky's reproof of his peers, Bourne also warned American intellectuals about the pitfalls of courting governmental influence. Jane Addams would also take Dewey to task with similar arguments, predicting that politicians would use experts as smokescreens for policies conceived without their help.

13. While the use of music, voices, and images in this section is extremely effective, literary scholars will notice that the "script" is implicit in the chapter from Dos Passos' novel *1919* (462-27). The theme of doughboy-as-victim is clearly the message of the chapter and the film. In some respects, *Goodbye Billy* makes the point with less anger and more subtlety than its literary original.

Works Cited

Black, Max. *The Labyrinth of Language.* New York: New American Library, 1968.

Caputo, Philip. *A Rumor of War.* New York: Holt, 1977.

Chomsky, Noam. *American Power and the New Mandarins.* New York: Random House, 1967.

Cimino, Michael. *The Deer Hunter.* Columbia, 1978.

Coppola, Francis Ford. *Apocalypse Now.* United Artists, 1979.

Creel, George. *How We Advertised America; The First Telling of the Amazing Story of the Committee on Public Information that Carried the Gospel of Americanism to Every Corner of the Globe.* New York: Harper, 1920.

Dickstein, Morris. *The Gates of Eden: American Culture in the Sixties.* New York: Basic, 1977.

Dos Passos, John. *1919, Second in the Trilogy U.S.A.* 1932. New York: Signet, 1969.

Dupuy, R. Ernest, and Trevor N. Dupoy. *The Harper Encyclopedia of Military History.* 4th ed. New York: HarperCollins, 1993.

Ehrhart, W. D. *Vietnam-Perkasie: A Combat Marine Memoir.* Jefferson, NC: McFarland, 1985.

Elder, Harris J. *Writing About Film.* Dubuque: Kendall/Hunt, 1977.

Fussell, Paul. *The Great War and Modern Memory.* New York: Oxford UP, 1975.

Griffin, Patrick. "Film, Document, and the Historian." *Film & History* 2.2 (1972): 1-5.

——. "The Making of *Goodbye Billy.*" *Film & History* 2.2 (1972): 6-10.

——. "Perspectives: Media in *The History Teacher.*" *The History Teacher* 6 (1972):107-8.

H(ome) B(ox) O(ffice). *Dear America: Letters Home from Vietnam.* Dir. Bill Couturie, 1988.

Heller, Joseph. *Catch-22.* New York: Simon and Schuster, 1961.

Hemingway, Ernest. *A Farewell to Arms.* New York: Scribner, 1929.

——. *The Sun Also Rises.* New York: Scribner, 1926.

Hill, George Roy. *Slaughterhouse Five.* Universal Pictures, 1972.

Hoffman, Frederick J. *The Twenties: American Writing in the Postwar Decade.* Rev. ed. New York: Free Press, 1962.

Hynes, Samuel. *A War Imagined: The First World War and English Culture.* New York: Atheneum, 1991.

Kovic, Ron. *Born on the Fourth of July.* New York: McGraw-Hill, 1976.

Krutch, Joseph Wood. *The Modern Temper: A Study and a Confession.* New York: Harcourt, 1929.

Kubrick, Stanley. *Full Metal Jacket.* Warner Bros., 1987.

Lasch, Christopher. *The New Radicalism in America, 1889-1916: The Intellectual as a Social Type.* New York: Knopf, 1965.

Levin, Harry. "Observations on the Style of Ernest Hemingway." *Kenyon Review* 13.4 (1951): 589-603.

Lippmann, Walter. *Public Opinion.* New York: Macmillan, 1922.

O'Brien, Tim. *Going after Cacciato.* New York: Dell, 1979.

Marshall, S. L. A. *World War I.* Boston: Houghton Mifflin, 1964.

Marx, Leo. *The Machine in the Garden; Technology and the Pastoral Ideal in America.* New York: Oxford UP, 1964.

Raack, R. C. "Clio's Dark Mirror: The Documentary Film in History." *The History Teacher* 6 (1973): 109-17.

Raack, R. C., Patrick Griffin, and William Malloch. *The Frozen War: America Intervenes in Russia, 1918-20.* San Francisco: Cadre Films, 1973.

———. *Goodbye Billy: America Goes to War, 1917-18.* Los Angeles: Churchill Media, 1971.

———. *The Stars and Stripes and You, 1917-1918.* San Francisco: Pox Productions, 1971.

Richards, I. A., and C. K. Ogden. *The Meaning of Meaning: A Study of the Influence of Language Upon Thought and of the Science of Symbolism.* 1923. New York: Harcourt, 1968.

Rollins, Peter C. "The Historian-Filmmaker's Contribution to the Study of Foreign Affairs." *Teaching International Politics in High School.* Ed. Raymond English. Lanham, MD: UP of America, 1989. 73-90. Also published as "Teaching International Politics: What the Historian-Filmmaker Has to Offer." *Film and History* 19.1 (1989): 2-14.

———. "The Historian as Filmmaker: The Use of Visual Language." *The Frozen War* (1973). Booklet distributed with *The Frozen War.*

———. "*Storm of Fire* (1978): Reflections of Cadre Films and the Historian as Filmmaker." *The History Teacher* 12.4 (1979): 539-48.
(Both films are available from the Audiovisual Center, Oklahoma State University, Stillwater, OK 74078; 405-744-9212.)

Stone, Oliver. *JFK.* Warner Bros., 1991.

———· *Platoon.* Orion, 1986.

Vonnegut, Kurt. *Slaughterhouse Five; or, The Children's Crusade, a Duty-Dance with Death.* New York: Delacorte, 1969.

11

CBS Reports:
Interpreting World War I
from the Mid-1960s

Richard C. Bartone

Late in 1963 John Sharnick, a producer of *Eyewitness to History*[1] at CBS News, proposed to the News Division a documentary series on World War I. Richard Salant, president of CBS News, and Blair Clark, general manager, refused to allocate twelve hours—twenty-six half-hour time periods—to history, preferring a contemporary subject. They doubted World War I was saleable. Sharnick approached Bud (Burton) Benjamin, executive producer of *The Twentieth Century* since 1957, and Isaac Kleinerman, producer, for support. At that time Salant and Clark were pleased with *The Twentieth Century*'s shift to judicious portions of history and emphasis on recent topics.[2] Benjamin and Kleinerman had strict parameters for developing historical compilation documentaries— they stressed World War II battles, social and political uprisings, and biographies. Both men welcomed the idea for a compilation series but were skeptical about the availability of actuality footage to support twenty-six episodes on the Great War. The results of preliminary film research by William Novik and Arthur Stevens in Europe allayed their fears.[3]

Sharnick's perspective on history differed from *The Twentieth Century*'s fact-laden, narrowly focused compilations with Walter Cronkite as "the voice of god." Sharnick envisioned World War I as the narrative structure, the framework, for a thematic investigation of the ideas, manners, mores, and culture that animated the world from 1900 through postwar Europe. In addition, Sharnick conceptualized the series through the looking glass of national and international issues in the 1960s. Benjamin backed *World War I* (September 22, 1964 to April 18, 1965).[4] Visually, the series differed from *The Twentieth Century*: It eschewed eyewitnesses, kept the narrator, Robert Ryan, off camera, extensively utilized still photographs as well as actuality footage, and had a more literary script, balancing descriptive language with an elegiac tone. By

197

March of 1964, with the support of William S. Paley, president of CBS, and Mike Dann, CBS programming director, the News Division approved the series under the auspices of Bud Benjamin.

Producing a Vision within an Institutional Structure

This essay examines the determinant factors and thematic points circumscribing *World War I*. Sharnick committed himself to *The Twentieth Century*'s production resources and mechanisms, including the vital network of European film researchers. Although Benjamin is listed as executive producer and Kleinerman and Sharnick as producers, Sharnick worked out of a different building and supervised production. The production process consisted of the following steps for each episode: 1) a written research report; 2) a review and blocking—literally, with pen— of the research report to isolate a narrative line and the actuality footage required; 3) screening of the footage compiled; 4) preparation of a treatment for the editors; 5) screening of the rough cut; 6) preparation by Sharnick of an outline script and direction notes for the writer (when Sharnick was not the writer);[5] 7) reviewing the final cut; 8) writing to the final film; 9) the mix. Benjamin and Kleinerman had creative input when screening footage in step 3, which, when necessary, resulted in a story treatment being realigned from the narrative outline. As a matter of policy, Kleinerman reviewed rough cuts, and Benjamin reviewed final scripts.

Sharnick's supervision over the production process, his distinct role, provides *World War I* with its unique vision, pacing, language, and ambiance. In this case, an established production system allowed Sharnick the role of auteur: he determined the themes, blocked the research report, wrote the treatment outline for the editors and script directions for the writers, reviewed all scripts, and rewrote sections of scripts written by others. The result was continuity of style and approach. This factor accounts for scripts written by Retired Brigadier General S. L. A. Marshall, Benjamin, and Sharnick as having the same qualities in the narration. Significantly, Sharnick became aware of Robert Ryan's style of reading and attempted to adapt sentence structure and language, encouraging a natural delivery.

Sharnick formulated an overriding vision of war's momentum that the public could understand, viscerally and cognitively. From his experience in World War II, Sharnick was struck by the unpredictability of wars, how "they take on a life of their own, a force of their own so that the objectives of wars usually have nothing to do with their outcome."[6] For Sharnick all twenty-six episodes are tied together by the unpredictable nature of war, and the consequences of ignoring this condition.

Once the military machine was accidentally set in motion, "a repeated, insistent pursuit of a course that represented a view of war and the human condition . . . prevailed at that time. . . . If you simply had a plan and carried it out you would arrive at an objective." This thesis was central to the success of *World War I* with CBS's executive hierarchy and the public. Television never dealt on an appropriate scale with World War I, Sharnick believed, probably because of the complexity of geography, strategy, tactics, and politics. Searching for a "form of communication . . . identifiable to Americans," Sharnick jettisoned the chronology necessary for this complexity but believed the military spirit, the visual "look" of war, and the social and cultural history of an era provided the necessary elements for his thesis.

Filtering the Past through Present Concerns

All history comes into existence through the interpretive process of an aesthetic consciousness. CBS's *World War I* came into existence through an interpretive process reflecting the sensibility of John Sharnick:

In the 1960s there was a gathering of a sense of doom, of things going out of control. We had just recovered from the jolt of the Cuban missile crisis. I started thinking about the series. The parallels were deliberate. I tried not to draw excessive parallels because history never repeats itself. It carries elements of the past with it. One idea is that the objectives of war are eventually overwhelmed. The objectives recede, and are never achieved in the form that the generals and politicians envisioned them. Consequences are vastly different from anything anyone envisioned. . . . To see people planning nuclear war seemed . . . horrible, [it] ignored . . . the WWI experience. . . . [And the current] changes in alliances and the hostilities . . . this occurred in WWI. The international situation of the 1960s was very much involved in planning the series. (Sharnick 1993)

World War I is as much about the conditions in the United States and the world in the mid-1960s as it is about World War I itself. The civil rights movement in 1963 comes out of a history of oppression, and World War I was one arena. In "Over There,"[7] the implications are direct: "Fretting at the chores assigned to them, some units volunteer for action. Among the first is the 15th Colored Infantry Regiment." In "Over Here" the war effort at home causes the movement of black Americans into the industrial northeast; unfortunately, these workers are met with hate and an angry white backlash. Even the French in occupied Germany place many "Negro colonials, whom they know the Germans will resent" on guard duty.

Two episodes on Russia establish the birth of Communist doctrine during World War I—"Revolution in Red" and "The Allies in Russia." The series correlates the war's progression with Russia's rise to political prominence and position as an international power. Arthur Danto suggests that every program (artwork) should be interpreted in its institutional context on a historical continuum. *Project XX*'s "Nightmare in Red" (December 27, 1955) and many episodes of *The Twentieth Century* produced in the late 1950s take a rigid anticommunist stand.[8] But in 1964-65 *World War I* tempers the irrational fear of communism and establishes the Soviet Union as a powerful nation. *World War I* also portrays the shock of a nation psychologically unprepared for the extreme consequences of its participation in World War I, and in the nuclear terror of the Cuban missile crisis.

Sharnick wanted the public to connect contemporary conditions with pivotal events in *World War I*. In "Year of Lost Illusions" Irish nationalism and the Easter Rising, the central event that gave rise to the IRA, reinforces war's ability to lay a foundation for future conflicts. The purpose of "The Promised Lands" is to raise the complex historical circumstances that formulated two of the most critical conflicts of our times: the settlement of Jews in Palestine (and the rise of Arab nationalism), and the creation of Yugoslavia. In "Over Here" the entrance of women into the economy foreshadows conditions in World War II and the increasing role of women in the work force in the early 1960s.

Two behavioral conditions repeatedly surface in *World War I:* the unpredictability of politicians and military leaders, and the potential callousness of a government toward its people. In the early 1960s the popularity of such novels as *Catch-22* (1961) and *Cat's Cradle* (1963) provided evidence of widespread concern about such conditions, especially the potential nightmare scenario between the governed and government, or the power elite. By the end of 1963, the unpredictable path of events in South Vietnam increasingly tugged at America, sending ominous signals of greater involvement, wittingly and unwittingly.

A Series Driven by the Inadvertent War Theory

The inadvertent war theory, succinctly announced in episode one, "Summer of Sarajevo," claims that World War I came about by "statesmen . . . overpowered by the workings of the military system." In both "Summer of Sarajevo" and "Clash of the Generals," Sharnick argues that the assassination of Archduke Francis Ferdinand and his wife, Sophie, set off a string of events with a momentum that military and political leaders could not stop. Certain historians, argues Marc Trachtenberg,[9] connect the inadvertent war theory with inflexible war plans, a commitment to the offensive, and pressure to mobilize first. In "Summer of Sarajevo," Austria and Germany "are now jointly committed to a fixed course, convinced that outsiders will back off." After attacking Serbia, the Czar is "persuaded that Germany is getting ready to strike. . . ." He orders full-scale mobilization and the momentum of offense continues. Using the metaphor of "a tangle of alliances and rivalries," Sharnick set up the principle characteristic of the inadvertent war theory: "If one of these strands should pull loose the whole thing may unravel." At times, Sharnick's thesis and his self-imposed parameters on military history did not compromise the representation of historical specificity. For example, central to the inadvertent war theory is the Schlieffen Plan. Formulated in 1905, this rigid military agenda—not tuned to conditions of 1914—is instituted without question. In "Clash of the Generals" the Schlieffen Plan "moves from crisis to mobilization to war." We follow its implementation, its failings, and finally the efforts of the German command to change the path of the juggernaut it set in motion.

Some historians conclude that there was little evidence for the inadvertent war theory. A separate bibliography was prepared by CBS researchers for each episode in *World War I* to assist Sharnick. On many of the bibliographies the same historical texts appear, such as works by Barbara Tuchman, Hanson Baldwin, George Kennan, and S. L. A. Marshall. One can extract from these works—especially Tuchman's popular text—support for the inadvertent theory; yet the bibliographies include texts arguing contradictory theories.[10] Alternative versions of history existed for the researchers and writers. Still these versions were not introduced or mentioned as possible explanations of a complex, large-scale war: Why? First, the theory relies on a broad-based, abstract concept that can embrace any actions and decisions by military or political leaders; for television, both a simple and open framework. Second, the theory connects directly to the anxieties of the American public in 1963, the kind of anxieties satirized in Stanley Kubrick's *Dr. Strangelove; or How I Learned to Stop Worrying and Love the Bomb* (1964).

The overwhelming momentum of the war that tyrannizes military leaders comes from interlocking mobilizations, a strategic approach most commanders are unprepared to physically handle and unable to strategically employ. In "Revolution in Red" Grand Duke Nicholas is "forced to strike before his armies are fully mobilized—forced by desperate calls for help." Some interlocking mobilizations are quickly demanded, haphazard, and disastrous. Once the plan begins, the vast, monumental scale of maneuvering reveals itself to the opposition, making the enormous military units vulnerable targets. Although "D-Day at Gallipoli" is known for its "vast scale, its ambitious aims, the

British command knows the enemy is prepared for them." Preparing for the "Battle of Argonne," General John J. Pershing must pull troops from allied sections. "The logistics of transport, of engineering are monumental." So "massive . . . it will prove a cumbersome machine on the advance, a target hard for enemy guns to miss."

World War I blindly accepts the strategy of "offense at all costs" without questioning its logic and validity or explaining its strategic roots. At these moments Sharnick's limits as an historian are evident. In "Verdun: The Inferno," General Joffre plans for an "all out offense" with disastrous results. In the "Battle of Jutland" Admiral Scheer calls his plan "total offense." In "The Trenches" the concept of offense takes on a deadly logic. Even when waiting in the trenches "generals cannot stand inactivity," they send raiders on the offense. The trenches are the zones where the military prepares for the "big push." It is appropriate that "The Trenches" conclude with the Somme offensive, where Sir Douglas Haig "will not call off the battle" and soldiers continue to go over the top to "feed" the maw of death. Even after the Battle of the Somme, Haig gets another chance for what he has been yearning: "a great offensive" in Flanders. In mid-July 1917 the Germans develop the "Friedensturm," the peace offensive . . . the blow that will end the war." This offensive is built with a "disdain" for secrecy. When the offense comes at Chateau-Thierry, the Allies are waiting in a massive ambush.

A Visual Strategy to Match Thematic Construction

Although the film researchers produced a wealth of moving images, Sharnick was struck by the expressive qualities of still images. The unit employed Howard Jensen to set up a camera that could film stills with precision—simultaneously panning, tilting, and zooming. The still image is central to a narrative strategy expanding two themes: the destruction from massive mobilization and the self-delusion of commanders and soldiers. Scenes composed of still photographs of military and political leaders in meetings are placed during and after moving images of battle and mobilization scenes. The faces of leadership reveal frustration, anger, defensiveness, elitism, introspection, and guilt. A slow zoom into a dazed face of a soldier in the trenches halts a series of moving images of mass troop movement. This strategy of juxtaposition jolts the viewer into recognizing that war's action and movement produces no discernible movement toward resolution. Still photographs are investigated by the camera, slowly panning and zooming in to reveal a detail, such as a broken bayonet, hands holding a cup, medals on a general's jacket, and the faces of politicians, military leaders, and soldiers. The camera consistently returns to faces, revealing a range of expectations of men in war.

Another dominant visual strategy resulted from film researchers uncovering long-takes of troops mobilizing, military equipment being moved through the countryside, trains carrying men and machines, and expanses of land, soon to be battlefields. Most of these images were composed in medium-long shot. Sharnick strategically employs these images to highlight war as a game of positioning and repositioning. Viewers become spectators to large alignments of troops and equipment that made little if any strategic gains. The striking images depict a military system on the move, but to little tactical avail.

A War Driven by Impulse and Delusion

Sharnick perceived *World War I* as an "extreme manifestation of the spirit of a society, of an age," and turned to statesmen, commanders, soldiers, artists and writers to drive the stories and themes, isolating them in the complicated landscape of military machinery. The "spirit" of the age is constructed from economic, social, and cultural forces. Many of these themes are expressed in war literature, including autobiographies of military leaders and statesmen, and the journals of soldiers. Sharnick argues that *World War I*'s literary perspective comes from integrating the writing produced during and after the war to explain the war. The bibliographies used by CBS reinforce this position. Consequently, the excessive language, the rhetoric of mobilization, and the "cult of the offense" (Trachtenberg 64) are consistent in contributing to the spirit of an age.

The narration evokes a self-propelled military machine that dictates to generals what they must do and turns individuals into cogs of a system. "Daredevils and Dogfights" begins by praising the airplane and the aces as the "last shred of private glory out of the vast mechanical slaughter grinding on below." The episode details development of aerial technology and personalizes aces from M. von Richthofen (who is pleasant, aloof, and writes his mother three times a week) to Albert Ball (who gardens and plays violin between missions). "Daredevils and Dogfights" concludes by announcing the Somaliland offensive, thus progressing from individualization to mechanization. The connection to Cubist art is intentional. War and art imitate each other.

World War I sets up a continuous contrast between an apparently indestructible war machine, and small, but insistent, miscalculations, navigation errors, communication breakdowns, and misdirections. When the mechanisms of the machine confront the impulse of the individual, the outcome is predictable. This concept is best illustrated by Pershing's advance on the Meuse-Argonne. He is bedeviled with details: "Wearing too many hats, taking on too many jobs, he administers a war zone and its strategy . . . while commanding a huge army engaged in desperate battle. The result is chaos. Signals missed and signals crossed . . . communication problems." Interestingly, the individual, the commanders, can only escalate problems within the path of mobilization. In "Clash of the Generals," General von Moltke says of himself, "I am too reflective."

With a sense of horrific witticism, Sharnick adds surreal characteristics to individual personalities responsible for the momentum into war. "The Doomed Dynasties" characterizes Kaiser Wilhelm the Second in the following terms: "Born with a severely deformed arm, he spends his life hiding it from the world and over-compensating for it." He "finds his wife stuffy and bourgeois," his children do not interest him and he "abuse[s] his leading ministers by kicking them . . . and calling them 'donkeys' and 'mutton heads' and noodles." Czar Nicholas the Second is a "moody hen-pecked husband at home, a vacillating autocrat to his subjects." The characterizations bolster the inadvertent war theory with a hint of the bizarre.

In a majority of episodes Sharnick tries to capture the psyche of ordinary troops, stressing how soldier and civilian are deluded by the goals and glory of war. People of the late Victorian era believed that victory was within human control, that man could control his environment. Episodes such as "The Trenches" and "Clash of the Generals" pose a question never directly answered in the series: Why did men continue to serve and face death? The French concocted a doctrine of elan: "The idea of elan . . . a spirit of ardor and impetuousness, expressed in simple, inspiring maxims: 'Offensive to the limit!' 'Whatever the circumstances . . . attack!' " ("Clash of the Generals"). In the battle of Soissons, the native soldiers speak of the "French dragoons in all their doomed, archaic glory. Doomed to slaughter in this attack, as in every one before" ("The Tide Turns"). For the Germans a commitment to total offense comes from the concept of "kultur," the advancement of Germanic civilization. With this concept in mind, even Thomas Mann embraced the war as a "purification, a liberation, an enormous hope" ("Summer of Sarajevo"). But kultur does not fully explain the rush toward death in the German psyche. Modris Eksteins in *Rites of Spring: The Great War and the Birth of the Modern Age* explains the German soldier's psyche in *Pficht*: "Death took on a creative function. Death became invigorating. War now held moral value of its own, without regard to foresight or hindsight. War became total" (Eksteins 198). *World War I* evokes the drive but never adequately explores its psychological underpinning.

"The language and literature of disillusionment would be on the whole a postwar phenomenon—everywhere," notes Sharnick, and the journals of soldiers provide a range of emotional reactions to the war. But even sketches and paintings suggest a strong sense of disillusionment in "Behind German Lines" from the artists Käthe Kollwitz, George Grosz, and Otto Dix. Ford Maddox Ford's *Parade's End* is used to conclude "Year of Lost Illusions" in relation to Flanders: "There will be no more Hope, no more Glory. Not for the nation, not for the world, I dare say. There will be no more parades."

After the war writers reacted against the inadequacy of hollow classic and romantic language to present the horrific, T. S. Eliot and e. e. cummings among them. In *A Farewell to Arms*, Ernest Hemingway preserved his indictment of patriotic abstractions: "I was always embarrassed by the words sacred, glorious, and sacrifice and the expression in vain. . . . I had seen nothing sacred, and the things that were glorious had no glory and the sacrifices were like the stockyards in Chicago if nothing was done with the meat to bury it" (184).

Sharnick attempted to give the overall tone of narration in *World War I* a literary style reflecting the Hemingway mood. In "The Promised Lands," "The Nationalist dream turned into a nightmare of struggling giants. And the dreamer trampled under foot." Instead of constantly writing exposition to images of twisted, muddy bodies, Sharnick found figures of speech and metaphors that would force the viewers to unravel in their minds the horrific experience of war. In "Verdun the Inferno," after five months of death Sharnick notes that "it is not just France that is bleeding. The inferno must be stoked, and it consumes whatever it is fed." In "The Days the Guns Stopped Firing," images of carnage end by acknowledging that "it will take the world's leaders five more weeks to shut down the engines of war." This writing style was a daring approach for a network compilation series.

The series' most popular episode, according to Sharnick, was "Tipperary and All That Jazz," presenting over twelve songs—American, British and French—from the war. Sharnick positioned the musical episode as nineteenth among the twenty-six programs. It had two intended functions: as evidence of the spirit of the time, melody, and lyric fueled the psyche of the beguiled; as a document broadcast in 1964-1965, it was aimed at millions of viewers as a reminder of how culture can turn a view of war into spirited nostalgia, cushioning the misery of the past. Only one song in the episode, censored during the war, matches the tone of Hemingway's voice—"Song of Craonne": "Goodbye to life, goodbye to love. We are all victims, doomed by a wretched war."

A Structure to Examine the Present through the Past

Sharnick wanted each episode of *World War I* to stand on its own. This meant that the narrative contain a dramatic flow of events with a clear beginning, middle, and end. If a viewer missed one episode, he would not be "historically" disoriented in the next episode. Many of the episodes end without a complete closure to the action. Several episodes, for example, end on the retreat of troops and the refugees left behind. Sharnik claims that his interest in "intellectual history" over "military history" contributed to the design of the series and the structure of episodes. In trying to present the war in a manner "identifiable for Americans" in the mid-1960s, Sharnick searched for a "common experience" between past and present. Besides the experiences of national and international issues, Sharnick raises moral issues. Leaving refugees behind poses moral questions common to past and present. When "Clash of the Generals" concludes with the failure of the high command, condemning "Europe to four bitter years in the trenches of the Western front," we are confronted with the moral responsibility of leadership. "The Day the Guns Stopped Firing" concludes with the following: "Tonight the final entry will be written in the French army's journal of communiqués: 'Closed because of victory.' The last word is 'victory'—not peace." In this series Sharnick did not opt for strict narrative closures that gave finality to events. He selected a narrative form that engaged the viewer in the moral problems posed by history. *World War I* re-opened many moral conflicts that existed in 1964—and still exist today.

Notes

1. *Eyewitness to History* aired from 1959 through 1963. It was the first half-hour network news program devoted to one news story, and led to the expansion of the *CBS Evening News* from 15 to 30 minutes.

2. *The Twentieth Century* was originally conceived as a compilation documentary series. It produced 17 compilation documentaries in the 1957-58 season; 18 in 1958-59; 20 in 1959-60; 9 in 1960-61; 14 in 1961-62; 12 in 1962-63; and 11 in 1963-64.

3. The series would not have been produced without the participation of the film researcher and director William Novik, working out of France and coordinating European research. Novik was supervising film research for *The Twentieth Century* since 1957 and had freelance film researchers throughout Europe. Only two footage shot lists still exist for the *World War I* series—listing the source for each piece of film—but frequently they have Novik's name as the source. He was instrumental in getting footage from private sources.

4. All references to statements and direct quotes from John Sharnick are from two interviews, conducted on August 17, 1982, and June 1, 1993, by the author.

5. John Sharnick wrote thirteen of the twenty-six episodes in the series.

6. Before considering the series, Benjamin asked Sharnick to produce a program on Verdun for *The Twentieth Century*. "Verdun: End of the Nightmare" aired on December 8, 1963.

7. All narration quotes are taken from the CBS scripts for each program. Quotes used were checked against the film for accuracy.

8. *The Twentieth Century* had a reputation for strong anticommunist rhetoric. Such programs in the series include "The Red Sell: The Propaganda Mill" (October 25, 1958), "The Red Sell: Report from the Targets" (November 2, 1958), "Czechoslovakia: From Munich to Moscow" (April 8, 1962), and "Germany: Red Spy Target" (November 4, 1962).

9. Marc Trachtenberg in *History and Strategy* (New Jersey: Princeton UP, 1991), provides a comprehensive summary in chapter 2, "The Coming of the First World War: A Reassessment," of historians advocating the inadvertent war theory, and the tactics that followed.

10. Other texts that Sharnick and the production unit had available for investigating alternative versions of history included John Dos Passos, *Mr. Wilson's War* (Garden City: Doubleday, 1962); Cyril Falls, *The Great War: 1914-1918* (New York: Capricorn, 1959); Pierce Fredericks, *The Great Adventure* (New York: Dutton, 1960); J. F. Fuller, *The Conduct of War* (New Jersey: Rutgers, 1961); Liddell Hart, *The Real War* (Boston: Little, Brown, 1931); Laurence Stallings, *The Doughboys* (New York: Harper, 1963); Richard Thoumin, *The First World War* (New York: Putman, 1964).

Works Cited

Baldwin, Hanson. *World War I*. New York: Harper, 1962.

Danto, Arthur C. *Beyond the Brillo Box: The Visual Arts in Post-Historical perspective*. New York: Farrar, 1992.

——. *The Philosophical Disenfranchisement of Art*. New York: Columbia UP, 1986.

Eksteins, Modris. *Rites of Spring: The Great War and the Birth of the Modern Age*. New York: Doubleday, 1989.

Hemingway, Ernest. *A Farewell to Arms*. 1929. Scribner, 1962.

Kennan, George F. *The Decision to Intervene*. Princeton: Princeton UP, 1958.

——. *Russia Leaves the War*. Princeton: Princeton UP, 1956.

Marshall, S. L. A. *World War I*. Boston: Houghton Mifflin, 1964.

Trachtenberg, Marc. *History and Strategy*. Princeton: Princeton UP, 1991.

Tuchman, Barbara. *The Guns of August*. New York: Macmillan, 1962.

12

The Moving Picture Boys in the Great War: The Making of a Documentary

Larry Ward

Twenty-two years ago, while still a graduate student at the University of Iowa, I participated in the production of a compilation film about the role of the motion pictures during World War I. It was entitled *The Moving Picture Boys in the Great War* (1975) and was produced as a part of the Post-Newsweek Television's American Documents series. Blackhawk Films in Davenport, Iowa, provided the production facilities as well as the irreplaceable services of producer David Shepard. Without his guidance and his encyclopedic knowledge of the silent film era, it is doubtful if *The Moving Picture Boys* would ever have reached the screen.

Working together with three fellow students (John Abel, Peter Dufour, and Robert Allen), we began our research into the motion picture record of the Great War. This essay will examine our efforts with the advantage of twenty-twenty hindsight, analyzing what we were trying to do; where we succeeded and failed; and what subsequent research suggests we might have done differently.

Methodology

Today *The Moving Picture Boys in the Great War* seems dated. In the wake of Ken Burns's wonderful films (*The Civil War* and *Jefferson*), perhaps many older compilation films look stodgy and old-fashioned in comparison. But one of the basic weaknesses of *The Moving Picture Boys* was entirely of our own making. From the very beginning of production, we made a conscious effort to limit ourselves to authentic materials from the World War I period. This decision extended not only to motion picture clips used in the film, but to magazine covers, theater slides, posters, newspaper headlines, and still photographs. Even the music track was to be constructed from period recordings, including piano rolls used to accompany films during the era, and wax cylinder recordings of war songs—most of which came from the audio archives

209

at Syracuse University. One obvious inconsistency was our building of elaborate sound effects tracks to "punch-up" the silent footage, a concession made as much for commercial reasons as for any other. Finally, even our off-screen narrator, Lowell Thomas, the long-time voice of the Fox Movietone Newsreel, was also from "the period." Even if we had wanted to employ on-screen interviews or subject experts, our budget would not have allowed it. To a great extent, our self-imposed limitation was simply a way of making the maximum use of limited resources.

Our motives were pure even if our aesthetic judgment was lacking. We wanted to write our documentary history with the films of the period, to let the images speak for themselves. In part, we were reacting to the tendency in compilation filmmaking to use the images primarily as illustrations for the narration. Too often narration describing an event like a major battle is accompanied by generic "battlefield footage," not film materials from the actual historical event. If the narrator was talking about "The Battle of the Somme," we wanted to use only footage that we could verify as being from that battle—not a montage of explosions, tanks, and men in the trenches drawn from any archival source. We also wanted to differentiate on-screen between newsreels and fiction films. We made this distinction by lightly tinting the theatrical film materials in *The Moving Picture Boys*, a relatively common practice in the silent film era. In fact, some of the first films we collected in our research were already tinted. Newsreels or other actuality materials were left in black and white. This color code would keep viewers informed about the nature of the footage on screen, thereby helping us to avoid the sleight of hand so common in network compilations—at the time and as recently as last-night's special on the *The History Channel.*

Working through film histories, trade magazines, and newspapers, we constructed an initial list of more than 450 war-related films made between 1914 and 1919. Only a small percentage of these films were still extant. (The common estimate that no more than 15 percent of the American silent film heritage has survived to the present is probably high for films made during the war years.) Still, even with our limited budget we collected a sizable sampling of films from a variety of film archives, film companies, and private collections. The final cut of the film contained clips from more than eighty different newsreels, theatrical films, and government motion pictures. These films were supplemented by still photographs, magazine covers, posters, and theater slides used to communicate reel changes or to provide other messages to audiences during the silent era.

The wealth of images and sound we accumulated was a two-edged sword. On one hand, we had more than enough material in our fifty-minute time frame to let the images "speak for themselves." On the other hand, our film database was incomplete for both budgetary and historical reasons. We did not, for example, have enough money to purchase the film rights to Charlie Chaplin's *Shoulder Arms* (1918). Other important films, such as *The Kaiser, the Beast of Berlin* (1917), were lost like so many films of the silent era.

Dating films proved difficult. Films obtained from the National Archives and Library of Congress were well catalogued, but other film materials, particularly actuality footage, were sometimes impossible to date or verify with total certainty. Our color-coding scheme, while generally consistent, was often difficult to implement. Should "faked" newsreel footage be tinted as fictional material, or should it be left as black and white? How was one to color-code a government-made trailer using actors and a script? On more than one occasion, I am also certain that we succumbed to the never-ending conflict between editing the images and writing the narration, slipping in a shot to make a visual transition flow more smoothly, or taking a shot out of context to underline some point in the narration. There is not too much of this kind of manipulation in the final film, but our best intentions turned out to be far easier in theory than in practice.

The Film Itself: Telling the Story

The Moving Picture Boys is chronological in structure. It begins with an overview of the American film industry prior to the beginning of European hostilities in 1914. It surveys the growing movie audience and the rise of the feature film before turning to the films made during the long period of American neutrality, 1914-1917. The next section of the film features pacifistic films such as Thomas Ince's *Civilization* (1916) and D. W. Griffith's *Intolerance* (1916) as well as a movie serial, *The Mystery of the Double Cross* (1916) and a cartoon, Winsor McKay's *The Sinking of the Luisitania* (1916), that capitalized on the submarine scare. Using newsreels, but also clips from several theatrical films, we showed how the movies dealt with the preparedness issue, and how the demand for war newsreels led to widespread reconstruction of war-related actualities. After the United States entered the war in April 1917, a flood of films dealing directly with the war were released. We were able to obtain far more films produced after the declaration of war than from the prewar period.

The next segment of *The Moving Picture Boys* shows the film work of the government's official wartime propaganda agency, the Committee on Public Information (CPI), and briefly describes the relationship between Hollywood and the government as the country mobilized for war. This section contains newsreel footage of popular film stars (Charlie Chaplin, Douglas Fairbanks, Mary Pickford) selling war bonds and clips from studio-produced trailers and informational shorts designed to enlist support for a myriad of government war programs. The film concludes with a long section focusing on theatrical Hollywood war films such as Warner's *My Four Years in Germany* (1918), Griffith's *Hearts of the World* (1918), Alan Holubar's *Hearts of Humanity* (1918), featuring Eric von Stroheim in his trademark role as a cruel German officer, and Mack Sennett's *Yankee Doodle in Berlin* (1919), with the Keystone Kops as a bungling platoon of German soldiers.

The *Moving Picture Boys* presents a reasonably accurate chronology, and it does not make too many simplistic assumptions about the relationship between film and American society during the World War I period. The film's point of view is unexceptional, if not timid: "Both the American film industry and American society came of age during the Great War." Unfortunately, some of the best cultural film histories (Jowett, Sklar, O'Connor and Jackson, Rollins) that might have helped us sharpen our approach as we developed *The Moving Picture Boys*, had not yet been written!

In retrospect, the greatest strength of *The Moving Picture Boys* resides in the sheer power of the images. The war posters, the theater slides, the covers of magazines such as *Leslie's Illustrated Weekly*, and the films themselves provide a vivid record of propaganda techniques and wartime attitudes. Too much of the time the film tends to bury analysis under an endless stream of images and audio recordings. As director-editor for the film, I deserve most of the blame for this overloading: I had the images and I was determined to use them. I know firsthand that this is the basic temptation of compilation filmmaking, trying to cram it all in, even to the point of overload.

One example of this error is the film's soundtrack. On several occasions, war songs with lyrics are run underneath silent film footage. This does an injustice to both; furthermore the lyrics change the way the viewer interprets the image; the war song was never meant to be used as the soundtrack for something like a half-baked historical music video. I still wince when I watch the scene of Robert Harron and Lillian Gish in Griffith's *Hearts of the World* with the words of the period war song "Good-bye Frenchie, Good-bye" playing beneath them. About the only thing that rings true in this juxtaposition is the setting—France. Everything else is wrong. While Harron gazes longingly at a wallet picture of his American girl (Gish), the song lyrics create a totally different (and confusing) image of an American soldier leaving his French girlfriend behind.

What else would I do differently? Additional research conducted long after the production of *The Moving Picture Boys* suggests at least three basic elements of the film that would be given a different emphasis or interpretation if I were making the film today: the effectiveness of World War I film propaganda; the scope and nature of the CPI film campaign; and the overall significance of the many efforts to employ motion pictures as a propaganda weapon during the Great War.

Film Propaganda in World War I

First, I believe now that it is unlikely that motion picture propaganda played as significant a role in influencing American public opinion during World War I as *The Moving Picture Boys* suggests. We were not alone, of course, in this perception. Contemporary observers made extravagant claims about the impact of motion picture propaganda during the war years, particularly during the three years of American neutrality. Prior to American entry into the war, both the Germans and the Allies attempted to solicit support in the United States with motion picture propaganda campaigns built around war newsreels. However, the effectiveness of these film campaigns in mobilizing American public opinion was undermined in several ways.

The newsreels of 1915 or 1916 were not hard news by modern standards. Most of the so-called "war films" from this period focus on training activities, equipment displays, and endless scenes of marching troops. Actual combat footage is extremely rare, a combination of military censorship and a cumbersome filmmaking process that worked against coverage of fast-breaking events. News footage shot in France had to be processed, edited, and then shipped across the Atlantic before it could appear in American movie theaters. Compared to the graphic and instantaneous coverage of the Gulf War in the video age, the newsreels of World War I tended to feature "news" with a long shelf-life: fashion shows, zoo tours, daredevil stunts, new inventions and biographies of the rich, the famous, the unusual. In general, many of the so-called "war films" of World War I are war newsreels without much war.

The difficulty of obtaining authentic war footage led some newsreel producers into practices that further undermined both the credibility and the propaganda value of their films. Some companies initially tried to create "war films" by simply re-editing footage from their film vaults of anything that marched or wore a helmet: the Swiss Army on maneuvers, or scenes of a local politician reviewing national guard troops. Archive footage could be passed off as current news for only so long and strict military censorship in Europe dampened the prospects of shooting new film. Even if an enterprising newsreel cameraman somehow overcame these obstacles, military authorities were generally reluctant to allow civilian photographers near the front—not only to protect them from the potential danger of enemy fire but as a means of restricting the release of photographs and newsreels for security reasons.

Unscrupulous film producers found a simple answer to this impasse. Armed with a few rifles, some actors and old uniforms, it was relatively easy to stage dramatic "war films" that far exceeded the quality of anything that could actually be shot at the front. In the early days of the war this practice was so widespread that the Universal Film Company's J. D. Tippet concluded that "anything you see in America of any consequence is fake" (50), a perception echoed by exposés that appeared in a number of newspapers and magazines (Smither 149-68). *The Literary Digest*, for example, took obvious glee in describing the Hollywood-style production of British war films: "As the charging 'Germans' reach the other bank and make straight for the 'British' machine guns, terrible explosions occur. . . . At the proper moment the fake mines are exploded by throwing a switch or pressing a button, thus sending clouds of smoke and a dummy figure or two into the air" ("Fake War Movies").

As a means of combating the general belief that all war films were fake, the Germans, the Allies, and even a few American newsreel companies began releasing so-called official films, newsreels obtained with the official sanction of either the government or the military in one of the European nations. These films were either purchased from military cinematographers or they were shot by commercial newsreel cameramen under the watchful eye of military advisors. They were not much of an improvement over the static stock footage that had spurred the fake newsreel epidemic. They seldom featured anything approaching battlefield action, but the fact that they had been secured "officially" gave American audiences at least some assurance that what they were watching had not been staged. Even the knowledge that these "official films" had been subject to heavy military censorship tended to increase their legitimacy. By 1916 most of the warring nations had begun to produce their own "official films" using photographers and film editors attached to the military. Still, given the long delays in getting war films to American theaters, the poor quality of the footage they contained, and the nagging questions raised about their authenticity, it is doubtful if such films could be considered a primary force in mobilizing American public opinion for entry into the war.

On the surface at least, war-related motion pictures released in the United States during the neutrality years do seem to mirror the country's transformation from a neutral nation to an active participant in World

"Authentic" battle footage—from New Jersey.

War I. It is questionable, however, if the on-screen transition from paci-fism to preparedness, from neutrality to a pro-Ally position is as smooth as *The Moving Picture Boys* suggests. Many of the most important paci-fistic films such as Ince's *Civilization*, Griffith's *Intolerance* and Herbert Brenon's *War Brides* were not even released until 1916. Furthermore, pro-German war newsreels were being shown in the United States until just weeks before the American declaration of war. More important, nei-ther war-related newsreels nor theatrical films dominated American movie screens during the two and one-half years of neutrality. Most of the films shown in American theaters during this period did what they had always done—provide inexpensive entertainment. It is significant that none of the major movie stars such as Charlie Chaplin, Mary Pick-ford, Douglas Fairbanks, or William Hart appeared in a war-related film during the neutrality years.

In retrospect, what *is* important is that both commercial filmmakers and U.S. government officials *thought* motion picture propaganda was effective. This belief led both private film interests and the government to develop a variety of schemes to employ the motion picture in an essentially new role—as a tool to persuade and inform.

Regardless of their effectiveness as propaganda, the "official" Euro-pean war films did pique the interest of at least a few American military leaders during the neutrality period. Some attended screenings of for-eign-made war films, and gave endorsements to films that they consid-ered supportive of greater American military readiness. Ironically, this kind of film activity underscored a surprising revelation about screen propaganda during the Great War: the films were probably no more important than the setting they were shown in. Packed with a large crowd, the movie theater itself was a propaganda weapon of consider-able value, an ideal place for patriotic speechmaking, fund-raising, song-singing and flag-waving. Later in the war, this concept found fruition in the Committee on Public Information (CPI), whose Division of Four-Minute Men, an organization of public speakers who delivered brief patriotic talks (supposedly four minutes or less in length) between reel changes in movie theaters throughout the United States.

By the time the United States entered the war, the credibility of motion picture propaganda was fairly well established. The War Depart-ment had provided nominal assistance to the producers of two prepared-ness-oriented films, *The Eagle's Wings* (1916) and *Uncle Sam Awake* (1916) (Ward 41-43). In fact, the two filmmakers responsible for those films, Rufus Steele and Laurence Rubel, both made significant contribu-tions to the U.S. government's official World War I propaganda cam-paign: Steele as head of the CPI's Division of Pictures, and Rubel as head of the CPI's Bureau of War Photographs. Despite this flurry of prewar activity, there is no evidence that either the government or the military made any plans to use motion pictures in the event of American entry into the war. Perhaps the uncertainty of American involvement encouraged procrastination. In any case, whatever interest motion picture propaganda may have raised in the neutrality years, it was not enough to spur contingency planning.

The CPI Campaign: Government Propaganda

A second area of possible revision concerns the scope and nature of the U.S. government's official film effort in World War I. *The Moving Picture Boys* does devote a section of the film to the activities of the CPI Film Division. By the time the war ended the CPI had produced a number of films, most of which have been preserved in the Library of Congress. This includes feature-length newsreel-style documentaries such as *Pershing's Crusaders* (1918), *America's Answer* (1918), and *Under Four Flags* (1918), and many issues of a weekly war newsreel entitled *The Official War Review* (1918). The quality of these films is not much different from the "official" European films of the neutrality period. With almost no prior preparation and with virtually no filmmaking experience, the CPI film effort grew as much out accident and circumstance as careful planning.

The Army Signal Corps' decision to produce a "pictorial history" of the Great War provided much of the impetus for the creation of a Film Division within the CPI. This was an entirely new assignment for the Signal Corps, and the difficulty of securing labs, production equipment, and trained personnel was constant source of frustration until the very end of the war (Mould 204). The character of these films is best explained by the Signal Corps' own term—"record photography." The Signal Corps was trying to build a photographic record of the war both for historical and future training purposes. This meant documenting every aspect of the American military effort, no matter how mundane, from buildings to equipment and training procedures. Most of this footage was static and could have been shot as easily, and probably as well, with a still camera. Later in the war when the CPI began using Signal Corps motion pictures in its own propaganda work, the Corps recognized the difference between shooting "record films" and shooting films for the government's propaganda effort. When photographing scenes for use in CPI productions, Signal Corps cameramen were encouraged to shoot from "some unusual viewpoint . . . to suggest local color or with something of local interest in the foreground ("Photographic Bulletin No. 4").

None of the CPI's films based on this footage will be mistaken for landmarks of cinematic art nor will they be remembered as shining examples of government documentary filmmaking. Indeed, the CPI film production effort developed so quickly and so haphazardly that it is a miracle that so many films were actually completed. To a great extent the Division of Films was at the mercy of Signal Corps cameramen who were shooting their film for entirely different purposes. It is not hard to envision the CPI film editing staff late at night, trying desperately to figure out some way to use a Signal Corps "record film" showing how the army recycled shoes.

Because these films were readily available, *The Moving Picture Boys* tends to draw heavily from the CPI film productions. Most of the CPI's films, of course, were produced too late in the war to have much impact on public opinion. The CPI's most significant achievements, however, were not in production, but in distribution and exhibition, areas for which there is virtually no film record that could have been put on the screen in *The Moving Picture Boys*.

Early in the war the CPI's Division of Films limited itself to free distribution of Signal Corps films to various patriotic and educational organizations. Writing in the 1920s, film historian Terry Ramsaye provided a perceptive analysis of the problems this kind of free distribution posed: a CPI press release was far different from a free government motion picture. The CPI's press corps could get a story published in any newspaper in the country, but the only way to be sure a CPI film message would reach the American public was for the film to be distributed and exhibited through commercial film industry channels (Ramsaye 783).

The appointment of Charles Hart, former advertising manager of *Hearst's Magazine*, as chairman of the Division of Films in April of 1918, signaled a turning point in the CPI film effort. Although he had no motion picture experience prior to the war, Hart quickly demonstrated some of the attributes of a fledgling movie mogul. Within a short time he greatly expanded and improved the CPI's ability to make and distribute films, and eventually branched out into film exhibition, staging special screenings of CPI films in commercial theaters across the country. Hart, clearly, was no longer bound by the CPI's initial policy to avoid direct competition with the private film industry. In fact, the CPI's growing film program demanded an even greater level of government-industry cooperation.

Using contacts in the private film industry, Hart first concentrated his attention on assembling a staff with professional filmmaking experience, including everything from production secretaries to former newsreel cameramen and film editors. A CPI liaison officer was sent to

France to coordinate and improve the quality of Signal Corps film production. Hart then turned his attention to distribution and exhibition. The CPI controlled all films shot by the Signal Corps, but the American Red Cross and the various Allied film services were still showing or selling their own war films in the United States long after American entry into the war. After some bitter negotiations, Hart forced the Red Cross and the British, French, and Italian film services to give control of their films to the CPI. Having obtained a virtual monopoly, the CPI initially tried to sell these war films to the established newsreel companies. When negotiations faltered, the CPI Division of Films decided to produce its own weekly newsreel, *The Official War Review*. What Hart needed now was a distributor rather than a newsreel production company.

After a heated bidding war, the powerful Pathé newsreel organization won the rights to distribute the official U.S. government newsreel. Pathé agreed to return eighty percent of the proceeds from the *Official War Review* to the Division of Films. Extra film not used in The *Official War Review* was sold to other newsreel companies for a dollar per foot of film (Creel 54). To facilitate the distribution and exhibition of its feature-length newsreel documentaries (*America's Answer, Pershing's Crusaders*, and *Under Four Flags*), the CPI staged "official" screenings in commercial theaters in the largest metropolitan areas. Using the advance publicity generated through these gala screenings, the CPI then sold its films to commercial distributors to ensure that they would be shown in the rest of the country.

The income from these efforts nearly enabled the Division of Films to break even, an amazing accomplishment since the CPI continued to furnish free films to nonprofit organizations and to the Foreign Film Service. Under Hart's aggressive leadership, the Division of Films far surpassed any previous government effort to use motion pictures in an official capacity. By the time the war ended, U.S. government films were being shown in every state in the union and over sixty-two hundred reels of government pictures had been shipped abroad (Creel 52-53).

In many respects the CPI's greatest success was not in making films but in getting them seen. Without the cooperation of the private film industry this would not have been possible. Without access to commercial movie theaters, most Americans would never have seen them, and the CPI film program would have been deprived of the income it desperately needed to expand its work at home and abroad.

Ripple Effects of the Film Campaign

A third area of potential revision in *The Moving Picture Boys* is a matter of emphasis—reassessing the significance of the various World

War I film campaigns. The success of the CPI's Division of Films did not herald a golden age of government filmmaking. Once the war ended and the CPI was disbanded, government filmmaking virtually disappeared until the mid-1930s and the work of Pare Lorentz and the short-lived U.S. Film Service. At best, the work of the Army Signal Corps and CPI Division of Films may have provided some valuable precedents for the film efforts of the Office of War Information and the Signal Corps Photographic Center during World War II.

In retrospect, the flurry of wartime film activity was of more lasting importance to the American film industry than to the United States government. Garth Jowett's social history of American film, *Film, the Democratic Art,* suggests a compelling explanation for the industry's behavior during the war—the film industry's long-standing quest for acceptance and recognition. The government's World War I film effort would seem to have posed a number of immediate threats to industry interests, raising the dreaded specter of government censorship and even the possibility of direct government competition. Through the enormous powers of wartime agencies such as the Fuel Administration and the War Trade Board, the government clearly possessed the means to force industry cooperation. The film business could have been declared a "nonessential industry," and the theaters could have been closed to conserve fuel. Although the CPI possessed no statutory authority to alter film content, a series of regulations and executive orders enabled the CPI to exert considerable pressure on filmmakers to alter the content of motion pictures. Through its use of War Trade Board export permits, the CPI exerted direct control over the content of films sent abroad. It is likely, of course, that the CPI's foreign film campaign actually helped the American film industry, particularly its attempts to drive German films off the neutral screens of Europe. The government also aggressively pushed American films into new foreign markets as a means of expanding its propaganda campaign, an effort with obvious benefits for the burgeoning American film industry. *The Moving Picture Boys* only mentions this in passing, but clearly this is an area that warrants further research.

Still, there is little evidence that the government had to employ these powers to gain the industry's assistance. If anything, the government had to fight off the volunteers, sifting through an endless barrage of motion picture publicity schemes and would-be government filmmakers. The industry's trade associations, war cooperation committees, and stars provided seemingly total support for the government's film effort. At their own expense, commercial film companies made short films to help sell war bonds, encourage enlistment, and explain the need for conserving food and fuel. Popular film stars criss-crossed the country, promoting patriotism and securing subscriptions for the government's Liberty Loan drives.

Robert Sklar has observed that the movies were the first medium of mass communications controlled by men "who did not share the ethnic or religious backgrounds of the traditional cultural elites" (27). Many of early film pioneers, William Fox, Samuel Goldwyn, Adolph Zukor, and Carl Laemmle, were fairly recent European immigrants who had gone from careers in the jewelry or clothing businesses to positions of prominence in the young film industry. For them, the Great War may well have intensified the motion picture industry's long-standing cultural inferiority complex, raising new questions about loyalty, patriotism, and public service.

From a point early in the war when representatives from Universal tried to arrange for their German-born president, Carl Laemmle, to simply shake hands with Woodrow Wilson, the situation had changed dramatically. Through its participation in the U.S. government's World War I film program, contact with government officials had become almost commonplace. Filmmakers now corresponded regularly with the President; actor Douglas Fairbanks gave President Woodrow Wilson a movie projector that was installed in the White House. After the war a number of Treasury Department officals who had worked closely with the industry during the Liberty Loan campaigns actually went into the film business. Treasury Secretary William McAdoo, Wilson's son-in-law, was offered the presidency of the new United Artists Corporation, a company formed by the stars of the loan drives: Charlie Chaplin, Mary Pickford, D. W. Griffith, and Douglas Fairbanks. McAdoo declined this offer, but did agree to serve as general counsel for United Artists. McAdoo's first assistant at Treasury, Oscar Price, was appointed to United Artists' board of directors, and Treasury's chief publicity engineer, Frank Wilson, later formed a motion picture finance company and produced educational films (Balio 24-25).

By the end of the war the film industry seemed to have achieved a degree of respectability and recognition that was previously unimaginable. The industry's war efforts were not the only reasons for these changes, but there is no question that industry's participation in the government's wartime film effort accelerated the industry's acceptance as a vital new communications medium.

Envoi

I had not looked at *The Moving Picture Boys in the Great War* for more than a decade when I began work on this essay. Seeing it again was not unlike finding a twenty-year-old college term paper—a source of some chagrin and embarrassment, of some pride and laughter, of some amazement at the naiveté. I am being unfair, of course. I can still remember the time and commitment the film required, and hindsight— even of the twenty-twenty variety—is ultimately unfair. *The Moving Picture Boys* won several film festivals in 1975. Working within the constraints of our budget and schedule, I know that we made the best film that we could have twenty-two years ago. I do have a greater appreciation for narration now than I did then. Used wisely, it has the potential to fill in the gaps that cannot be filled any other way. In the end, there really is a difference between writing a history and making a compilation film. Despite these thoughts about rewriting, revising, and re-editing, *The Moving Picture Boys* will not be changed. Like the films of World War I, it, too, is now a part of the historical record.

Works Cited

Balio, Tino. *United Artists: The Company Built by Stars*. Madison: U of Wisconsin P, 1976.

Creel, George. *The Complete Report of the Chairman of the Committee on Public Information, 1917, 1918, 1919*. Washington: GPO, 1920.

"Fake War Movies." *Literary Digest* 3 Oct. 1914: 50.

Jowett, Garth. *Film, the Democratic Art: A Social History of American Film*. Boston: Little, Brown, 1976.

Mould, David. *American Newsfilm 1914-1919: The Underexposed War*. New York: Garland, 1983.

The Moving Picture Boys in the Great War. Dir. Larry Ward. Post-Newsweek Television. Sun Valley, CA: Blackhawk Film Library, 1975.

O'Connor, John, and Martin Jackson, eds. *American History/American Film: Interpreting Hollywood Images*. New York: Ungar, 1979.

"Photographic Bulletin No. 4." *Headquarters of the AEF, Office of the Chief Signal Officer, Photographic Division*. 6 Aug. 1918. File 004.5, Records of the AEF, R.G. 120, N.A.

Ramsaye, Terry. *A Million and One Nights*. New York: Simon and Schuster, 1926.

Reid, Hal. Letter to Joseph Tumulty. 22 Apr. 1915. Wilson Papers. Ser. 4. File 72. Reel 199.

Rollins, Peter, ed. *Hollywood as Historian: American Film in a Cultural Context*. Lexington: UP of Kentucky, 1983.

Sklar, Robert. *Movie-Made America: A Cultural History of American Movies*. New York: Random House, 1975.

Smither, Roger. "A Wonderful Idea of the Fighting: The Question of Fakes in 'The Battle of the Somme.'" *Historical Journal of Film, Radio, and Television* 13.2 (1993): 149-68.

Tippet, J. D. "All War Pictures Fake." *Moving Picture World* 3 Oct. 1914: 50.

Ward, Larry. *The Motion Picture Goes to War: The U.S. Government Film Effort during World War I*. Ann Arbor: UMI Research P, 1985.

Wilson, Woodrow. Letter to Douglas Fairbanks. 13 Jan. 1919. Wilson Papers. Ser. 5B. Reel 289.

13

Coming Home from the Great War: World War I Veterans in American Film

James I. Deutsch

Ever since the early 1970s, the alienated and disaffected veteran of Vietnam, unable to readjust to civilian society after the war, has been a familiar figure in American culture. As depicted in American film and fiction, this veteran returns from overseas with serious physical and emotional wounds of war, the result of traumatic combat in jungles and rice paddies, only to incur new—and sometimes even more debilitating—wounds of readjustment upon his postwar encounter with civilians at home. Vietnam veterans and their sympathizers often assume that these representations of Vietnam are *sui generis*, as if the movies and novels about earlier combat veterans, by contrast, always showed them coming home to celebratory parades and optimistic outlooks for the future. What many in the Vietnam generation seem to have forgotten, however, is that the same basic themes, formulas, and characterizations of the alienated and disaffected veteran were likewise employed in the cinematic and fictional depiction of Americans returning from Korea, World War II, and (in its most influential formulation) World War I.

This essay examines the representations in American film of the World War I veteran's return and readjustment to civilian society. Its central thesis is that in these films were established five archetypal narratives, which have persisted essentially intact in the cinema of the United States ever since. Primarily for reasons of box-office sales but also, in part, to help both veterans and civilians cope with the often-difficult transition from war to peace, the formulas for the disaffected and alienated veteran were firmly set in place in the movies and novels that followed World War I, and then never seriously amended—in spite of the profoundly dissimilar historical aftermaths for each of America's twentieth-century wars.

Just as narratives describing the problems faced by combat veterans did not begin with Vietnam, neither did they originate in the period after World War I. Disaffected veterans of the Trojan War, for instance, are the

225

central protagonists in the epic legends of both the Greeks and the Romans: Homer's *Odyssey* (ca. 850 BCE) and Vergil's *Aeneid* (ca. 30 BCE). Likewise, in the Bible, particularly the books of Joshua, Judges, and I and II Samuel (ca. 200 BCE), many of the stories chronicle not only the wars that were fought in the land of Israel, but also the surviving veterans of those battles, including Joshua, Judah, Gideon, Samson, Saul, and David. Similarly, the popular legends in the Middle Ages of King Arthur and his Knights of the Round Table—notably the romances of Lancelot and Perceval attributed to Chrétien de Troyes (ca. 1170)—can also be viewed in part as narratives about the problems faced by veterans of combat, home from the war.

This sweeping summary of ancient and medieval world literature is intended only to suggest that the veteran is a universal character found in many of the most important cultural artifacts produced by a variety of civilizations from around the globe, and that the problem of the veteran's return to peacetime society after battle is a topic that has long concerned the creators and shapers of dramatic narrative. Nevertheless, there are several compelling reasons why it is logical to begin an analysis of veterans' homecomings to the United States with the First World War. For one thing, World War I was the first time that large numbers of American veterans returned home after extended combat overseas. The wars in Mexico during the 1840s and Cuba during the 1890s were relatively close to home, so it was not until the doughboys came back from "over there" in 1918-1919 that the United States first experienced a large-scale demobilization of veterans from a distant foreign war. Secondly, World War I was the first time that contemporary feature-length motion pictures were produced in the immediate aftermath of a war. Obviously, there was no such thing as the cinema at the time of the U.S. Civil War, and none of the roughly one hundred short documentary-like films produced after the Spanish-American War told a story about the return of those soldiers (Niver 495).

The Trauma of World War I

Consequently, the depictions of World War I veterans on film are the first that any contemporary movie audience would have seen. A third and final reason is that World War I marks a profound shift in the nature of warfare that distinguishes it (and its postwar aftermath) from all previous episodes of combat. "Many wars have been fought in modern times," Alfredo Bonadeo has noted, "but never before World War I did so many nations meet on the battlefield, never before were the resources of the combatants so fully engaged, and never before was human life destroyed on such a vast scale" (vii). Although this new mode of warfare did not necessarily create a new breed of veteran, its indelible impact on those who survived the combat was unprecedented, particularly in the way it transformed their identities and personalities (Leed 1-38). Accordingly, it was known at the time not by what we call it today—World War I, which "defines the event as merely the first in a series of global apocalypses"—but as the Great War, "the war of wars" (Gilbert and Gubar 259).

In terms of battlefield hardships and loss of life, the American experience in World War I was relatively mild compared with that of the other principal combatants. During the nineteen months (April 1917 to November 1918) when it was in a state of war, the United States was fighting intensely for only the final twenty-five weeks, sustaining 116,516 service-related deaths (more than half of them victims of disease rather than battle), while in four years of fighting, there were 2.3 million Russian dead, 1.6 million German, 1.45 million Austro-Hungarian, 1.35 million French, and 950,000 British (U.S. Department of Commerce 1140 and Ferro 227).[1]

Nevertheless, the Great War had an enormous impact on American opinion, "all of it negative." By the 1920s and 1930s, the consensus was that "American entry into the war had been a mistake, the consequence of undue influence of either Allied propaganda or American arms manufacturers. . . . The war was seen as a futile aberration of American foreign policy that ended in diplomatic failure, divided the nation, betrayed American liberal promise, and resulted in a mood of disillusion and cynicism that 'spread like a poison gas, to every part of the social body'" (Wynn xv). Having entered the war with "high hopes, high dreams, and high resolve," the Americans returned home thoroughly disillusioned, descending down "a sorry slide into bitterness, isolation, and a lost generation" (Moeller 87). These feelings of bitterness and disillusionment found their fullest expression in the 1920s literature written by members of what has become known as the lost generation.

The Lost Generation Vision:
Dos Passos, Fitzgerald, Hemingway, Faulkner

The passage of some seventy years has created a more critical view of the lost generation writers, especially many of the novelists, who "were not so hopelessly alienated as they chose to pretend," in part because they received "a surprising amount of support from the public they denounced" (Cunliffe 325). But during the interwar period, the cynicism and disillusionment of the lost generation became the attitudinal model to be followed by nearly every writer who aspired to be taken seriously. Not surprisingly, the futility of war and the inability of veterans to readjust successfully to civilian society were two of the topics most favored by the writers of the lost generation. Although a large number of works and writers could be cited here, only a few of the most representative examples will be discussed, specifically those written by four major U.S. authors: John Dos Passos, F. Scott Fitzgerald, Ernest Hemingway, and William Faulkner.

As the oldest of the quartet and the one who saw combat the earliest, Dos Passos was also the first to make it into print with a novel that reflected the cynicism and despair of the nascent Lost Generation. The three protagonists in *Three Soldiers* (1921) are not only crushed by the oppressive machine of war; they continue their tragic descent even after the Armistice, unable to find sanctuary in postwar society. Dan Fuselli, sick with a venereal disease, is court-martialed into permanent K.P. duty with a labor battalion; "Chris" Chrisfield, filled with hatred, deserts the army after murdering the officer who has been his constant nemesis; and John Andrews, also a deserter, though the most sensitive and intelligent of the three, is arrested at the novel's conclusion by the military police, leaving his unfinished musical composition to be scattered by the wind.

Defeat is also the end result for many of the veterans of World War I in F. Scott Fitzgerald's fiction. Perhaps the best example is Gordon Sterrett, a twenty-four-year-old graduate of Yale, recently returned from France but already down to his last dollar, without a job and needing money to pay off the mercenary young woman he has made pregnant. This "spiritless" veteran is the central character in Fitzgerald's short story "May Day" (1920), which begins with Sterrett pathetically seeking (and being denied) a loan from a former college friend, and ends twenty-four hours later with his firing "a cartridge into his head just behind the temple" (64, 125). In between these events, there is a lavish fraternity party at Delmonico's where the "pitiful and wretched" Gordon is snubbed by an ex-girlfriend (90), followed by a riot sparked by a mob of drunken veterans at the office of a socialist newspaper, resulting in the death of one of the veterans. "The soldiers don't know what they want, or what they hate, or what they like," one of the socialists explains (106).

Although other World War I veterans appear in Fitzgerald's later novels—most notably Nick Carraway and Jay Gatsby in *The Great Gatsby* (1925), and Tommy Barban in *Tender Is the Night* (1934)—it would be stretching the point to discuss these works as narratives about the problems faced by veterans of combat, home from the war. However, those problems are addressed much more directly in the fiction of Ernest Hemingway, Fitzgerald's friend and rival, particularly his early stories and novels, such as "Soldier's Home" (1925) and *The Sun Also Rises* (1926), in which the physical and emotional wounds of war figure prominently in the cynicism and alienation of the protagonists. In the confines of his Oklahoma "soldier's home," Harold Krebs, a former Marine, is truly one of the lost. He is not only apathetic and bored with his postwar existence but also disgusted with everything in life, particularly the lies that seem to him inherent to the human condition. However, when Krebs tries to stop lying, telling his mother that he does not love her—indeed does not love anybody—he realizes that "It wasn't any good. He couldn't tell her, he couldn't make her see it. It was silly to have said it" (76). The only solution for Krebs is to move away, to avoid further complications, to keep from hardening like the piece of bacon fat on his breakfast plate that morning.

Jake Barnes, the protagonist of *The Sun Also Rises* shares with Krebs a sense of apathetic alienation. But whereas Krebs's wounds (i.e., his feelings of nausea and disgust) are emotional only, the wounds borne by Barnes are both physical (an injury to the groin that has rendered him sexually impotent) and emotional. "Che mala fortuna!" he is told by a commiserating Italian colonel in a military hospital. "You have given more than your life" (31). Indeed, Barnes has given up on life, enduring sleepless nights and spiritless alcoholic days (except for occasional pleasures at the running of the bulls and the reeling of the fish), all the while displaying the correct composure in conformance with the Hemingway version of a lost generation's ritualistic code. The novel's concluding sentences underscore Barnes's ability to maintain that appearance in spite of his inability to consummate anything in life. Watching a "mounted policeman in khaki . . . raise his baton," Jake responds to his companion's remark that they "could have had such a damned good time together" with a chilling expression of detached disillusion: "Yes. Isn't it pretty to think so?" (259).

Although William Faulkner is not usually cited as belonging to the lost generation, his debut novel and several of his early stories—written before he turned in a more inspired way to his fictional world of Yoknapatawpha County—share much of the same postwar despair and disillusionment already seen in the works of Dos Passos, Fitzgerald, and Hemingway. As early as 1919, Faulkner had begun to develop in poetry and prose what would become *Soldiers' Pay* (1926), the story of a hero in the Royal Air Force who returns home to Georgia with not only a "dreadful scar" across his "tortured brow," and a "drawn and withered" right hand, but also manifesting early signs of blindness and the mark of death about him (25, 27). Indeed, Donald Mahon is so horribly disfigured by the war that his fiancée faints when she first sees him and later, after much agonizing, breaks off their engagement. Although Mahon then marries Margaret Powers, a sympathetic woman widowed by the war, the novel ends bleakly with the disfigured veteran dying just a few weeks later, his final moments filled with the traumatic memory of being wounded in combat, when he saw "his bared bones" and heard "something gnawing through his frontal bone, like mice" (294).

Soldiers' Pay deals more with the varied reactions and feelings of the characters around Donald Mahon than with the readjustment problems of the wounded aviator himself. However, in Faulkner's "Victory," a short story written about the same time, the emphasis is placed on the veteran, Alec Gray, a lower-class Scotsman whose battlefield pluck (and luck) have gained him not only medals but also somewhat amazingly the rank of captain during the war. After the Armistice, "with his cards and his waxed moustache, his sober correct clothes and his stick carried in a manner inimitable," Gray tries to carry on as an English gentleman, failing to realize that postwar society has a different caste system than the military (455). The story chronicles his gradual but inexorable descent into destitution and derangement, selling matchboxes on the street in his "threadbare clothes . . . freshly ironed," staring at passersby "with eyes that were perfectly dead" (463).

In short, as depicted in the American fiction written after World War I, the returning veteran is thoroughly and irredeemably disillusioned by his combat experiences. He carries with him—sometimes visibly (as in a physical disfigurement), but more often not (as in a psychological scar)—the debilitating wounds of war. The veteran's reception by members of postwar society may vary from sympathy to indifference to antipathy, but that is usually of lesser importance to him, seeking as he does "a separate peace" for himself in the postwar world.[2] Nevertheless, his search for peace is almost always doomed to fail; there is no place for the alienated veteran. If not fortunate enough to have died in action, the veteran may later kill himself (like Gordon Sterrett), drift into poverty and insanity (like Alec Gray), end up in jail (like John Andrews), or simply endure his suffering with cynicism and nihilism (like Jake Barnes). Rarely if ever does any hope for the future exist. The veterans of World War I, at least in the fiction of the most famous American authors of the postwar period, are perpetual members of the lost generation, their dues having been paid in full.

The Films: Five Upbeat Formulas

In several respects, the veterans depicted in the U.S. motion pictures that followed World War I resemble their literary counterparts. They return from combat with identical wounds of war, such as disfiguring scars and shell shock. They share a similar sense of disillusionment and alienation, not really caring what becomes of them in the postwar world. And their welcome home covers the same spectrum from sympathy to indifference to antipathy. But the typical denouement for World War I veterans on film is dramatically different from that found in the fiction. Instead of ending, as do most of the novels, with suicide, insanity, and further suffering, the World War I veterans in the movies are almost invariably able to resolve their problems satisfactorily. Either their wounds of war are healed (sometimes miraculously), or their previously bleak situations are suddenly improved.

Most of the roughly 150 U.S. motion pictures depicting the return of World War I veterans to civilian society were produced within the first decade after the war. And by focusing on the narrative or dramatic conventions at work in these films, there emerges from the mass just a handful of formulas, which can be seen as representative or prototypical of the whole. Briefly stated, these five formulas are as follows:

1. The veteran returns with a visible wound of war (such as blindness or a disfiguring scar) that he fears will mark him as pitiable or undesirable, an outcast from society. However, with the help of another person (frequently an attractive woman who loves him), he either comes to understand that there is indeed a place for him in the postwar world, or he experiences a dramatic healing of his wound.

2. The veteran returns suffering from shell shock, often in association with spells of amnesia, which thereby prevent him from readjusting normally to civilian society. However, through a fortunate chain of events (often with the help of a friend or loved one), the veteran is cured of his affliction in the end.

3. The veteran returns to find that his wife or girlfriend has been unfaithful while he was fighting overseas. Depressed and disillusioned, the veteran drifts about until he finds an authentically true love in the end, and realizes that the unfaithful woman was unworthy of him.

4. The veteran returns to find himself the victim of a nefarious plot, sometimes accused of a crime he did not commit, sometimes cheated out of personal property or employment. In the end, however, he succeeds in clearing his name and/or regaining his rightful possessions.

5. The veteran returns with no visible scars nor diagnosable psychoneuroses, only with a vague sense of alienation and disillusionment, which often leads to crime or poverty. In the end, however, often as the result of a chance encounter or occurrence, his perspective on life suddenly brightens into renewed faith and confidence.

Although not all of the 150-plus films depicting World War I veterans fall neatly into one of these five categories, the vast majority do, even sometimes combining several formulas into a single dramatic structure. A few examples should suffice.

In *The Stolen Ranch* (1926), Frank Wilcox and "Breezy" Hart return from the trenches with a friendship cemented when Breezy shared his gas mask after Frank's sprung a leak. Although the horrors of war have left Frank in a state of shell shock, his "nerves near the breaking point," the two buddies head west to claim the Lazy-Z Ranch, willed to Frank by his uncle. But in the meantime, a crooked lawyer and the ranch foreman are scheming to keep the Lazy-Z for themselves. After Frank one day tumbles off a rock in a panic when hearing a gunshot, the villains get the idea to "put Wilcox out of the way quick" by firing their guns, thinking this will scare him away for good. But Frank stoutly stands his ground and fights, until Breezy comes to the rescue with the original will that proves the veteran's claim to the ranch. In the end, both Frank and Breezy have found female companions, but only Frank can exclaim, "The shell shock is gone. I'm cured" (quotations from the film's intertitles).

Indeed, in nearly every case of cinematic shell shock, the veteran is suddenly and conclusively healed. Even if the shell shock is associated with some other debilitating ailment—e.g., with amnesia in *The Skyway-man* (1920), *Wandering Fires* (1925), *Closed Gates* (1927), *Absent* (1928), and *Three Live Ghosts* (1929); with deafness in *Puppets* (1926); or with cowardice in *Shootin' for Love* (1923) and *Cross Breed* (1927) —the cure is just as certain. Similarly, many of the veterans who return home blinded from the war are likely to find their sight restored by the picture's conclusion, as in *The Jilt* (1922), *The Sixth Commandment* (1924), and *Remember* (1926); while in *Humoresque* (1920) and *Lucky Star* (1929), it is a crippling or paralyzing injury that is overcome in the end. The most miraculous cure of all, however, occurs in *The Enchanted Cottage* (1924), in which a horribly disfigured veteran is transformed (through the magic of the movies as much as by the enchantment of the cottage) from disfigurement to handsomeness—at least in the eyes of his loving wife.

Of course, not every war injury is healed so dramatically. There are no cases, for example, of amputated limbs suddenly regenerating, though that is not to say that the veteran in the movies who has lost an arm or leg is unable to come to terms with his affliction. Perhaps the best known instance of amputation occurs in *The Big Parade* (1925), in which the wealthy Jim Apperson goes off to war insouciantly. Eventually embittered by combat, Apperson returns home not only minus a leg, but also to discover that his fiancée has fallen in love with his own brother. The cold stare on his face, while sitting in a car, smoking a cigarette, is a brilliant visual representation of the veteran's alienation. And when Apperson's deceitful brother claims, "You look great, Jim, old man," the one-legged veteran snarls, "Don't try to kid me. I know what I look like." Nevertheless, *The Big Parade* concludes on the usual upbeat note, with Apperson returning to France, happily hobbling up a hill with a cane and prosthesis to embrace his true love, a French peasant girl.

Indeed, in the movies made after World War I, it was not uncommon for the veteran to return home and find that his wife or girlfriend has been unfaithful. In *Paris Green* (1920), for example, a veteran named Luther "Paris" Green returns to his small rural village only to be rejected by his girlfriend. Depressed, he drifts to the city of New York, where he is startled to see Ninon Robinet, the French lass he had befriended in Paris after the war. When Ninon is abducted by villainous kidnappers, Luther rides a horse to the rescue—and a happy ending. More serious examples of infidelity include *Sorrell and Son* (1927), based on Warwick Deeping's 1925 novel, in which a former captain returns to his London home to find that his wife has run off with another man, leaving him with their infant son; *The Mating Call* (1928), about a Florida farmer who after the war learns that his wife has had their marriage annulled in order to marry a wealthier man; and *Wolves of the Air* (1927), in which the veteran returns to discover not only that his former assistant has married his sweetheart, but that the same dastard has gained control of his family's airplane factory.

Although losing control of the family factory is a rather unconventional plot complication, it corresponds closely to one of the most common screen formulas after World War I: the veteran who returns from the war to find himself cheated out of the ranch that is rightfully his. In addition to *The Stolen Ranch* (discussed earlier), other examples, some with slightly varied action, include *Catch My Smoke* (1922), *The Pride of Palomar* (1922), *Headin' West* (1922), *Four Hearts* (1922), *The Galloping Ace* (1924), *Riding Double* (1924), *The Fighting Boob* (1926), and *West of the Rainbow's End* (1926). In nearly every case, the denouement is identical: the veteran thwarts the villain(s), regains the ranch, and gets the girl.

The same resolution occurs in a slight variant on this cheated-out-of-the-ranch formula, one in which the veteran is accused of (or oftentimes framed for) a crime he did not commit. Although momentarily depressed over this obvious injustice, the veteran quickly rallies to his own defense, often in league with an attractive woman who has also been victimized by the villains. Examples include *Clarence* (1922), *Four Hearts* (1922), *Find Your Man* (1924), *Cactus Trails* (1925), *Transcontinental Limited* (1926), and *The Action Craver* (1927).

In the final category of films, the veteran actually may be guilty of a crime, though, if so, it is almost always the result of his war-induced disillusionment. Or if he is not exactly a criminal, the veteran-protagonist may be living very close to the edge, drifting aimlessly after the war, sometimes as a gambler or con man, sometimes as a hobo, tramp, or bum. But whatever his sorry state may be, the veteran invariably sees the errors of his ways, and is reformed to a more wholesome life. Some examples include *The Struggle* (1921), *The Back Trail* (Universal Pictures, 1924), *Under the Rouge* (1925), *Burning Bridges* (1928), and *Square Shoulders* (1929).

A principal message found in all five categories of films is that the postwar environment to which the veteran returns in 1918 and 1919 is not the same one he left in 1917 on his way to make the world safe for democracy. The ranch, the job, and/or the loved ones he was expecting to find at home are no longer his. As a result of the war, the veteran's ideals have been shattered, occasionally along with his sight, hearing, appearance, mobility, and mental health. Not surprisingly, these are the same situations that the novels of the 1920s depicted for returning veterans of World War I. But in the movies of the same decade, the veteran's disappointment, disillusionment, and often even his disability, are shown to be transitory. The films end not with defeat, despair, and death, but with confidence and optimism in a brighter-looking future.

The Persistence of Formula in the 1930s

These same patterns persist in American film throughout the 1930s. *Born to Love* (1931), for example, recycles the ever-popular "Enoch Arden" theme, in which the veteran returns home years after being reported missing in action. Naturally, the story ends happily when the wife's postwar husband conveniently dies, thereby awarding the original couple custody of the child they conceived shortly before the veteran disappeared behind German lines. An even better example from the same period is *Girl of the Port* (1930), in which the veteran-protagonist returns from the war as an alcoholic (known as Whiskey Johnny) who is fearful of fire, the result of a traumatic combat incident involving German flame-throwers. Describing the horror some years later, the veteran graphically recalls how

the fire came hissing, curling, like water, twenty, fifty feet, and whatever it touched, it burned, flesh and bone and brain. I saw them burn. The boys beside me, just boys, most of them crying like children, calling on God to end them, wrapped in fire. We cried "God on the right," only God wasn't with us that time. I came through alive, the only one alive. Lying in a shellhole, with my leg broken under me, watching the others crisp up and die, hearing them die, seeing the fire draw nearer, nearer, seeing it all around me. Oh, God, don't let the fire get me! Don't let the fire get me!

As if this horrifying wound of war were not enough, *Girl of the Port* borrows from another of the five formulaic patterns by making the veteran the victim of an unfaithful girlfriend. "I was going to marry a girl," he explains. "A cousin of mine, frightfully good looking. She swore she'd help me fight that fear, the fire fear, you understand." But in the week before the wedding, the veteran discovers that instead "it was my friend she loved, my best friend. She despised me because of the fear, just a poor coward, only fit to give her the things she wanted, while she laughed behind my back, in my friend's arms. My best friend, laughing together at my fear of the fire." However, by the end of the film, when challenged to participate in the fire-walking rites of Benga Island, the veteran miraculously overcomes his fears, enabling him in just a few minutes of screen time to defeat the villain, arrange a marriage with the woman who has befriended him, and rejoin his wealthy aristocratic family.

One of the best-known films of the 1930s about World War I veterans, *Heroes for Sale* (1933), is still another example of the standard cinematic formula at work, casting a suffering protagonist into the depths of despair before inevitably resolving his problems in the end. Tom Holmes returns from the war addicted to the morphine prescribed to allay the pain of his combat wounds, thus necessitating his committal to a state narcotics farm. After his cure, Tom achieves prosperity by investing in laundry machinery, only to be unjustly imprisoned for leading a mob into battle against the police, and subsequently banished from town upon his release. Ignored by an ungrateful society, Tom "joins the army of unemployed transients, riding the freights across the country in search of work. He too has become a fugitive, hunted and persecuted, chased out of towns and herded into boxcars. Voicing the indignation of the forgotten man, he tells a policeman, 'We're not tramps. We're ex-servicemen'" (Roffman and Purdy 85). If *Heroes for Sale* were like most of the novels about the veterans of World War I, it would end at that point, or perhaps with Tom committing suicide in despair. But in the realm of the movies, the veteran's salvation is nearly always assured. Despite his years of suffering and humiliation, Tom still has faith in the system. The fearless inaugural address of President Franklin D. Roosevelt, combined with the gospel of Christian sacrifice and martyrdom, bring Tom renewed hope and an upbeat resolution.

Certainly there are exceptions to these generalizations, for film as well as fiction. Just as not every novel about a World War I veteran concludes pessimistically in lost generation despair—Zane Grey's *The Call of the Canyon* (1924), for instance, ends with the veteran being reunited with his fiancée—so, too, not every film ends with unalloyed buoyancy. One well-known picture, *I Am a Fugitive from a Chain Gang* (1932), concludes with the unjustly hunted veteran retreating back into darkness and despair, where he has "no friends, no rest, no peace," and survives only by stealing. Similarly, the film version of Hemingway's "Soldier's Home"—which, significantly, was a non-Hollywood production—does not deviate from the short story's conclusion; Harold Krebs leaves home rather than face any of life's complications. But as exceptions, these relatively rare instances prove the rule: both literary and film narratives for returning veterans are bound less by historical circumstances and more by convention and formula.

Historical Comparisons with World War II

Perhaps the best test of this hypothesis is to compare the cinematic depictions of veterans from two contrasting historical periods. Take, for instance, the veterans of World War II, who like the doughboys of World War I, had journeyed overseas to fight, in some cases on the same European ground against a renascent German enemy, and who likewise returned home as victorious veterans of the war. But there the historical similarities largely cease. The demobilization of U.S. troops after the sudden cessation of hostilities in November 1918 was not particularly well planned or administered. At the time, there was "no American precedent worth following and few European examples to emulate," which meant that the Army was left "stumbling toward the most expeditious solution it could find" (Noggle 9-10). The problem was compounded by the varying—if not also conflicting—postwar objectives sought by representatives of labor, business, government, and the military. In addition, many of the nation's leaders, "who could have given reality to at least a few economic and social improvements, were silent or preoccupied with international ideals, and the majority of the citizens followed the same course" (Mock and Thurber 30).

By February 24, 1919, when the U.S. Congress finally awarded a bonus of sixty dollars for every officer and enlisted man, nearly 1.3 million veterans had already been mustered out, and the sixty dollars was, in any case, "a paltry sum" (Wecter 312 and Ross 12). To make matters worse, these multitudes of men were being "discharged into a labor market which was already glutted with unemployed war workers and former government employees" (Mock and Thurber 39). In contrast, the demobilization of World War II troops had been planned for more than a year, and was built around the bountiful provisions of the Servicemen's

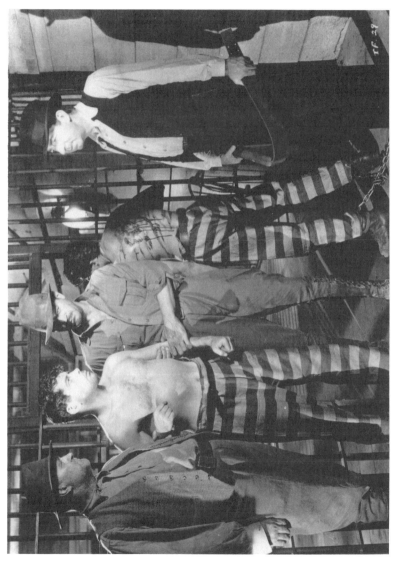

The World War I veteran is accused of a crime he did not commit—Paul Muni as James Allen in *I Am a Fugitive from a Chain Gang*. Credit: The Film Archive

Homer Parrish, Peggy Stephenson, Fred Derry, Milly Stephenson, Al Stephenson, and (above) Butch Engle are back together after World War II in *The Best Years of Our Lives*.

Credit: The Film Archive

Readjustment Act of 1944 (better known as the GI Bill of Rights). Consequently, the veterans of World War II—unlike their predecessors who had marched on Washington in a vain effort to receive war bonuses—received extraordinarily generous benefits for hospitalization, disability allowances, home and farm loans, education, employment, and more. A second important difference is that whereas World War I stopped with an armistice, a word that proved all too prophetic—in that the suspension of hostilities lasted not much more than twenty years—World War II ended in surrender, final and unconditional, bringing a long-lasting peace, if not also an enduring alliance, among the nations that had once fought so bitterly against each other. Although there were fears in 1945 that a new war against the Soviet Union would soon be in America's future, there were no doubts that the Axis Powers had been conclusively defeated.

But for all the differences in the historical aftermaths of World Wars I and II, the depictions in American film of combat veterans coming home from those two wars are remarkably alike. Rooted in the very same formulas and conventions established after World War I, the veteran-protagonists of World War II received the same treatment in the movies, even as they were receiving a substantially different treatment at home. Perhaps the best example of this phenomenon is the most celebrated film of the World War II-veteran genre, *The Best Years of Our Lives* (1946), in which nearly every one of the five dramatic formulas from World War I can be found.

A Comparative from World War II:
The Best Years of Our Lives

The veteran who returns with a visible wound of war that he fears will mark him as pitiable or undesirable is epitomized by Homer Parrish, who returns home from the Navy without any arms below the elbow—the result of a fire on board his ship—and must try to readjust with steel hooks instead of hands. In spite of the skill with which he uses his hooks, Homer feels extremely self-conscious about his disability, believing that people either regard him as a freak or are pitying him. In one particularly chilling scene, Homer crashes both hooks through a glass window, angrily thinking that the children watching outside have been making fun of him. However, by the end of the film, Homer has come to terms with his disability, and has found his place in the postwar world. As per the usual formula, Homer's conversion is effected by the unwavering support of his fiancée, who sees the veteran at his most helpless moment, after his hooks and harness have been removed for the night, but reassures him nevertheless, "I love you and I'm never going to leave you. Never."[3]

The veteran who returns suffering from shell shock, which prevents him from readjusting normally to civilian society, is epitomized by Fred Derry (played by Dana Andrews), a former bombardier in the Army Air Forces. On his first night back home, Fred wakes up screaming, vividly recalling (not unlike Whiskey Johnny in *Girl of the Port*) a traumatic incident from the skies over Berlin:

This is it. She's on fire, she's on fire. Out at two o'clock. Number three engine smoking. Watch it. Fire's spreading. It's Gadorsky. There goes number four. She's breaking formation. Watch out for fighters. It's spreading to the wing. The wing's on fire. She's out of control, she's out of control. Bail out! Jump! Get out of there! Bail out, Gadorsky! Gadorsky, get out of that plane!

Gadorsky, however, did not survive the crash; and Fred's nightmares continue throughout the film, causing his wife to doubt his sanity. "Can't you get those things out of your system?" she asks in her characteristic insensitive way. "Maybe that's what's holding you back. You know, the war's over. You won't get anyplace until you stop thinking about it. Come on, snap out of it." Naturally, by the end of the film, Fred finally does snap out of it.

Fred Derry also epitomizes the veteran who returns to find that his wife or girlfriend has been unfaithful. While Fred was overseas winning the Distinguished Flying Cross for "heroism, devotion to duty, professional skill, and coolness under fire," his wife, Marie, was working in a nightclub. When Fred asks her about other men while he was away, she replies, "I knew lots of people. What did you think I was doing all those years?" However, as per the usual formula, Fred realizes that Marie is unworthy of him, and finds in Peggy Stephenson an authentically true love in the end. Finally, the veteran who returns with no visible scars nor psychoneuroses, only a vague sense of alienation and disillusionment, is epitomized by Al Stephenson (played by Fredric March), a former Army sergeant. Although he comes home all in one piece to his loving wife, Milly, and a promotion at the Cornbelt Loan and Trust Co., where he worked before the war, Al is troubled by his return to postwar society. His children have matured almost beyond recognition, and his employers are so intent on making money that they are reluctant to grant loans to needy veterans. Al's uneasiness is momentarily alleviated by alcohol, but by the end of the film, he has stood up to his superiors at the bank and is ready to face the future with renewed faith and confidence.

Conclusion

These same formulas are followed in nearly every other film about the return of veterans from World War II (see Deutsch for numerous other examples). And if a cinematic formula proves successful for the ex-servicemen of World Wars I and II, the enterprising but cautious film-makers in Hollywood are much more likely to recycle it for subsequent veterans from Korea and Vietnam than they are to take a risk and try to deal with a new set of circumstances, even though the historical after-maths of Korea and Vietnam wars were obviously different.

Of course, all veterans who return home from battle must undergo the difficult transition from soldier to civilian. To some extent, the cine-matic continuity from one war to another in the veteran's narrative is a reflection of age-old concerns regarding the return from battle to peace-time society of the warrior, a near-universal character who can be found in narratives from around the globe. Veterans of all wars and from all cultures may be the only group of people permitted to enter the forbid-den realm where the killing of other human beings is (temporarily) sanc-tioned by society. The transition from soldier to civilian is often a diffi-cult passage therefore, frequently fraught with tensions and anxieties not only for the veterans themselves, but also for their noncombatant friends and families. What may be needed for many such individuals is a cathar-tic release in both body and mind of the contaminations wrought by war. Such cultural needs may account in part for the consistency of cinematic representations from one war to the next.

However, it is also clear that the commercial exigencies of motion-picture production frequently rely on time-tested and box-office-proven formulas. Whether for westerns, musicals or returning veterans, these generic forms are repeated so frequently that they are able to transcend the events and circumstances of chronological history. If a formula proves successful for the veterans of World War I, the enterprising but cautious filmmakers in Hollywood are much more likely to recycle it for the veterans of World War II (or Korea or Vietnam) than they are to take a risk and try to invent something new. Thus it is that the formulas and conventions that were established for the films about U.S. veterans in the wake of the World War I have found repeated resonance in the after-maths of not only a "Great War" but even a "Good War," a "Forgotten War," and a "Debated War."

Notes

An earlier version of this essay was first presented at the International Association for Media and History conference in Amsterdam, July 1993. For access to many of the films described, I would like to thank the National Endowment for the Humanities for a Travel to Collections grant, and particularly the staff members at both the Wisconsin Center for Film and Theater and Research and the Motion Picture, Broadcasting, and Recorded Sound Division at the Library of Congress.

1. It should be noted that these figures do not include deaths occurring after 1918 that may be attributable to injuries or illnesses incurred during the war. For instance, Clark estimates an additional "60,000 to 65,000 post-war deaths, caused by the War," among U.S. servicemen (184).

2. This well-known phrase is first found in Ernest Hemingway, chapter 6, *In Our Time* (81): "You and me we've made a separate peace," says a wounded Nick Adams to Rinaldi; and then repeated by Frederic Henry in *A Farewell to Arms* (New York: Scribner, 1929): "I did not want to read about the war. I was going to forget the war. I had made a separate peace" (260).

3. In a casting move very unusual for the time, Homer Parrish was portrayed on the screen by Harold Russell, an actual Army veteran who had lost his hands in an explosion while training in North Carolina on D-Day, June 6, 1944. For his performance, Russell won two Academy Awards, one of which he recently sold at auction (Purdum).

Works Cited

The Best Years of Our Lives. Prod. Samuel Goldwyn. Dir. William Wyler. RKO, 1946.

The Big Parade. Prod. Irving Thalberg. Dir. King Vidor. Metro-Goldwyn-Mayer, 1925.

Bonadeo, Alfredo. *Mark of the Beast: Death and Degradation in the Literature of the Great War*. Lexington: UP of Kentucky, 1989.

Born to Love. Prod. Pathé. Dir. Paul L. Stein. RKO, 1931.

Clark, John Maurice. *The Costs of the World War to the American People*. New Haven: Yale UP, 1931.

Cunliffe, Marcus. *The Literature of the United States*. 4th ed. New York: Penguin, 1986.

Deutsch, James I. "Coming Home from 'The Good War': World War II Veterans in American Film and Fiction." Diss. George Washington U, 1991.

Dos Passos, John. *Three Soldiers*. New York: Doran, 1921.

Faulkner, William. *Soldiers' Pay*. New York: Boni and Liveright, 1926.

——. "Victory." *These Thirteen*. New York: Cape and Smith, 1931. Rpt. in *Collected Stories of William Faulkner*. New York: Random House, 1950.

Ferro, Marc. *The Great War*. Trans. Nicole Stone. London: Routledge, 1973.

Fitzgerald, F. Scott. "May Day." *Smart Set* July 1920: 3-32. Rpt. in Fitzgerald, *Tales of the Jazz Age*. New York: Scribner, 1922.

Gilbert, Sandra M., and Susan Gubar. *No Man's Land: The Place of the Woman Writer in the Twentieth Century*. Vol. 2: *Sexchanges*. New Haven: Yale UP, 1989.

Girl of the Port. Dir. Bert Glennon. RKO, 1930.

Hemingway, Ernest. "Soldier's Home." *In Our Time*. New York: Boni and Liveright, 1925. Rev. ed., New York: Scribner, 1930.

——. *The Sun Also Rises*. New York: Scribner, 1926.

Heroes for Sale. Prod. Hal Wallis. Dir. William Wellman. Warner Bros., 1933.

I Am a Fugitive from a Chain Gang. Prod. Hal Wallis. Dir. Mervyn LeRoy. Warner Bros., 1932.

Leed, Eric J. *No Man's Land: Combat and Identity in World War I*. Cambridge: Cambridge UP, 1979.

The Mating Call. Prod. Howard Hughes. Dir. James Cruze. Paramount, 1928.

Mock, James R., and Evangeline Thurber. *Report on Demobilization*. Norman: U of Oklahoma P, 1944.

Moeller, Susan D. *Shooting War: Photography and the American Experience of Combat*. New York: Basic, 1989.

Niver, Kemp R. *Early Motion Pictures: The Paper Print Collection in the Library of Congress*. Washington, D.C.: Library of Congress, 1985.

Noggle, Burl. *Into the Twenties: The United States from Armistice to Normalcy*. Urbana: U of Illinois P, 1974.

Paris Green. Prod. Thomas H. Ince. Dir. Jerome Storm. Famous Players-Lasky, 1920.

Purdum, Todd S. "His Best Years Past, Veteran in Debt Sells Oscar He Won." *New York Times* 7 Aug. 1992: A10.

Roffman, Peter, and Jim Purdy. *The Hollywood Social Problem Film: Madness, Despair, and Politics from the Depression to the Fifties*. Bloomington: Indiana UP, 1981.

Ross, David R. B. *Preparing for Ulysses: Politics and Veterans During World War II*. New York: Columbia UP, 1969.

Soldier's Home. Prod. David B. Appleton. Dir. Robert Young. American Short Story, 1977.

Sorrell and Son. Prod. Joseph M. Schenck. Dir. Herbert Brenon. United Artists, 1927.

The Stolen Ranch. Prod. Carl Laemmle. Dir. William Wyler. Universal, 1926.

U.S. Department of Commerce, Bureau of the Census. *Historical Statistics of the United States: Colonial Times to 1970*, Part 2. Washington, D.C.: GPO, 1975.

Wecter, Dixon. *When Johnny Comes Marching Home*. Boston: Houghton Mifflin, 1944.

Wolves of the Air. Prod. and dir. Francis Ford. Sterling, 1927.

Wynn, Neil A. *From Progressivism to Prosperity: World War I and American Society*. New York: Holmes, 1986.

14

The Great War Revisioned:
A World War I Filmography

Gerald Herman

Note: All of the dramatic films listed below appear in the following way: *Title* (release date-language if other than English-length at release/edited length-16mm rental source/video source) alternate title. Video sources are always preceded by a slash (/) even if no 16mm rental source has been discovered by the author. Given the volatility of this industry, the source listings should be regarded as accurate at the time the text was written and should be viewed as starting points for searches thereafter.

Dramatic Films: Prelude

A British television series, *The Fall of Eagles* (1976), dramatized the dynastic intrigues and failures that resulted in the wartime collapse of the Hapsburg, Hohenzollern, and Romanov regimes. The series begins with Bismarck and the death of Kaiser Wilhelm I and ends with the abdication of his grandson in 1918. C. L. Sulzberger wrote a companion volume with the same title for the series.

Port Arthur (1983-Japanese-140 min.-/Video City Productions) is a Japanese epic on the Russo-Japanese War and on generals Nogi and Kodama's strategy for capturing the city.

The covert activities that accompanied the diplomacy and arms race of the pre-war era is explored in the early episodes of the twelve-part Thames-PBS Masterpiece Theatre production of *Reilly, Ace of Spies* (1987-672 min.-/HBO Video—an 80-minute theatrical condensation of its early episodes has also been released and is available from Facets Multimedia) that deal with the shady and sometimes self-serving activities of Rosenblum (Reilly's real name). These activities were on behalf of the British Secret Service to safeguard the Persian oil discoveries of William D'Arcy, to provide British ally Japan with needed information about Port Arthur's defenses at the outbreak of the Russo-Japanese War, and to secure for Britain German Naval designs by making sure that post-war Russian fleet rebuilding orders were placed with the German shipbuilding firm of Blohm and Voss (for whom Reilly worked) so that German designs could be stolen for the British—that the British Vickers firm failed to get the contract was a source of embarrassment for munitions magnate Basil Zaharoff, who plotted against Reilly.

Much less successful as a prewar spy was Austro-Hungarian Colonel Alfred Redl whose extravagant expenditures and promiscuous homosexual affairs opened him to Russian offers of money for information. His treason, discovery, and suicide in 1913 is the subject of István Szabó's *Colonel Redl* (1985-Hungarian/German-149 min.-/Facets Multimedia) inspired by John Osborne's 1965 play *A Patriot for Me.* Klaus Maria Brandauer's Colonel is more sympathetically portrayed in the film than he has been in history.

Riddle of the Sands (1984-102 min.-/Vid America) is based on the 1903 Erskine Childers novel about two young Englishmen who discover, while sailing off the coast of Germany in 1901, a plot to invade England. It is ironic that Childers, though a Protestant Englishman who fought on the western front in 1914, was a committed Irish nationalist who planned the running of German guns into Ireland in preparation for the Easter Uprising, fought the British in the aftermath of the war, and was executed by the Free State government near the end of the sectarian Troubles in 1922.

Rocambole Contre Services Secret (1962-French-96 min.), based on Ponson du Terrail's novel, transposes the novel's Victorian-era setting to London in 1903 to tell its story about how the con man Rocambole helps the British Secret Service compromise a German diplomat.

A Nazi era German film, *Ziel im den Wolken* (1937-German without subtitles-101 min.-/International Historic Films), is a film about a young German cavalry officer who battles against the conservative bureaucracy for military aviation in the prewar period.

Pascali's Island (1988-101 min.-/Live Home Video) uses the growing prewar tensions in a story of intrigue and betrayal on a Turkish-controlled Greek island in the last days of the Ottoman Empire.

Joseph Conrad's 1907 novel, *The Secret Agent,* about an agent provocateur who, caught between his Russian and British handlers, persuades his brother-in-law to commit an anarchist act of violence, formed the basis for Alfred Hitchcock's *Sabotage* (1936-76 min.-Kit Parker Films/Video Yesteryear) also known as *A Woman Alone,* and, under its original title, has been made into a Masterpiece Theatre series (1992-180 min.) and a theatrically released feature film (1996-105 min.).

The assassination of Austro-Hungarian Archduke Francis Ferdinand and his wife Sophie by Serbian-trained Bosnian nationalists is recreated in *The Day that Shook the World* (1978-111 min.-/Vid-America).

When Russia signed the humiliating treaty of Portsmouth, it was the last straw for many Russians suffering under Tsarist oppression. The resulting 1905 revolution and its aftermath are the subjects of portions of *The Fall of Eagles* and of *Nicholas and Alexandra* (see below). Learning Corporation of America has excerpted this part of the movie in *Nicholas and Alexandra: Prelude to Revolution-1904-1905* (1976-29 min.-Kent State University Audio Visual Rentals).

Several Soviet films deal with these events including the Stalin era docudrama *Revolutionists* (1936-Russian-107 min.-Corinth Films) and the two versions of Maxim Gorky's 1907 novel, *Mother*, about revolutionaries in an industrial town. Vsevolod Pudovkin made the classic silent version (1926-87 min.-Kino International/International Historic Films) and it was remade as *1905* (1955-Russian-92 min.-Corinth Films) to commemorate the revolution's fiftieth anniversary.

The most famous film of the 1905 revolution is Sergei Eisenstein's *Potemkin* (1925-Russian-silent-67 min.-Films Inc./Facets Multimedia—a restored version [65 min.-/Facets Multimedia] is also available) about the mutiny of the Black Sea fleet. Its Odessa Steps sequence—one of the most famous (and copied) in cinema history—is available separately from the Museum of Modern Art.

The industrial conditions that followed the Revolution, as its hard-won reforms were one-by-one withdrawn or subverted, are the subject of Eisenstein's first film, *Strike* (1924-Russian-silent-66 min.-Kino International/Facets Multimedia), and of the first two parts of Grigori Kozintsev and Leonid Trauberg's, *Maxim Trilogy, The Youth of Maxim* (1934-Russian-80 min.-Corinth Films) and *The Return of Maxim* (1937-Russian).

Several films deal with the Siberian monk who, by controlling the Tsarevitch's hemophilia, was able to exert enormous influence over the boy's mother, the Tsarina Alexandra. *Rasputin and the Empress* (1932-125 min.-Films Inc.), *Nights of Rasputin* (1960-Italian-95 min.-Films Inc.), *Agoniya/Rasputin* (1978-Russian-104 min.-/Facets Multimedia), and *Rasputin* (1996-120 min.-/HBO Home Video) are examples of this minor, somewhat lurid, and not terribly accurate genre.

Dramatic Films and the Wartime Propaganda War

Films of the Great War began being made during the war itself and the history of attitudes toward the war can be traced by studying the moods of its movies both during the war and thereafter. Beginning with such films as *England Expects* (1914), films made in the various combatant nations reflected the war-aims and passions of those countries. In Germany, the "war heroine"—the woman who bravely endured the separation and sacrifices demanded by the Fatherland—was particularly extolled and the actress Henny Porten became the quintessential representative of the type in such films as *Die Ehe der Luise Rohrbach* [*The Marriage of Luise Rohrbach*] (1916-silent) and *Die Faust des Riesen* [*The Iron Fist*] (1917-silent), based on Rudolf Stratz's novel. The fact that Porten's own husband, actor-director Kurt Stark, was killed at the front only added to her tragic aura.

Initially, American films either proclaimed neutral abhorrence of war—D. W. Griffith's *Intolerance* (1916-silent-208/123 min.-Films Inc./Video Yesteryear) is the greatest of these—or feigned hatred of war while pointing squarely at its villains—though Thomas Ince's *Civilization* (1916-102 min.-Museum of Modern Art/Video Yesteryear) projects an overtly pacifist message and was credited with helping Woodrow Wilson win his "he kept us out of war" 1916 presidential campaign; the warmongers of the fictional kingdom are so clearly Germanic that the film was banned in neutral Sweden.

J. Stuart Blackton's *Battle Cry of Peace* (1915) was based on Hudson Maxim's (brother of the machine gun inventor) *Defenseless America*, endorsed by Theodore Roosevelt, made a fortune in wartime Britain, and became a rallying symbol for the American preparedness movement. Yet when war came to America, the film was considered too tame and was re-released in an edited form as *The Battle Cry of War*. A sequel, *Womanhood, the Glory of the Nation* was also produced.

Once war was declared by the United States in 1917, American films quickly adopted the country's wartime stance and, under the watchful eye of the Creel Committee, helped to whip the country into a war frenzy.

Robert Goldstone, the man whose company provided the costumes for D. W. Griffith's 1915 epic *Birth of a Nation,* was inspired by that involvement to produce an epic of his own on the American Revolution. His film, whose British villains perpetrate the Wyoming Valley Massacre, was released in the summer of 1917 as *The Spirit of '76* (1917-only some single reels are known to exist). In the hysteria of war, which by then had engulfed the country, Goldstone (a Jew of German extraction) was convicted of violating Title IX of the Espionage Act, despite the fact that the court conceded that there was no evidence of German involvement and that the film's portrayal of historical events was accurate. He was fined and given a ten-year prison sentence for sowing disloyalty among the Armed Forces. In 1919 President Wilson commuted the sentence, but the fine and legal fees bankrupted him.

Cecil B. DeMille's *The Little American* (1917-80 min.-Festival Films/Grapevine Video) with Mary Pickford, and D. W. Griffith's

British commissioned (and partly shot in England and France) *Hearts of the World* (1918-122 min.-Kit Parker/Facets Multimedia) with Lillian and Dorothy Gish are the best of the pro-war genre.

Winsor McCay's *Sinking of the Lusitania* (1918-19 min.) represents an early animated film and a powerful piece of wartime propaganda.

Many propaganda films of lesser quality, but of equal or greater hysterical passion, ranging from *My Four Years in Germany* (1918-Budget Films) based upon and made in cooperation with U.S. Ambassador James W. Gerard, and *The Kaiser, the Beast of Berlin* (1918), to Raoul Walsh's *The Prussian Cur* (1918), whose blatant encouragement of lynching as the appropriate punishment for disloyal German Americans caused the film to be withdrawn. Another film, *The Eagle's Eye* (1918-presumed lost), based on retired U.S. Secret Service Chief William J. Flynn's memoir, tells the story of pre-American entry, German sabotage and espionage activities in the U.S., focusing on the work of Captains Franz von Papen (later to become German Chancellor and ally of Hitler) and Karl Boy-Ed.

American film stars including Mary Pickford, Douglas Fairbanks, Sr., and Charlie Chaplin made nationwide Liberty Bond drive appearances and Chaplin made a short film called *The Bond* (1918-11 min.-Filmic Archives/Video Yesteryear) encouraging American support. His *Shoulder Arms* (1918-42 min.-/Fox Video), released just before the armistice, is one of the few comedies and the most enduring film of this period. Though many of the conventions of wartime propaganda were used in the film, and Charlie himself captures Kaiser Bill, it all turns out to be the dream of a new recruit. Chaplin was warned by Cecil B. DeMille that a war related comedy might be in bad taste, but when the film was released it became an instant success.

The Interwar Years: Memories of Wartime Experiences

The World War I films of the 1920s and early 1930s provided recollections—some nostalgic, some horrific, some tinged with antiwar sentiment—of the often futile heroism and comraderie of the war. The first of these was Rex Ingram's *The Four Horsemen of the Apocalypse* (1921-silent-114 min.-Swank), based on Vincente Blasco-Ibañez's 1916 novel about a family whose sons fight one another in the war. It was the film that made Rudolph Valentino a star. It was remade in a World War II setting (1961-153 min.-Swank/MGM-UA Home Video), but the original is better.

In 1922, Irish director I. G. Eppel made *Irish Destiny*, a love story set against the background of "The Troubles." It features the burning of the Dublin Customs House.

Two films, one, King Vidor's *The Big Parade* (1925-silent-126 min.-Swank/Facets Multimedia) based on a story by Laurence Stallings (who, as a Marine, had lost his leg in battle, which was recreated in the film), and the other, Stallings (and Maxwell Anderson's) antiwar play *What Price Glory?* (1926-silent-120 min.-Museum of Modern Art/Critics Choice Video), were the best of this period. The latter film's director, Raoul Walsh, softened the antiwar content of the play in favor of the broad comedy of the Captain Flagg/Sergeant Quirt confrontations (lip-readers find a whole new dimension in these). The recreation of the Battle of Belleau Wood is quite realistic. Early in the sound era, Walsh made a sequel called *The Cock-Eyed World* (1929-118 min.) about the two protagonists continuing their private war on a south-Pacific island after the war. John Ford remade the original (1952-111 min./Key Video) with James Cagney and Dan Dailey.

The other silent epic of this period is former Lafayette Flying Squadron combat pilot William Wellman's *Wings* (1927-139 min.-Films Inc./Key Video), which extensively employed the services of the U.S. Army and Army Air Corps in its story of two typical American boys, in love with the same girl, who join the Army Air Corps and fight in France. Its climax was a full-scale reconstruction of the Battle of St. Mihiel, filmed near San Antonio, Texas. Despite the advent of sound, *Wings* (released with recorded sound effects, but no spoken dialogue) won the first best picture Academy Award.

The dogged and romantic glory of the air war became a popular topic for movies thereafter: *Lilac Time* (1928-silent-90 min.-/Critics Choice Video), the story of an English flyer (Gary Cooper) who falls in love with a French farm woman (Colleen Moore) on whose land sits the aerodrome from which he flies into combat, is one example of this genre. Howard Hughes's *Hell's Angels* (1930-125 min.-Swank/Facets Multimedia) is another—its early technicolor ball sequence has recently been rediscovered.

The two versions of John Monk Saunders's *The Dawn Patrol* (1930-95/82 min.-/MGM-UA Home Video), directed by Howard Hawks, and its more famous but inferior remake (1938-103 min.-Swank/Facets Multimedia) are a third. Saunders and Wellman joined forces to make another air war epic, *Legion of the Lost* (1928-silent-82 min.) with Gary Cooper and Fay Wray. As with many silent films released in the midst of the sound revolution, no print of this film currently exists.

Michael Curtiz, who had made a number of Biblical epics in his native Hungary before coming to the United States, directed *Noah's Ark* (1929-transitional-135/100 min.), based on a Darryl F. Zanuck script. It tells the story of two Americans who rescue a German woman from a train wreck while traveling in Europe in 1914. After the onset of war, the two young men join the army, experience the horrors of the trenches, and find themselves trapped in a cellar (with the German woman and a minister) by an exploding shell. While there, the minister compares their situation to that of Noah and the great flood, which introduces a spectacular, if somewhat tangential, flashback to Biblical days. Note that Robert Youngson produced an abbreviated version of the film for theatrical rerelease (1957-75 min.), but the complete film is in the final stages of restoration and should be available shortly.

Today We Live (1933-113 min.-/MGM-UA Home Video), whose screenplay by William Faulkner was based on his story "Turn About," tells the tale of a British woman (Joan Crawford), whose shifting affections cause a rivalry between a naval officer (Robert Young) and an American flyer (Gary Cooper). Faulkner's original story centered on the inter-service rivalry and had no love interest as its cause.

On the other side, *Crimson Romance* (1934-70 min.) portrays two flight-crazed Americans who join the German Air Force, find themselves oppressed by a sadistic commander (Erich von Stroheim) and confronting their fellow countrymen.

Two revisionist classics were made in 1930, one in the United States, the other in Germany. Lewis Milestone's *All Quiet on the Western Front* (1930-Transitional-both sound and silent with sound effects versions were released-140/105 min.-/MCA Home Video), based on Erich Maria Remarque's 1929 antiwar novel, followed the growing disillusionment of a group of high school students who become front-line soldiers. Responding to Nazi and other right-wing pressure, the film was banned by the Weimar Republic in 1931 and rereleased there only after its studio, Universal, agreed to excise scenes that called into question German manhood, patriotism, or military prowess from prints released elsewhere in the world as well as in Germany. For over two decades, such "sanitized" versions were seen by viewers around the world. The film was banned entirely in other European countries and, once the Nazis assumed power, in Germany (and Austria) as well. French censors, who demanded that the scene showing the death of the French *poilou* be trimmed for its initial silent release in 1930, banned the film entirely in 1938 as France began rearming for war. The story was remade for television (1979-150 min.-Swank/CBS-Fox Video) in a more literally complete but less imaginatively inspired version.

G. W. Pabst's *Westfront 1918* (1930-German-98 min.-Museum of Modern Art/Facets Multimedia), based on the novel *Vier von der Infanterie,* dwells on the desolate landscape that war produces as emblematic of its human costs.

German pacifist writer Leonhard Frank's novella *Karl und Anna*, about two German prisoners of war who escape from a Siberian lead mine during the chaos of the Russian Civil War, one of whom falls in love with the other's wife, was produced by Erich Pommer as *Heimkehr* (*Homecoming*) (1928-German-silent-74 min.-/German Language Video Center). The film's production company, UFA, which had just come under the control of right-wing industrialist Alfred Hugenberg, undermined the novella's moral to remove "Bolshevist tendencies" from the film and added a happy ending. Both Pommer and the film's director, pioneer filmmaker Joe May, would flee Germany following the Nazi takeover.

The same fate befell Karl Grune's pacifist film *At the Edge of the World* (1927-silent), though it was completed before the Hugenberg takeover. The film told the story of a miller who retains his love of humanity through the brutality of war and UFA demanded that a tag line be placed at the end of the film calling it a "A Film for Tomorrow." Grune demanded that his name be removed from the released version of the film. He emigrated to England in 1933.

In keeping with its political orientation, UFA then produced a group of Russian emigré films including *The White Devil* (1929/30), based on Tolstoy's novella *Hadji Murad*. At the same time, G. W. Pabst's film, *The Love of Jeanne Ney* (1927-silent-105 min.-/available on Laser disc from Image Entertainment as part of its "Golden Age of German Cinema" set) based on a novel by Soviet writer Ilya Ehrenburg about a French woman who falls in love with a Russian Revolutionist in the Crimea at the time of the Bolshevik assumption of power, had its ending changed by order of the studio. The novel ended tragically in a depressed and decadent post-war Paris, but the film, which borrowed many of its techniques from contemporary Soviet cinema (under the terms of Weimar-Soviet cooperation agreements, trade between the two was encouraged), ends happily.

Four Sons (1928-silent-100 min.) is one of several revisionist films made by John Ford during this period. It is the melodramatic story of a Bavarian widow whose sons fight on both sides during the war. It was remade early in World War II (1940-89 min.), substituting a Czech mother for the German one.

With screenwriter Dudley Nichols, Ford made *Seas Beneath* (1931), which follows a confrontation between an American Q-boat crew and a German U-boat crew (whose dialogue is in German with English intertitles). The film was remade in a World War II setting at the height of the Cold War (1959) with a good German, bad (that is Nazi) German subplot.

American director Henry King's first sound movie, *She Goes to War* (1929-50 min.-/Nostalgia Family Video), tells the story of a spoiled rich woman who discovers the horrors of war when she volunteers to work in a canteen near the front lines in France.

British director James Whale, who had come to America because of the lack of sufficient sound equipment at home and who helped Howard Hughes with *Hell's Angels*, made *Journey's End* (1930), based on World War I veteran R. C. Sherriff's play about the war's effects on the common men who fought it.

Anthony Asquith's *Tell England* (1930), from Ernest Raymond's novel, also dealt with the theme, though it is more famous for its spectacular scenes of the Gallipoli landings of 1915.

Ford and Nichols's *Pilgrimage* (1933-95 min.) tells a story about a woman who breaks off her son's romance by turning him in to the Draft Board. After he dies in combat, she finds redemption by visiting her son's grave in France and helping another young man resist his domineering mother to follow the course of true love.

Erich Pommer's *Farewell Again* (1937) follows a group of British soldiers on a one-day London layover before leaving for France. This story makes an interesting parallel to *Urlaub auf Ehrenwort* (see below).

Arnold Zweig's 1928 novel about the cynical disregard of the Military bureaucracy for human values and lives, *The Case of Sergeant Grischa* (1930), was also filmed.

Ernest Hemingway's 1929 semiautobiographical novel based on his service in the volunteer ambulance corps in Italy, *A Farewell to Arms,* was filmed in 1932 (78 min.-Filmic Archives/Video Yesteryear) with Gary Cooper and Helen Hayes and again in 1957 (152 min.-Budget Films). *Force of Arms* (1951-100 min.-/Critics Choice Video), later reissued as *A Girl for Joe,* sets the same story in World War II. The theatrically released docudrama *In Love and War* (1997-115 min.-/New Line Home Video) focuses on Hemingway's own wartime service during which he was wounded by an Austro-Hungarian trench mortar and machine gun and, while recuperating in a Red Cross hospital in Milan, fell in love with Agnes von Kurowsky, a young nurse who became the model for Catherine Barkley in the novel.

The only American film that dealt directly with American disillusionment with the war is *Private Jones* (1933) about a wartime draftee. This was a low budget satire that failed at the box office.

Two Irish films deal with the war for independence from Britain. *Guests of the House* (1932-silent), based on a Frank O'Connor short story, deals with the relationship that develops between two captured British Soldiers and their Irish Republican Army captors (the movie's cast were all members of Dublin's Gate Theatre company). *The Dawn* (1936) is based on Irish Republican Army activities in County Kerry during the Black and Tan war.

The German film *Morgenrot* (1933-German but no subtitles-75 min.-International Historic Films), about a noble but doomed submarine crew, is a peculiar blend of patriotism and antiwar sentiment. It was completed and released just as Hitler came to power and is often seen as symbolic of the transition from Weimar to Nazi filmmaking.

Several other German films from the late Weimar period, *Niemandsland* (1931) released as *Hell on Earth*, and *Berg in Flammen* (1931) released as *The Doomed Battalion*, dealt with the survival of humane values and comradeship under the stress of war as did Pabst's *Kameradschaft* (1931-German-87 min.-Kit Parker/International Historic Films), which transposed to 1919 a real 1906 incident in which German miners came to the assistance of their French co-workers when a disaster engulfed them at Courrieres, near the German border. A comparison of its values to those of *Patrioten* (see below) is most instructive.

The Last War and the Next

The World War I films made in Nazi Germany, chiefly by Karl Ritter, portray the *Völkische* nobility of the German soldier, as in *Operation Michael* (1937) or *Patrioten* (1937-German-97 min.-/German Language Video Center), betrayed by evil forces working to undercut the German war effort at home. This is the juxtaposition portrayed in *Urlaub auf Ehrenwort* (1937) and resurrected by the Nazis as with *Pour La Merite* (1938), which ends with the Nazi recreation of the German air force.

Many films of the 1930s romanticized the war through a nostalgic haze. An example is the melodramatic American film *Captured* (1933-72 min.), based on a novel by Sir Philip Gibb, which turns its German prisoner-of-war camp locale into a *Grand Hotel* (1932) setting in which a group of British, French, and American inmates work out their personal problems. Two French features made in the same year, Jean Renoir's *La Grand Illusion* (1937-French-111 min.-Films Inc./CBS-Fox Video) about the attempt to maintain chivalric values in the face of modern war in a German prisoner of War Camp, and Abel Gance's sound remake of his 1918 silent film *J'Accuse* (1937-French-95 min.-Biograph Entertainment/Facets Multimedia) about a French soldier driven mad by the horrors of war, are true antiwar classics.

The equilibration of the two wartime adversaries achieves its most complete form in the French film *Les Otages* (1939-French) in which French hostages of German occupying forces are presented unheroically, while their captors, trying to discover the murderer of a fellow officer, are equally human. This sort of equivocation would later make the France's surrender and its Vichy aftermath easier to bear.

In the early 1930s, Hollywood made a large number of World War I espionage adventure stories, usually involving beautiful women, often with shady pasts, who either ensnare idealistic naïve young men or re-establish prewar relationships with lovers on the enemy side. The only one of these currently available is *Dishonored* (1931-91-min.-/MCA-Universal Home Video) with Marlene Dietrich as an Austro-Hungarian spy in love with a Russian agent (Victor McLaglen) who dies to save her.

As the war clouds gathered in the late 1930s, World War I personalities, events, and attitudes were made to serve the ends of the new preparedness. Two British films about coerced wartime espionage were released in 1937. *Secret Lives* (1937-79 min.), based on a novel by Paul de Sainte Colombe and also known as *I Married a Spy,* is about a German-born French spy who is tried and convicted of treason on the basis of forged evidence. *The Windmill* (1937-62 min.) is the story of a German-born Belgian woman who is forced by the Germans to spy on British operations. No print of either film currently exists. Alexander Korda adapted a novel by J. Storer Clouston about a German World War I U-boat commander sent to infiltrate a British naval base in the Orkney Islands with the assistance of a beautiful spy and an apparently turncoat British naval officer. The film, directed by Michael Powell and written by Emeric Pressburger, premiered in Britain as *Spy in Black* (1939-82 min.-/Nostalgia Family Video) and was released in the United States as *U Boat 29.*

In the United States, in the midst of the 1938 Munich crisis, Fox released John Ford's *Submarine Patrol* (1938-95 min.), adapted from Ray Millholland's history of *The Splinter Fleet of the Otranto Barrage* and made with U.S. Navy support about the training and wartime work of sub-chasers.

Thunder Afloat (1939-94 min.), another film about World War I antisubmarine warfare made with the U.S. Navy's cooperation, was completed in June but held back at the request of the Roosevelt Administration so that it might have an impact on the preparedness debate that was to resume in Congress in the fall. The film was released in late September, after the outbreak of the Second World War in Europe.

Howard Hawks's *Sergeant York* (1940-134 min. Swank/Facets Multimedia—a colorized version also exists) is a somewhat rationalized "biopic" of the pacifist Tennessee farmboy who won the Congressional Medal of Honor for capturing 132 German soldiers almost single-handedly. Gary Cooper won an Oscar for his performance and John Huston helped write the script.

Another film, *The Fighting 69th* (1940-90 min.-Swank/Facets Multimedia—a colorized version exists), is a comic-heroic portrayal (by James Cagney and Pat O'Brien) of Irish-American soldiers in action in World War I.

The Propaganda War Revisited:
The Lessons for World War II Warriors of World War I

James Cagney's prettified biopic of the composer/performer/producer George M. Cohan, *Yankee Doodle Dandy* (1942-126 min.-Swank /CBS-Fox Video-two colorized versions, one edited for TV exist), sets the story into an envelope of President Roosevelt rewarding Cohan for his World War I patriotic service in the midst of World War II mobilization.

The film of the wartime Broadway review *This Is the Army* (1943-121 min.-Kit Parker/Video Yesteryear) is built on a reunion of the soldiers who had staged *Yip Yip Yaphank* during their army training in 1917 on Long Island, to recreate the show with their sons who are preparing to embark for combat in World War II. Irving Berlin (the 1917 show's author) played himself in the film (as he had in the smash Broadway review on which it was based) and George Murphy played Ronald Reagan's father.

The Iron Major (1943-85 min.-/Turner Home Entertainment) is a wartime inspirational biography of football coach and Great War hero Frank Cavanaugh.

Captain Eddie (1945-107 min.), about the American air ace Eddie Rickenbacker, is another inspirational wartime biography. This story is told in flashbacks as he and his companions await rescue after their plane crashed in the Pacific in 1942.

The wartime biography of the World War I president, *Wilson* (1944-154/119 min.-/Fox Video), emphasized the tragic idealism and missed opportunities of the earlier period as a salutary lesson for Americans beginning to think about the next peace.

Despite their age, many of these feature films can be used to convey information and images not only about the war itself, but about wartime and post-war attitudes about it. In addition, films like *Wings* and *Hell's Angels* contain spectacular air combat scenes staged by men who were actually there. *The Big Parade* contains some of the most panoramic ground assault images ever recorded.

Aspects of World War I in Dramatic Films:
The Western Front

A number of films concern the war on the western front. In the 1920s, a series of mostly British melodramas was produced using various specific western front battles and place names as their backdrops. These include *Zeebrugge* (1924), *Ypres* (1925), *Mons* (1926), *The Somme* (1927), and *The Guns of Loos* (1928).

The film that uses the songs and statements of the front-line soldiers themselves to set forth the war's futility and savagely satirize its sanctimonious and self-serving staff officers is Richard Attenborough's *Oh! What a Lovely War* (1969-139 min.), based on Joan Littlewood's blackout play and adapted for the screen by John Mills and Len Deighton. Its set pieces about Britain's wartime military elite are held together by the thread of the members of the Smith family—everypersons—who are affected by those activities and decisions.

Biographies: Siegfried Sassoon (1971-60 min.) is a National Educational Television dramatized account of the British soldier/poet's rebellion against the war in 1918. Rather than court martial Sassoon (who was a hero), the army incarcerated him in a Scottish mental hospital. Recognizing the futility of his protest, Sassoon returned to the front.

King of Hearts (1966-102 min.-Swank/MGM Home Video) is about a Scots soldier who finds himself in a western front village abandoned by everyone but the inmates of an insane asylum.

Thomas L'imposteur (1965-French-93 min.), based on a Jean Cocteau story, also dealt with wartime illusion and reality.

A 1915 French army mutiny and its punishment, on which Humphrey Cobb's 1935 novel was based, is the subject of Stanley Kubrick's *Paths of Glory* (1957-87 min.-Swank/MGM Home Video).

Bertrand Tavernier's *Capitaine Conan* (1996-French-129 min.-Kino International) tells the story of a career officer more interested in not wasting the soldiers under his command than obeying the orders of his superiors.

The ordeal of Anzac troops on the western front, belittled and abused by their European commanders, is the subject of *Mutiny of the Western Front* (1928-/Baker and Taylor).

1917 (1968) is Stephen Weeks's short-subject about an incident on the western front.

Joseph Losey's *King and Country* (1964-90 min.-Ivy Films) concerns the legal defense of an accused deserter on the western front.

Between Wars (1977-101 min.-/Nostalgia Family Video) is an Australian film about an Army Medical Corps doctor who works with shell-shock victims in a military hospital. There he meets a German prisoner of war, also a doctor, who introduces him to Sigmund Freud's psychoanalytic theories and practices, considered disreputable by the medical establishment. After the war, the doctor returns to Australia and takes up a rural practice to avoid notoriety, but conflict develops there as well.

How Many Miles to Babylon (1980-111 min.-/CBS-Fox Video) tells the story of two friends in the army, one of whom must organize the other's execution for desertion.

A five-part British Masterpiece Theatre production dramatized the wartime experiences of Vera Brittain as a VAD (Voluntary Aid Detachment) nurse in England, on Malta, and on the western front. It is based on her 1933 memoir, *Testament of Youth* (1980-290 min.).

The Secret War

Director Herbert Wilcox made two films about Edith Cavell, the British nurse in Belgium who was shot by the Germans for hiding Entente soldiers and for espionage in 1916. The first was *Dawn* (1928) and the second was *Nurse Edith Cavell* (1939-108 min.-Kit Parker/ Kartes Video Communications).

I Was a Spy (1933-88 min.) is a British film based on the story of a Belgian nurse (played by Madeleine Carroll) who spied successfully on the Germans who had overrun her country.

The most famous—and ineffectual—accused spy of the war was Margareta Gertruda Zelle, the subject of *Mata-Hari: The Red Dancer* (1928-German); *Mata Hari* (1932-90 min.-Swank/MGM-UA Home Video) with Greta Garbo; *Mata Hari: Agent H-21* (1964-French) with Jeanne Moreau; and *Mata Hari* (1985-108 min.-Swank/MGM-UA Home Video) with Sylvia Kristal. Rex Ingram's *Mare Nostrum* (1926-silent) was based on the Mata Hari story.

Inside the Lines (1930-73 min.-/Video Yesteryear) sets the story of the female German spy in wartime England, and Blake Edwards's spy spoof *Darling Lili* (1970-136 min.-/Facets Multimedia) is a takeoff on this story.

Stamboul Quest (1934-88 min.) and *Fräulein Doktor* (1968-102 min.) piece together the story of the unknown woman who was Germany's most effective spy.

The Divine Emma (1979-Czech-111 min.) [*Božska Ema*] is a loosely fact-based docudrama about a world-famous soprano who returns to Bohemia at the outbreak of war, is confined to her estate and forbidden to perform because she is (incorrectly) suspected of being a spy.

Though the German wartime exploits of Britain's most famous spy, Sidney Reilly, are all but ignored in the British produced Masterpiece Theatre series about him, the fictionalized and heavily censored adventures of British author W. Somerset Maugham, who served as a military intelligence operative in France, Switzerland, Russia, and Italy, *Ashenden* (1928), was quirkily filmed by Alfred Hitchcock as *Secret Agent*

(1936-86 min. Kit Parker-/Facets Multimedia). Four of the stories ("The Dark Woman," "The Tailor," "Mr. Harrington's Washing," and "The Hairless Mexican") detailing Maugham's growing disillusionment with this secret war (and incorporating details from Maugham's own experience) were made by the BBC and the Arts and Entertainment cable network as a television drama called *Ashenden* (1992-108 min.).

The War in the Air
The air war on the western front is the subject of such recent films as the fact-based *Von Richthofen and Brown* (1971-97 min.-Swank) also known as *The Red Baron* about the head of the German Flying Circus and the Canadian pilot who probably shot him down.

Three fictional air stories are *The Blue Max* (1966-156 min.-/CBS-Fox Video), *Lafayette Escadrille* (1958-93 min.-/Warner Home Video), and *Zeppelin* (1971-101 min.-/Facets Multimedia).

The War at Sea
Several postwar films glorified aspects of the war at sea. These include John Ford's *Submarine Patrol* (1938-95 min.).

C. S. Forester's novel *Brown on Resolution* about a British seaman rescued by a German warship, who escapes and snipes at it until British warships show up to sink it, is the subject of *Forever England* (1935), also known as *Brown on Resolution*. It was remade, in a World War II setting and absent some of the melodramatic elements, as *Sailor of the King* (1953-83 min.).

Italy and Points South: The Near East and Africa
The war's southern fronts are portrayed in a number of films. Mario Monicello's black comedy *The Great War* (1959-Italian-118 min.-/Facets Multimedia) was the first Italian film to demystify the Italo-Austrian war, showing the reality behind the heroic facade.

A late Weimar-era German film, Luis Trenker's *Berg in Flammen* (1931-German-97 min.-/Scholar's Bookshelf), released abroad as *The Doomed Battalion,* is set among Austro-Hungarian soldiers defending a Tyrolean mountaintop against attacking Italian forces.

The last of Hungarian director István Szabó's *Mitteleuropa* trilogy, *Hanussen* (1988-Hungarian/German-115 min.-/Columbia Tristar Home Video), begins with ex-Variety performer Klaus Schneider suffering a head wound on the Italian Front while fighting in the Austro-Hungarian army. It follows the true story of his discovery of telepathic and clairvoyant powers while recovering from that wound, his decision to adopt the stage name Eric Jan Hanussen, and his successful stage career in postwar Vienna, Czechoslovakia, and Weimar-era Berlin, and ends with his prediction of the *Reichstag* fire and subsequent murder by the Nazis in 1933.

The Entente's abortive 1915 Dardanelles campaign is the subject of *Gallipoli* (1984-110 min.-Films Inc./Paramount Home Video) and of the made-for-television movie *Anzacs: The War Down Under* (1987-240 min.-/Celebrity Home Video). Taking advantage of the popular enthusiasm that the Gallipoli landings created, an Australian company produced a fictional film entitled *The Hero of the Dardanelles* (1915) in which the amphibious assault was restaged at Tamarama Bay near Sidney.

The Arab revolt against the Turks is the subject of David Lean's epic *Lawrence of Arabia* (1962-222/202 min.-Films Inc./Columbia Tristar Home Video), re-released theatrically in 1989 and on video shortly thereafter in the version intended by its director (available both on video tape from Columbia Tristar Home Video and on a Voyager Video Disc set in a "letterbox" format).

The PBS drama *A Dangerous Man* (see below) picks up Lawrence's career where the Lean film's wartime action leaves off.

Franz Werfel's 1934 novel about the Turkish genocide of the Armenians is the source for *40 Days of Musa Dagh* (1985-120 min.-/Video City Productions).

The Lighthorsemen (1987-128/111 min.-October Films/Facets Multimedia) is an Australian film about the Australian Light Horse Brigade in the Palestinian campaign, culminating in the cavalry charge at Beersheba. It was produced by the nephew of the general who ordered the charge.

The same story about the British-Australian defense of the Suez Canal (with a strong admixture of anti-Nazi propaganda) is the subject of *Forty Thousand Horsemen* (1941-84 min.-/Facets Multimedia).

The British Campaign in Mesopotamia is the setting for John Ford's *The Lost Patrol* (1933-73/65 min.-/Turner Home Entertainment Video). With shifting locales the same story formed the basis for the 1939 western *Bad Lands* (70 min.-Swank/Facets Multimedia) and the World War II drama *Sahara* (1943-97 min.-Modern Sound Pictures/Columbia Tristar Home Video).

A fictional film set its story in the context of French Foreign Legion operations during World War I. *Man of Legend* (1971-95 min.-/United Home Video) was filmed in Morocco and tells the story of a German soldier who joins the Legion and falls in love with the daughter of a Rif chieftain.

The 1929 version of *King of the Khyber Rifles* is set during the First World War in India.

Les cavaliers de l'orage (1983-French-87 min.), based on Jean Giono's novel *Deux cavaliers d'orage*, is the story of two wrestlers competing for the affection of a young nurse. All three of them, plus the younger brother of one of the wrestlers, are mobilized and in June 1917 are sent to the Salonika front.

The war in Africa forms the setting for such films as *Black and White in Color* (1977-French-90 min.-Corinth/Facets Multimedia) about the war's outbreak in West Africa.

John Huston's *The African Queen* (1951-105 min.-Films Inc./CBS-Fox Video) is based by James Agee on C. S. Forester's novel about the East African war.

Shout at the Devil (1976-144/119 min.-/Live Home Video) is an inferior fictional account of the hunt for a German battle cruiser in East Africa by an Irish poacher, his daughter, and an expatriate Englishman at the outbreak of the war

The Royal African Rifles (1953-75 min.) is a story about a cache of machine guns stolen from the British in East Africa in 1914.

The early Nazi-era German film *Der Reiter von Deutsch-Ostafrika* (1934-German-89 min.-/Scholar's Bookshelf) tells a story about two friends—one German, one British—who find themselves on opposite sides of the East Africa campaign. Because the British friend is treated sympathetically in the film, the Nazis banned its further distribution when war broke out in 1939.

Portions of the film made from Karen Blixen's [Isak Dinesen's] autobiography, *Out of Africa* (1985-160 min.-Swank/MCA Home Video), and the British seven-part Masterpiece Theatre series made from Elspeth Huxley's *The Flame Trees of Thika* (1981-366 min./Signals Video), also portray the war in Africa.

The Eastern Front and the Collapse of the Russian Empire

Several American silent films from the period just before the February/March revolution dealt with Tsarist Russia. Their plots generally involved young women who became revolutionaries after being forced to suffer at the hands of (usually Cossack) government authorities, avenged themselves upon their oppressors, and escaped to the United States. These include *The Nihilists* (1905), *The Girl Nihilist* (1908), *Lost in Siberia* (1909), Edwin S. Porter's *Russia, Land of Oppression* (1910), and *The Cossack Whip* (1916).

Early in the provisional government period that followed the February/March revolution, a number of short films were made in Russia to discredit the Romanovs. They had titles such as *Dark Forces: Grigorii Rasputin and His Associates; The Trading House of Romanov, Rasputin,*

Sukhomlinov, Miasoedov, Protopopov, and Company; and *Mysterious Murder [of Rasputin] in Petrograd on December 16.*

Just after the February/March revolution, two strange films about the end of the Romanov dynasty were released. In both of these, Rasputin was the central protagonist. *The Fall of the Romanoffs* (1917) pitted the evil monk against an erstwhile follower and competitor, Sergei Mikhailovich Trufanov, who took the name Iliodor. He had come to the United States in the wake of the revolution and collaborated on (and played himself in) the film before disappearing into obscurity. Both this film and a competing one, *Rasputin the Black Monk* (1917), ascribed the February/March revolution to Rasputin's connivance with the German-born Tsarina to betray Russia to the Germans.

During the Soviet era, the war on the eastern front and the Russian revolutions that were, in part, precipitated by it were the subjects of some of the classic films of the Soviet cinema and of three American epics. *Arsenal* (1929-Russian-silent-65 min.-Kino International/Facets Multimedia) tells the story of the Ukraine during the war and the revolutions.

Sergei Eisenstein's first film, *Strike* (1924-Russian-silent-66 min.-Kino International/Facets Multimedia), portrays the Tsarist government's repression of worker unrest just before the revolution.

Dostigayev and Others (1959-Russian-99 min.-Corinth Films) is based on a Maxim Gorky play about counterrevolutionary plots during the Kerensky period.

Baltic Deputy (1937-Russian-95 min.-Corinth Films/Facets Multimedia) is the story of a Duma deputy's conversion to the Bolshevik cause.

Sergei Eisenstein's epic *October* (1927-Russian-silent-102 min.-Kino International/Video Yesteryear-MPI Home Video has released a 77 min. version that Orson Welles narrated), also known as *Ten Days That Shook the World*, based on American radical journalist John Reed's book of the same name, and Vsevolod Pudovkin's *The End of St. Petersburg* (1927-Russian-silent-74 min.-Kino International/Facets Multimedia), dramatize the Bolshevik Revolution in Petrograd. Both were made in honor of its tenth anniversary. Eisenstein was later forced by the Stalin regime to cut scenes of Trotsky's participation in the revolution from his film.

Lenin in October (1937-Russian-93 min.-Corinth Films), made to commemorate the revolution's twentieth anniversary, is a Stalinist version of the Bolshevik Revolution, aggrandizing Stalin's role at the expense of Trotsky. Its sequel, *Lenin in 1918* (1939-Russian-153 min.), conveys the same message about the Lenin-Stalin relationship as the two, with the aid of Maxim Gorky, work to bring order from chaos, war, and famine. Boris Shchukin, who played Lenin in both films, closely studied newsreels and voice recordings of Lenin to prepare for the role.

Portrait of Lenin (1965-95 min.-Corinth Films), also known as *Lenin in Poland,* is a Soviet film that uses the medium of an interior monologue to convey Lenin's thoughts as he considers how to escape his Austrian exile at the war's outbreak.

The impact of the war, revolutions, and ensuing civil war on the lives and beliefs of Russian soldiers and civilians is the theme of the Soviet film *Fragments of an Empire* (1929-Russian-silent-103 min.-Museum of Modern Art) about the adjustment a soldier must make to the new revolutionary order.

Chapayev (1934-Russian-101 min.-Corinth Films/International Historic Films) is a film about the Caspian region guerrilla leader. It is based on Dmitri Furmanov's novel and was directed by Sergei and Gregori Vasiliev. *Battle for Siberia* (1937-Russia-90 min.-Corinth Films), by the same directors, is about Siberian partisans. Its music was composed by Dmitri Shostakovich.

Alexei Tolstoy's novel *Ordeal,* about two sisters' experiences in the war, revolutions, civil war, and early 1920s, became a Soviet film trilogy: *The Sisters* (1957-Russian-145 min.-Corinth Films); *1918* (1958-Russian-120 min.-Cinecom International/Facets Multimedia); and *Bleak Morning* (1959-Russian-120 min.-Corinth Films).

Mikhail Sholokhov's epic 1934 novel *And Quiet Flows the Don* (1957-Russian-245/107 min.-both versions are available from Kino International) chronicles the lives of Don Cossacks through the upheavals of war and revolution.

The Civil War and Entente intervention is the subject of *The Forty-First* (1956-Russian-100 min.-Corinth Films), a Soviet film about a woman Red Guard and a White soldier trapped together on an island.

Miklos Jancso's *The Red and the White* (1968-Hungarian-92 min.-Kino International Film and Video) is a film about the war in Central Asia.

Pudovkin's *Storm over Asia* (1928-Russian-silent-73 min.-Kit Parker/Facets Multimedia) portrays the Mongolian resistance to the British occupation of Siberia.

Shors (1931-Russian-90 min.-Corinth Films) is about a Ukrainian partisan hero of the Civil War.

We Are from Kronstadt (1936-Russian-93 min.-Corinth Films) is about the 1919 defense of Petrograd against the White forces of General Yudenich.

Reduced to much more human terms is Alexander Askololov's long banned *The Commissar* (1967-Russian-released in 1980-170 min.-New

Yorker Films/Facets Multimedia) about a pregnant Bolshevik commissar who is taken in by a poor Jewish family and is thus confronted by both her own choices and her own prejudices.

Jancso's *Silence and Cry* (1968-Hungarian-79 min.-Kino International Film and Video) tells the story of a Bolshevik soldier who sacrifices himself to save his family.

Western films on this period include *Nicholas and Alexandra* (1972-183 min.- Kit Parker/Columbia-Tristar Home Video), a somewhat overly sympathetic portrait of the last Russian monarch and his family both before and during this period, and David Lean's epic film of Boris Pasternak's 1957 banned novel *Dr. Zhivago* (1965-193 min.-Films Inc. /MGM-UA Video).

Warren Beatty's film *Reds* (1981-200 min.-Films Inc./Paramount Home Video), about the American radical newspaperman John Reed who died of typhus at Baku in 1920 and lies buried in the Kremlin as a hero of the revolution, contains documentary interviews with Reed's contemporaries.

Knight without Armour (1937-107 min.-/Sultan Entertainment) is the story of a British journalist caught in the 1917 upheavals.

The core of the British Masterpiece Theatre production, *Reilly, Ace of Spies*, the "Mr. Harrington's Washing" segment of the *Ashenden* made for cable series, and episodes of *The Fall of Eagles* deal with the three monarchies' destruction in the Great War and revolution.

Boris Savinkov, Socialist revolutionary and, with Sidney Reilly, anti-Bolshevik conspirator, was the subject of a Soviet film *Krakh* (*Collapse*) (1969).

Tempest (1928-102 min.-Kino International/Facets Multimedia) is a turnabout romance set during the revolution.

Volker Schlöndorff's *Coup de Grace* (1976-German-96 min.-Kit Parker/Facets Multimedia) is a film of Marguerite Yourcenar's novel about an illicit affair during the Russian Civil War.

The recently (1988) rediscovered Italian version of Russian emigre Ayn Rand's 1936 novel *We the Living,* entitled *Noi Vivi* (1942-Italian-173 min.-/Angelica), is set in the Russian Revolution. It starred Rossano Brazzi and Alida Valli and was banned by Mussolini.

A Chef in Love (1997-French) tells the story of a Frenchman who prospers during the brief interlude of Georgian independence and suffers when the Bolsheviks take over in 1921.

A Slave of Love (1978-Russian-94 min.-Kit Parker/Facets Multimedia) is a film about a movie crew attempting to finish a silent melodrama in the wake of the Bolshevik Revolution and the changes in belief that occur during the filming.

Siberiade (1978-Russian-190 min.-Kino International/Facets Multimedia) is Andrei Konchalovsky's epic about two Russian families—the proletarian Ustyuzhanins and the aristocratic Solomins—struggling to survive the revolution, Stalinism, war, and "thaw." The film reaches its climax in a struggle over Siberian oil.

Two films, *Anastasia* (1956-105 min.-/Fox Video) and *Anastasia: The Mystery of Anna* (1986-200 min.-/Facets Multimedia), a two-part television movie based on Peter Kurth's book, *Anastasia: The Riddle of Anna Anderson*, explore the mystery of the woman some believe to be the survivor of the Bolshevik Ekaterenburg execution/massacre of the Russian royal family.

The Home Fronts

The impact of the war on the home fronts is the subject of such films as *Waterloo Bridge* (1931-81 min.), remade early in World War II (1940-103 min.-Swank/MGM-UA Home Video), and again as *Gaby* (1956-97 min.) set in World War II. All three are based on a play by Sherwood Anderson.

The Englishman Who Went Up a Hill But Came Down a Mountain (1995-99 min.-Swank/Miramax Home Video), based on director Christopher Monger's story, is set in 1917 as a Welsh town fights to keep its distinction as "the first mountain in Wales." Hugh Grant plays a young English surveyor seconded from the British Army because he was shellshocked on the western front.

British author Catherine Cookson's *The Cinder Path*, about familial conflicts that reach their climax on the western front, has been made into a three-part British Masterpiece Theatre production (1994-180 min.-/BFS Video).

Carrington (1996-122 min.-/PolyGram Video) begins in 1915 and its first episodes follow Lytton Strachey's resistance to World War I and his publication of *Eminent Victorians* in 1918 as he permits artist Dora Carrington into his heretofore homosexual life, causing her public break-up with fellow artist Mark Gertler.

A sexually frank three-part British Masterpiece Theatre production, *Portrait of a Marriage* (1992-210 min.), dramatizes the unconventional and mutually destructive relationship between diplomat and writer Harold Nicolson and novelist poet (and garden designer) Vita Sackville-West. Based on their son Nigel's 1980 book, the story is told through an extended flashback to the First World War (when Nicolson revealed his homosexuality to his wife and she began an affair with her childhood friend Violet Keppel) and to the postwar period.

Egon Schiele: Excess and Punishment (1995-German-90 min.) is the biography of the Austrian painter whose explicit nudes shocked Vienna and who died in the swine flu pandemic of 1918.

Days of Hope (1975) was a British dramatic television series that followed a working-class family from the establishment of conscription in 1916 through the 1926 general strike.

The short-circuiting of Irish home rule by the war and the availability of German and American aid inflamed the Irish independence movement. The resulting Easter 1916 Rebellion forms the background for Sean O'Casey's play *The Plough and the Stars* (1936-72 min.).

David Lean's *Ryan's Daughter* (1970-206/176 min.-Films Inc./ MGM-UA Home Video) sets its story of love and betrayal against the 1916 rebellion.

The life of the Sinn Fein rebel leader and negotiator of the treaty that created the Irish Free State in the aftermath of the war, only to be assassinated in the civil war that followed, is dramatized in *Michael Collins* (1996-117 min.-/Warner Home Video).

The Treaty (1991-109 min.-/Movies Unlimited) focuses more closely on the Anglo-Irish negotiations and Irish ratification process that resulted in the creation of the Irish Free State.

The Story of Adrien (1980-French-95 min.) sets the story of a rural French farmboy against the turmoil of the war.

102 Boulevard Haussmann (1991-102 min.) is Alan Bennett's dramatization of a wartime incident in the life of Marcel Proust.

Devil in the Flesh (1946-French-112 min.-/Facets Multimedia), based on Raymond Radiguet's autobiographical novel, deals with a young woman who has an affair with a 17-year-old schoolboy while her husband is away fighting at the front. The nonjudgmental tone of the film caused great controversy when it was released. It was remade more explicitly and in an updated, altered, more Freudian context in Italy (1987-Italian-110 min.-/Orion Home Video).

Cupid's Bow (1988-Polish-/Facets Multimedia), based on Juliusz Kaelen-Bandrowski's 1919 novel, *The Bow*, sets its story of decadence and sexual awakening in wartime Cracow, then a part of Austro-Hungarian Galicia.

An Australian docudrama, *Land of Hope* (1986-51 min.), portrays the domestic social and labor unrest that World War I brought to a head through the lives of the Patty Quinn family.

The American experience is the subject of Horton Foote's semiautobiographical *On Valentine's Day* (1986-106 min.-Angelika Films/Lorimar Home Video), also known as *Story of a Marriage* about Texas small-town life in 1917, and *1918* (1984-94 min.-Angelika

Films/CBS-Fox Video), about the 1918 swine flu pandemic's effect on that same town. Both were part of Foote's nine-play *Orphans' Home* cycle and were shown on the PBS American Playhouse television series.

The Killing Floor (1984-117 min.-/Orion Home Video) is a television movie about an interracial attempt to organize a Chicago meatpacking plant still under wartime government regulation. The script is partly based on federal hearing transcripts.

Legends of the Fall (1994-133 min.-Films Inc./Columbia Tristar Home Video) is an epic that traces a Montana family's confrontation with the prospect of war as its patriarch, who had experienced war at firsthand, tries to dissuade his idealistic sons from enlisting in the Canadian Army in 1914. It is based on a magazine story by Jim Harrison.

Francis Hodgson Burnett's story of World War I-induced separation, courage, and triumph, *The Little Princess*, has been filmed twice— once with Shirley Temple (1939-91 min.-/Facets Multimedia) with the plot thrown back into the Victorian period, and again (1995-97 min.- /Warner Home Video) set before and during the Great War.

The moods of impotence and despair produced by the war are visible in the novel Franz Kafka began to write in 1916-1917. His warning of faceless impenetrable bureaucracy was updated to a contemporary setting in Orson Welles's expressionistic film *The Trial* (1963-118 min.- University of Texas-Dallas/Goodtimes Home Video).

The same fatalism can also be seen in George Bernard Shaw's wartime play *Heartbreak House* (1985-120 min.-/Facets Multimedia), a PBS Great Performances program that starred Rex Harrison and Amy Irving.

At the other end of the spectrum, from the Portuguese countryside, where even in 1917 the war seems very far away, *The Miracle of Our Lady of Fatima* (1952-102 min.-/Warner Home Video) brought comfort and hope to a war-torn world. In the 1952 film, the miraculous sighting by three children is unsuccessfully suppressed by an atheistic radical republican government that stands in for the Cold War era Soviet Union.

Post World War I World: Immediate Aftermath

The November 1918 armistice that ended the war is the subject of Granada television's *Gossip from the Forest* (1979-54 min.-Wombat Films and Video).

Bertrand Tavernier's *Life and Nothing But* (1989-French-135 min.- /Facets Multimedia) follows an officer whose job it is to find and identify the war dead just after the war ended.

Signum Landis (1980-Czech) tells the story of an Austro-Czech soldier who refuses to surrender at the war's end.

The origins of the Spartacist revolt that followed in its wake is the culmination of Margarethe von Trotta's film biography of its leader *Rosa Luxembourg* (1986-German-122 min.-New Yorker Films/Facets Multimedia).

The Banner (1977-German-122 min.) tells the story of the foredoomed attempt of an idealistic Austrian officer to salvage his honor as Austria-Hungary collapses into chaos at the end of the war.

Lamb of God (1970-Hungarian-91 min.) tells the story of the Bela Kun revolution in Hungary.

Two Nazi films by Herbert Maisch cover this immediate postwar unrest: *Men Without a Fatherland* (1937-104 min.-/Scholar's Bookshelf), a film about a Latvian-German nobleman in the Baltic at the end of the war who finally decides to cast his lot with a *Freikorps* unit and dies heroically in its service, and *Strong Hearts* (1937), based on an anti-Bolshevist incident in the Hungarian revolution. The latter's antirevolutionary attitude insufficiently differentiated between left- and right-wing violence in its condemnations and was barred by Nazi censors prior to its release. It was banned again by the Allied Military Commission after the war in deference to Soviet feelings and was not finally released (as *Strong Hearts in the Storm*) until 1953 when anti-Soviet attitudes had solidified in West Germany.

The Fifth Day of Peace (1972-Italian-95 min.-/Prism Entertainment) tells the true story of two men executed by the German Army for desertion after the Entente had forbidden all such actions.

The growing unrest within Canadian Expeditionary Force units, billeted in Wales in January 1919 and restlessly awaiting transport home while influenza ravages their bodies and rumors of corruption and anti-Bolshevik missions enflame their minds (and their officers' fear of "Bolshies in their midst" color their reactions), is the story told in *Going Home* (1986-100 min.-/Image Home Entertainment). It is a CBC/BBC Wales co-production based on then newly released Canadian government records of mutiny and bloodshed in these camps.

Richard Attenborough's *Gandhi* (1982-188 min.-Films Inc./Columbia Tristar Home Video) recreates the 1919 Amritsar massacre and the Indian and British reactions to it.

A Dangerous Man (1992-120 min.-/Pacific Arts Video), a British television drama broadcast in the United States as part of the PBS Great Performances series, traces T. E. Lawrence's efforts on behalf of the Arabs at the Paris peacemaking.

Unsettled Land (1987-109 min.-/Facets Multimedia), an Israeli production, portrays the struggles of early postwar Jewish settlers in Palestine.

March or Die (1977-104 min.-/CBS Fox Home Video) follows a French Foreign Legion unit, led by a cynical and war-weary American expatriate major (Gene Hackman) on a suicide mission to Morocco in 1919 to protect archaeologists bent on looting its ancient treasures.

The Irish "troubles" are the subject of such films as those made from Liam O'Flaherty's novel *The Informer*. A 1929 version was filmed in England. John Ford made the classic version (1935-91 min.-Films Inc./VidAmerica), and an updated version called *Uptight* (1968-104 min.-Films Inc.) transposes the story to a U.S. black ghetto.

Celtic Revival patron and independence supporter Lady Gregory's one-act play about the rescue of an Irish Republican Army fighter from prison in 1921 is the last part and provides the title for an Irish film trilogy called *The Rising of the Moon* (1957-81 min.) performed by the Abbey Players, directed by John Ford, and introduced by Tyrone Power. It is also known as *Three Leaves*.

Other examples include Carol Reed's *Odd Man Out* (1947-115 min.-/Paramount Home Video), its updated version, *The Lost Man* (1969-122 min.-Swank), *The Gentle Gunman* (1952-86 min.), *Shake Hands with the Devil* (1959-110 min.-Swank/Facets Multimedia), *A Terrible Beauty* (1960-85 min.) also known as *Night Fighters*, and *The Dawning* (1988-97 min.-/Live Home Video), an unreleased theatrical film.

Fools of Fortune (1990-104 min.-/Columbia Tristar Home Video) traces one Irish family through the stresses of civil war.

Sean O'Casey's plays about the early republican days are 1924's *Juno and the Paycock* (1930-85 min.-/Facets Multimedia), directed by Alfred Hitchcock, and 1926's *The Plough and the Stars* (see above).

An idealized and fictional portrayal of the compromise that divided Ireland is the subject of *Beloved Enemy* (1936-86 min.-/Facets Multimedia) with Brian Aherne and Merle Oberon.

Broken Harvest (1995-101 min.) is an Irish film that explores, through a series of intergenerational flashbacks, the long-term effects of the war for independence, "the troubles," emigration, and politics on a small village in County Cork through the 1950s.

The Hebrew Lesson (1972-30 min.), an unsuccessful television pilot, is set in Cork in 1921 where a Jewish man (Milo O'Shea) shelters an Irish Republican Army fighter on the run from the Black and Tans and each learns lessons from the other.

Two Nazi-era films, *The Fox of Glenarvon* (1940) and *My Life for Ireland* (1941), sublimate the atrocities then being committed by the Nazis onto the British in their handling of the Easter Uprising and "the time of troubles."

Irish Whiskey Rebellion (1972-93 min.) tells the prohibition era story of young men who smuggle liquor into the U.S. to raise money for the Irish Republican Army.

The revolution in Turkey in the aftermath to World War I forms the backdrop for the adventure-comedy *You Can't Win 'Em All* (1970-97 min.).

Ju Dou (1990-Chinese-94 min.-/Live Entertainment) sets a melodrama of traditional obligation, love, and betrayal into the context of China in 1920. It is one of a number of films made in last decade in the People's Republic of China that deal with the political and personal struggles that resulted from the May 4th movement. Most of the films are set in the 1930s and 1940s rather than in the immediate aftermath of the First World War.

The widespread fear of anarchy and revolution that characterized postwar America is reflected in *Sacco and Vanzetti* (1971-Italian-120 min.-Kit Parker/United Home Video). Maxwell Anderson's play *Winterset* (1936-78 min.-Kit Parker/Hollywood Home Theater) is loosely based on this as well.

Long Term Effects and Residues

The longer term effects of the war, both on its veterans and on the society, are the subjects of a wide variety of films. D. W. Griffith's last independent production, *Isn't Life Wonderful* (1924-115 min.-Museum of Modern Art/Facets Multimedia), showed German postwar conditions (shot on location at Potsdam, Berlin, and elsewhere) under the strains of defeat and reparations demands. In deference to American feelings, its hero-lovers are Poles.

Soldiers' postwar physical debilities are the subjects of such films as the 1924 version of Arthur Pinero's play *The Enchanted Cottage*. It was remade in a World War II setting (1945-92 min.-/Facets Multimedia). Other examples include those made from James Hilton's 1941 novel about an amnesiac soldier, *Random Harvest* by Mervyn LeRoy (1942-124 min.-/Swank/Facets Multimedia) and Robert Redford (1997), the film of Rebecca West's first novel, *The Return of the Soldier* (1981-101 min.-/HBO Home Video) about a soldier whose memory is restored after twenty years, those made from Ernest Hemingway's 1926 novel *The Sun Also Rises* (1957-129 min.-Films Inc.) and its inferior two-part television remake (1984-200 min.), and those from W. Somerset Maugham's 1944 novel *The Razor's Edge*, made twice (1946-146 min.-/Facets Multimedia) and (1984-128 min.-/Columbia Tristar Home Video).

The film made by Dalton Trumbo from his 1939 antiwar novel, *Johnny Got His Gun* (1971-111 min.-/Media Home Entertainment), gets inside the head of a quadriplegic war veteran as he silently meditates about the war and its effect on him.

The psychological effects of the war on its participants and their loved ones are portrayed in *Reveille* (1924).

G. W. Pabst's *The Joyless Street* (1925-German-silent-90 min.-Kit Parker/Video Yesteryear), also known as *The Street of Sorrow*, is set in postwar Vienna. (This expressionist classic starred Greta Garbo, had Marlene Dietrich as an extra, and indirectly inspired the camera work and sets of King Vidor's *The Crowd*.)

The film made from Erich Maria Remarque's tale of postwar Germany is *Three Comrades* (1938-98 min.-Swank/Facets Multimedia) co-scripted by F. Scott Fitzgerald, and a postwar sequel to Remarque's *All Quiet on the Western Front*, entitled *The Road Back* (1937-97 min.), follows his *All Quiet* veterans home to frustration-filled lives.

A British Masterpiece Theatre production *To Serve Them All My Days* (1982-13 parts-754 min.), based on R. F. Delderfield's 1974 novel, follows a wounded war veteran's experience as a schoolteacher in postwar Britain.

James Hilton's 1934 novel, *Goodbye, Mr. Chips*, includes a teacher's reaction to his students being sent off to war. It was filmed in 1939 (114 min.-Swank/MGM-UA Home Video), in a musical version (1969-151/133 min.-Swank/MGM Home Video), and in a British Masterpiece Theatre version (1987-3 parts-174 min.).

Another Masterpiece Theatre production, *Sorrell & Son* (1987-5 parts-290 min.), based on Warwick Deeping's 1933 novel, portrays a war veteran's sacrifices for his son.

Chariots of Fire (1981-123 min.-Swank/Warner Home Video) tells the true story of the competition among British athletes preparing, in the wake of the war, for the 1924 Olympics.

Enchanted April (1992-98 min.-Films Inc./Facets Multimedia), based on a 1921 novel by Elizabeth von Arnim, sets its story of a renewing vacation in an Italian castle against a British society whose values were set adrift in the aftermath of the Great War.

J. R. Carr's novel, *A Month in the Country* (1987-97 min.-/Warner Home Video), tells a story about the recovery of a shellshocked veteran,

Ernest Hemingway's short story "Soldier's Home" (1977-41 min.-/Facets Multimedia) has also been filmed as part of the PBS American Short Story series.

François Truffaut's *Jules and Jim* (1961-French-104 min.-Films Inc./Facets Multimedia) explores the stresses of war through the lives of three friends.

The Burning Secret (1988-108 min.-/Vestron Video), based on a Stefan Zweig story, is set at an Austrian spa in 1919 where a young boy and his mother fall under the spell of an Austrian war veteran nobleman.

The Busby Berkeley Depression-era musical, *Gold Diggers of 1933* (1933-96 min.-Swank/Facets Multimedia) featured Joan Blondell in a starkly poignant production number, "Remember My Forgotten Man," about the plight of the World War I veteran in the wake of the violently dispersed bonus march on Washington.

This subject is more extensively explored in William Wellman's *Heroes for Sale* (1933-73 min.-Swank/MGM-UA Home Video) about a wounded war veteran (Richard Barthelmess) who suffers from morphine addiction and unemployment, but continues to survive.

British director Derek Jarman created a visual experience to illuminate Benjamin Britten's op. 66, *War Requiem* (1989-99 min.-/London CD Video). It contains Sir Laurence Olivier's last screen performance. Britten wrote the requiem for the consecration of the rebuilt Coventry Cathedral in 1962. It is a mass whose words are taken from the "Missa pro Defunctis" of the British soldier poet Wilfred Owen who was killed at the front late in 1918. The poet is the subject of a documentary entitled *Wilfred Owen: The Pity of War* (58 min.-/Films for the Humanities & Sciences).

Actuality Films: Prelude

One program in the Europe: The Mighty Continent series covers *The Years 1904-1914—The Drums begin to Roll* (1976-52 min.-University of Missouri).

One of A. J. P. Taylor's BBC How Wars Begin lecture series concerns *The First World War* (1977).

The first program in the PBS series The Great War and the Shaping of the Twentieth Century series, *Explosion* (1996-60 min.-/PBS Video), is an overview of European life in the first decade of this century with an emphasis of those factors that led to the outbreak of a Europe-wide war.

Two of CBS television's World War I series use archive film and Robert Ryan's narration to portray the *Doomed Dynasties of Europe* (1965-26/16 min.-Iowa State University) and the *Summer at Sarajevo* (1965-26/16 min.). Shortened "forum versions" are available from Encyclopedia Britannica Educational Corporation (the latter titled *Assassination at Sarajevo*), while the CBS Video Library has reissued the full versions on a videotape entitled *Seeds of War*.

The first part of Coronet MTI's World War I series explores *Background Tensions* (n.d.-second edition-13 min.-University of Minnesota) as does *The Smell of War* (1984-20 min.-/Films for the Humanities & Sciences).

A program in the British series The Century of Warfare presents an overview of the factors that combined as *The World Goes to War: 1900-1914* (1994-52 min.-/Time-Life Video).

The Engines of War (1983-24 min.-Pennsylvania State University) is a BBC documentary focusing on the strains within the Austro-Hungarian Empire and on its leaders' proposed solutions to the nationalist threat.

On a more general level, *Myth of Nationalism* (1976-30 min.- International Film Bureau) traces the growth of nationalism from 1870 to 1914.

Churchill and British History, 1874-1918 (1974-29 min.-Indiana University) places Churchill's early career against the backdrop of British history.

Prewar Russia is the subject of *Last Years of the Tsars* (1969-19 min.-Pennsylvania State University) and *Russia: Czar to Lenin* (1966-25 min.-Pennsylvania State University).

Newly available archival and forensic evidence combined with post-Soviet curiosity about (and perhaps nostalgia for) the Tsarist period to produce two recent documentaries on the last of the Romanovs: a National Geographic program entitled *Russia's Last Tsar* (1996-54 min.-/National Geographic); and the two-part *Last of the Czars* (1996-150 min.-/PBS Home Video), a Discovery cable channel production.

A number of the documentaries on the Russian Revolution itself begin with a survey of prewar life and conditions.

Wartime Propaganda

Military cameramen began shooting film of the war from almost the very beginning. The Central Powers originally gave civilian cameramen (including Americans) much freer access to the front than did the Entente. Both newsreel and documentary features were produced and distributed during the war, many as propaganda under official government auspices. Though few of these wartime productions are widely available—and some, including American documentaries made on the Central Powers' side while the United States was neutral and were seized as treasonable once the United States entered the war—have disappeared completely. The large amount of film shot during the war has provided the raw materials for a number of later compilation documentaries.

The Imperial War Museum in London (IWM) has packaged together the two most famous wartime official documentaries, *The Battles of the Somme and Ancre* (1993, IWM and DD Video). An IWM staff-prepared viewer's guide to *The Battles of the Somme and Ancre* is available separately. *The Battle of the Somme* (1916-82 min.-/Battery Classics or Films for the Humanities & Sciences) is available by itself with a viewers' guide prepared by the staff of the Imperial War Museum and a memoir by one of its principal photographers, Geoffrey Malins. One of the earliest projects of the then newly created German military dominated film unit, BUFA, was a partly actuality, partly staged response to the British film. Called *Bei unseren Helden an der Somme* [*With Our Heroes on the Somme*] (1917), it was considered a lost film until a copy recently turned up at the Bundesarchi/Filmarchiv, Berlin. It it not yet commercially available.

Other video compilations and oral histories available from the Imperial War Museum include *Voices from the Western Front* and *War Women of Britain: Women at War 1914-1918*.

The Interwar Years: Adjusting Memory to Justify War

Early post-war documentaries combined actuality footage, studio reconstructions, animated models and maps into such British recreations as *The Battle of Jutland* (1921), *Zeebrugge* (1924), *Ypres* (1925), *Mons* (1926), *Battle of the Coronel and Falkland Islands* (1927), *The Somme* (1927-not to be confused with the first full length British documentary *The Battle of the Somme*), *The Guns of Loos* (1928), and *Q Ships* (1928-/Discount Video).

U.S. Army Signal Corps film of the war was compiled into a documentary in 1927. This film has been re-released as *Americans Over There: The United States in World War I, 1917-18* (1996-72 min.-/Filmic Archives).

One German company produced *The Emden* (1927) and another, UFA, produced a three-part documentary featuring animated maps, archival footage, and scenes filmed "in the documentary mode," called *Der Weltkrieg* (1927), directed by Leo Lasko and released abroad as *The Great War as Seen through German Spectacles*. The film extolled the achievements of the German army during the war, was favorably viewed by Gustav Stresemann, and at the studio's direction was shown three times a day during that year's national meeting of the *Stalhelm*—a right-wing veterans' organization that was later absorbed into the Nazi *Sturm Abteilung*.

A French director, Leon Poirier, produced an emotionally charged compilation entitled *Verdun-Visions D'Histoire* (1927).

And in 1931, Richard Oswald produced, revised at the request of film censors, and finally released a re-enacted pseudo-documentary about the coming of the war called *1914: The Last Day Before the World Conflagration* placing into the mouths of its actors the diplomatic statements published by the German government in 1926 to make its revisionist point.

Douaumont—Die Holle von Verdun (1931-German-84 min.) used recreated battle scenes, animated maps, spoken dialogue, and some authentic wartime footage to comprehend the horror from the German side.

Just before the outbreak of World War II another, more comprehensive documentary was produced entitled *Over There: 1914-1918* (1939-90 min.-New Yorker Films/Films for the Humanities & Sciences).

And as the United States drew closer to the British side, Time Inc. released Louis de Rochemont's *The Ramparts We Watch* (1940-90 min.-Syracuse University/Facets Multimedia) as a March of Time special, using newsreels and enactments to compare American attitudes toward the last crisis to those about the current one.

Post World War II Actuality Presentations: Overviews

After the Second World War, two expansive television documentary series were produced on the First World War. The BBC produced *The Great War* (1964) and CBS produced *World War I* (1964-65-twenty-two 26 min. episodes-/CBS Video has released the full episodes on a five videotape boxed set with several episodes on each tape, Encyclopedia Britannica Educational Corporation offers so-called forum editions of some of them, each about 18 min.). Both of these are excellent, but flawed by the use of unauthentic newsreel footage, unauthenticated scenes from older secondary sources, the addition of sound or even (in the case of the British series) use of dramatic film materials as newsreel. But both provide extensive coverage of both the fighting and home fronts on both sides during the war.

Most recently, to commemorate the 70th anniversary of the establishment of the Veterans' Day holiday, KCET and the BBC in association with the Imperial War Museum produced an eight-part series entitled The Great War and the Shaping of the Twentieth Century (1996-480 min.-/PBS Video). Its individual sixty-minute programs are *Explosion* about the origins and outbreak of war, *Stalemate* about the transformation to war of attrition on the western front, *Total War* about the new technologies of war that increased the importance of, and danger to, home front populations and resources, *Slaughter* about life in the trenches, *Mutiny* about the French near collapse and the Russian collapse in 1917, *Collapse* about the last year of the war, *Hatred and Hunger* about the immediate post-war world, and *War without End* about the longer-term consequences.

Other general overviews of the war include the program in The Mighty Continent series entitled *This Generation Has No Future* (1976-

52 min.-University of Missouri), an NBC retrospective *The Great War-Fifty Years After* (1968-25 min.-/Social Studies School Service Video), and *World War I* (n.d.-3 parts-15-18 min. each-Coronet Films/Video, second edition) whose parts are *Background Tensions, Fighting on Two Fronts*, and the *Politics of Peacemaking*.

Films for the Humanities & Sciences offers three videos on the war, *Stalemate: History in Action, The Smell of War: History in Action* (1984-20 min. each), and a short overview, *World War I* (25 min.).

The British War File series contains a two-part program entitled *The Great War: The Story of World War I* (1991-50 min. each-/Video Treasures). The first part covers 1914-1916, while the second deals with the 1916-1918 period.

Aspects of the War: Prosecution

Barbara Tuchman's history of the first month of the war has been made into a feature-length documentary entitled *The Guns of August* (1965-99 min.-Swank/International Historic Films).

Several programs in the British PolyGram Century of Warfare series cover military aspects of the war. These include *Blood and Mud: Trench Warfare in the West, 1914-1918, War of the Eagles: The Eastern Front 1914-1918, Aces High: Air Warfare 1914-1918, Battlefleets and U Boats: Naval Warfare 1914-1918*, and *War to End All Wars? 1918 and the Aftermath* (1994-52 min. each-/Time-Life Video).

Verdun: End of a Nightmare (1965-26 min.-Indiana University) and *The Battle of Verdun* (1988-26 min.-/Films for the Humanities) detail the bloody but unsuccessful attempt by the Germans to capture the fortress town. Two-thirds of a million casualties made the name Verdun synonymous with the futility of war.

The Somme: 1916—Hell on Earth (1993-50 min.-/Cromwell Films) uses excerpts from the wartime documentary along with maps, dramatic readings, and historians' commentary to explain what happened and why.

The Battle of the Somme: 1916 (120 min.-/Films for the Humanities & Sciences) also uses footage from the official film to explore its wider significance.

Mutiny on the Western Front (1996-90 min.-/Mastervision) follows the bloody experience of Australian soldiers, after the Dardanelles debacle, on the western front where, misused and exhausted, many rebelled against their British and French officers in 1918.

Fifty Fathoms Deep: The Story of the Lusitania (1962-45 min.), a BBC production in association with NBC News, is scuba diver-photographer John Light's investigation of the remains of the ship and was the deepest underwater television photography project yet attempted (the wreck lies some 300 feet beneath the surface off the southern coast of Ireland). From his survey of the hull, Light concluded that the *Lusitania* was armed (though, he asserted, British Admiralty divers had removed the guns themselves prior to his visit) and that the secondary explosion that caused its sinking was caused by contraband munitions or munitions raw materials (aluminum powder) being secretly carried on board. *Exploring the Lusitania* (1994), a National Geographic film of a 1993 expedition utilizing both manned and robot submersibles from the Woods Hole Oceanographic Institution refutes both claims, asserting that what Light correctly identified as gun mounts on the ship's superstructure never actually held guns (the British Admiralty justified its loans to subsidize the ship's construction by requiring that it be easily convertible to an auxiliary cruiser in wartime—hence the gun mounts) and ascribes the secondary explosion to coal dust that had accumulated in the bunkers, which by that point in the ship's trans-Atlantic crossing were nearly empty. *Shipwreck: The Lusitania* (1997-26 min.) is a brief Discovery cable television overview of the disaster. *Aces: The Story of the First Air War* (1996-93 min.-/Videofinders) and *The Cavalry of the Clouds* (52 min.-/Films for the Humanities & Sciences) cover the air war.

Aspects of the War: American Entry and Role

The American intervention is the focus of the NBC Project XX program *The Great War* (1956-54 min.-University of Missouri/Fusion Video) and the subject of the Wolper film *The Yanks Are Coming* (1974-52 min.-University of Colorado), of *World War I: A Documentary of the Role of the U.S.A.* (n.d.-27 min.-University of Missouri/Zenger Media), of The American Experience program *The Great War-1918* (1989-58 min.-/PBS Video), of *Doughboys: Heroes of World War I* (1995-41 min.-/Filmic Archives), and of the Cadre Film *Goodbye Billy: America Goes to War, 1917-18* (1972-25 min.-Churchill Films/Video) made by R. C. Raack, Patrick Griffin, and William Malloch in association with the American Historical Association History Education Project.

Men of Bronze (1977-58 min.-/Facets Multimedia) is the story of the U.S. Army's 369th Infantry Regiment—the unit of African Americans that served longer in action (part of the time in French Army uniforms) than any other American unit.

The Pershing Story (n.d.-29 min.-International Historic Films) is a U.S. Army Big Picture biography focusing on his First World War command. It is packaged with *The American Siberian Expeditionary Force* (n.d.-29 min.-/Fusion Video).

Chaplin urges a Wall Street crowd to buy war bonds.   Credit: National Archives

The early part of *American Caesar* (1985-270 min.-/Embassy Home Entertainment), based on William Manchester's biography, covers General Douglas MacArthur's World War I experience as Rainbow Division Commander.

One program in Alistair Cooke's America series covers *The Promise Fulfilled and the Promise Broken* (1975-52 min.-Kent State/ Ambrose Video) about World War I and the interwar period.

Homefront, 1917-1919—War Transforms American Life (1967-17 min.) covers American life and attitudes during the war.

Aspects of the War: The Propaganda War

The roles of propaganda and of those who recorded the war are subjects of John Terraine's *The First Casualty* (1974-55 min.-Pennsylvania State University) about British wartime propaganda, of *The Moving Picture Boys in the Great War* (1986-52 min.-Modern Sound Pictures/ Facets Multimedia) narrated by Lowell Thomas, of *Cameramen at War* (26 min.-/Facets Multimedia), produced by the British Ministry of Information about the British Film Unit Newsreel Cameramen during both World Wars, and of the episode of Hollywood, The Silent Years entitled *Hollywood Goes to War* (1979-54 min.-/HBO Home Video).

The French postwar documentary *Pour la Paix du Monde* was dedicated to the six French cameramen who were killed on active duty and even includes the shots taken while one was killed.

Aspects of the War: National Self-Determination

The Armenian Case (1975-43 min.-University of Texas-Dallas) narrated by Mike Connors is a documentary setting forth the facts of the Turkish genocidal massacres of the Armenians in 1915 and proclaiming the continuing Armenian national claims.

Episodes of Robert Kee's series Ireland, a History concern *1916, Michael Collins and the Black and Tans,* and *Civil War* (1980-54 min. each).

The Easter Rising is Irish documentary filmmaker George Morrison's compilation based upon the photographic holdings of the National Gallery of Ireland. In 1959 and 1960, Morrison assembled the surviving newsreel footage of the Irish struggle for independence in two 90-minute gaelic documentaries, *Mise Éire* and *Saoirse?*

The first episode of The Struggles for Poland, *Once Upon a Time (1900-1921)* (1988-60 min.-/PBS Video), tells the story of the wartime struggle for Polish national rebirth.

Collapse, Revolution, and Civil War in the Russian Empire

The Decline of Tsardom (1989-30 min.-/Filmic Archives) surveys the military defeats and social unrest that led to the collapse of the Romanov dynasty.

The most sweeping coverage of the Russian Revolution is the British Broadcasting Corporation's *The World Turned Upside Down* (1967-80 min.), produced with the cooperation of Soviet authorities and narrated by Leo McKern. It surveys Russian history from the end of the eighteenth century to the death of Lenin.

Slanted in a markedly anti-Soviet direction and as interesting as a document of the Cold War as it is as a history of the Soviet Union and Communism is the NBC Project XX program *Nightmare in Red* (1955-55 min.-Modern Sound Pictures).

The four-part Russian Revolution series (1971-20 min. each-Kent State University) covers *Russia in World War I, Last Years of the Tsar, Lenin Prepares for Revolution,* and *The Bolshevik Victory.*

Two excerpts of the docudrama feature *Nicholas and Alexandra* are subtitled *War and the Fall of the Tsar: 1914-1917* and *The Bolshevik Victory: 1917* and are available as free standing programs (1976-27/26 min.-/Learning Corporation of America).

One video in the History's Turning Points series covers *The Russian Revolution* (1995-30 min.-/Filmoc Archives).

Red Dawn (1974-20 min.-Films for the Humanities & Sciences) traces the provisional government/soviets stage of the revolution from the abdication of the Tsar to the Bolshevik takeover, while *The October Revolution and After* (26 min.), *Lenin's Funeral* (52 min.), and *Trotsky* (58 min.), all from the same source, carry the story into the 1930s.

Several Soviet documentaries or docudramas cover the revolutionary era. Ester Shub's *The Fall of the Romanov Dynasty* (1927-101 min.-silent-Museum of Modern Art/Facets Multimedia) covered the February/March revolution in commemoration of its tenth anniversary. It is a classic of the documentary filmmaker's art. Virtually simultaneously, she completed *The Great Road* (1927-silent-140 min.) commemorating the Bolshevik victory.

A PBS Nova series program, *Anastasia Dead or Alive* (1995-54 min.-/WGBH Video), investigates the newly uncovered remains of the deposed Tsar, his family, and their retainers, documents from the Kremlin archives, and comparative DNA profiles to test the claim of Anna Anderson Manahan that she was the Russian Grand Duchess. It concludes that she was not Anastasia and probably was Franzisca Schanzkowska, a Polish factory worker who had disappeared from Berlin just before Anna was rescued from a canal there.

Kino Pravda #21 (1929-25 min.-Museum of Modern Art/Facets Multimedia) and *Three Songs about Lenin* (1934-Russian-68 min.-Kino International/Facets Multimedia) are two of Dziga Vertov's agitprop films linking Lenin to the Russian people.

Revolution in Russia, 1917 (1967-19 min.-Kent State University) is a CBS documentary on the revolution.

Lenin's Revolution (1970-20 min.-Utah State University) also covers the subject.

Lenin (1978-39 min.-Learning Corporation of America) is a British Granada Television biography narrated by journalist James Cameron.

The last of A. J. P. Taylor's BBC lecture series Revolutions and Revolutionaries covers "Russia 1917: The Last European Revolution" (1978).

And a program in John Kenneth Galbraith's The Age of Uncertainty series covers the economic impacts of both the war and the revolution in *Lenin and the Great Ungluing* (1977-57 min.-University of California EMC).

A U.S. Army documentary, *The American Siberian Expeditionary Force* (29 min.-/International Historic films), a Cadre Films production, *The Frozen War-America Intervenes in Russia, 1918-20* (1973-30 min.-Churchill Films), and an episode of the CBS World War I series, *The Allies in Russia* (Forum title, *Soviet Union: Civil War and Allied Intervention*), cover these aspects of the revolution.

Lenin and Trotsky (1964-27 min.-Kent State University) is a CBS documentary on the two men's relationship and on Trotsky's failure to succeed Lenin upon his death.

Aftermath and Effects

The war's conclusion and aftermath are the subject of several of the CBS and BBC World War I series programs. The CBS programs include *Armistice* (Forum title, *The Day the Guns Stopped Firing*), *Wilson and Peace,* and *Aftermath of World War I.*

Two of A. J. P. Taylor's How Wars End lectures cover *World War I: Armistice* and *The Peace Conference* (30 min. each-/Films for the Humanities & Sciences).

Men in Crisis: Wilson Versus the Senate (1964-27 min.) covers the U.S. treaty ratification attempt.

Versailles—The Lost Peace (1978-26 min.-University of Minnesota) looks more broadly at the treaty and its impact.

The War That Failed to End Wars (14 min.-/Films for the Humanities & Sciences) identifies some of the problems left over from World War I that would lead to World War II.

The League of Nations: The Hope of Mankind (1976-54 min.-University of Minnesota) looks at Wilson's dream and its inadequacies.

A program in the British The Century of Warfare series, *Enter the Dictators: 1920-1935* (1994-52 min.-/Time-Life Video), covers long-term political effects of the war.

Another program in historian John Terraine's Europe: The Mighty Continent series is *The Results of War: Are We Making a Good Peace* (1976-52 min.-/University of Missouri).

The Shadow of Béalnabláth (1989-104 min.-/Rego Records and Tapes) is a four-part Radio Telefis Eireann (RTE) investigation by Colm Connolly of the still controversial death of Irish Free State military commander Michael Collins in August 1922.

Several of Robert Hughes's Shock of the New programs cover the artistic changes accelerated or aggravated by the war. These include *The Powers That Be, The Threshold of Liberty,* and *The View from the Edge* (1980-60 min. each-University of California EMC/Ambrose Video).

A Museum without Walls program called *Germany-Dada* (1986-52 min.-/Kartes Video) incorporates the art, poetry, and film of Dadaist artists as well as their reminiscences.

More broadly, the changes brought with the technologies of mass slaughter introduced in or made visible by the First World War is the subject of one of Bill Moyers's Walk through the Twentieth Century programs, *The Arming of the Earth* (1984-58 min.-/PBS Video).

And the changes in leadership by the war's end is the subject of the introductory program in the Leaders of the Twentieth Century series entitled *The End of the Old Order: 1900-1918* (1979-24 min.-Coronet/Landmark Films and Video).

Contributors

Robert Baird teaches film at the University of Illinois English Department. There he administers the integration of multimedia technology in the classroom and the Department's web page: http//www.english. uiuc.edu. His research and writing attempt to translate recent discoveries in neurology and cognitive psychology into a revised psychology of visual spectatorship.

Richard C. Bartone is a senior associate editor of the journal *Film & History* and a member of the editorial board of *The New Jersey Journal of Communication*. His research activities include visual autobiography as a form of historical evidence. He teaches in the Communication Department of William Paterson University, New Jersey.

Michael Birdwell teaches American history at Tennessee Technological University and is involved in cataloging the personal papers of Sgt. Alvin C. York for the Sgt. York Historical Association.

James I. Deutsch is an associate professorial lecturer in American civilization at George Washington University, and occasional consultant for the Smithsonian Institution and National Council on the Aging. Recent publications have included works on American film and folklore.

Gerald Herman teaches history at Northeastern University, where he also serves as special assistant in the office of the University Counsel. He teaches European cultural history, history and film, and a media production course in the department's public history program. He is the author of *The Pivotal Crisis: A Comprehensive Chronology of the First World War, 1914-1919*, and is currently completing *An Historian's Guide to Media*.

Michael T. Isenberg, who died in 1994, was an associate professor of history at the United States Naval Academy. His publications include *War on Film: The American Cinema of World War I, 1914-1918; Puzzles of the Past: An Introduction to Thinking About History;* and *John L. Sullivan and His America*. His essay on *The Big Parade* originally

283

appeared in *American History/American Film*, edited by John E. O'Connor and Martin A. Jackson.

Andrew Kelly is a film historian. His book on the antiwar cinema of World War I, *Cinema and the Great War*, was published by Routledge in June 1997. He is also the author of *Filming T. E. Lawrence: Korda's Lost Epics*. He is currently writing the history of the film *All Quiet on the Western Front* and is researching a biography of the film director Lewis Milestone.

Daniel J. Leab is professor of history at Seton Hall University, managing editor of *Labor History*, general secretary of the Historians of American Communism, and treasurer of the International Association for the Study of Media and History (IAMHIST). His books include a study of blacks in American movies, a monograph on the organization of white-collar newspaper workers, and (with his wife, Katharine Kyes Leab) a handbook to auction houses worldwide. He has published numerous articles on Cold War movies, in both German and English. Forthcoming is a book on the life and times of Matt Cvetic, the eponymous hero of the film *I Was a Communist for the FBI*.

Martin F. Norden teaches film as a professor of communication at the University of Massachusetts-Amherst. His articles on moving-image media have appeared in many journals and anthologies, including three volumes of Popular Press's Beyond the Stars series. He is the author of *The Cinema of Isolation: A History of Physical Disability in the Movies* and *John Barrymore: A Bio-Bibliography*.

John E. O'Connor is professor of history at New Jersey Institute of Technology and Rutgers University-Newark. Founder and, for 20 years, editor of the journal *Film & History*, he is the author or editor of eight books, most recently *Image as Artifact: The Historical Analysis of Film and Television*. The American Historical Association has honored him by the creation of its annual John E. O'Connor Award for best film/video production about history.

Dominick A. Pisano is a curator in the Aeronautics Division, National Air and Space Museum, Smithsonian Institution, Washington, D.C. He is coauthor of *Legend, Memory, and the Great War in the Air*, a catalog based on the exhibition of the same name at the National Air and Space Museum, published by the University of Washington in 1992.

Peter C. Rollins is regents professor of English and American and film studies at Oklahoma State University and the current editor-in-chief of *Film & History*. His film *Will Rogers' 1920s* was awarded a CINE Golden Eagle; his *Television's Vietnam(s)* were broadcast over PBS and WTBS. Publications include *Hollywood as Historian* and *Hollywood's Indian,* also with John E. O'Connor. With James Digital Media, he has recently completed a CD-ROM for all 26 years of *Film & History*. (See http://h-net2.msu.edu/~filmhis)

Larry Ward is a professor in the Department of Communications at California State University, Fullerton, where he teaches film history and aesthetics and a variety of film and video production courses. His recent scholarship has focused on the impact of digital technologies on all aspects of filmmaking.

James M. Welsh teaches at Salisbury State University in Maryland and is the editor of *Literature/Film Quarterly*. His last book was *Peter Watkins: A Guide to References and Resources*. He co-authored *Abel Gance* with Steven Philip Kramer and *His Majesty the American: The Cinema of Douglas Fairbanks, Sr.* with John C. Tibbetts. He coordinated a workshop on Colonial America at the movies with John O'Connor at Colonial Williamsburg, and he has also published in *Film & History; The Historical Journal of Film, Radio, and Television; Sight & Sound; Film Comment; American Film; Cinema Journal; The Journal of Popular Film and Television;* and *Cinéaste*.

Thomas Winter teaches part-time at the University of Cincinnati, Xavier University, and Northern Kentucky University. His work focuses on middle-class definitions of manhood and the cultural construction of class in the Gilded Age and the Progressive Era. He currently is at work on a book-length study titled *Making Manly Men: The YMCA, Manhood, & Class, 1872-1921.*

General Index

287

Film/TV Index